SOVIETICA

MONOGRAPHS

OF THE INSTITUTE OF EAST-EUROPEAN STUDIES

UNIVERSITY OF FRIBOURG / SWITZERLAND

Edited by

J. M. BOCHEŃSKI

SOVIET THEORY OF KNOWLEDGE

THOMAS J. BLAKELEY

Department of Philosophy, Boston College, Boston, Mass., U.S.A.

SOVIET THEORY OF

KNOWLEDGE

D. REIDEL PUBLISHING COMPANY / DORDRECHT-HOLLAND

TABLE OF CONTENTS

INTRODUCTION   VII

CHAPTER I   THE DEVELOPMENT OF SOVIET THEORY OF
            KNOWLEDGE AND ITS MAIN REPRESENTATIVES   1

   1. Beginnings   1
   2. Current Events   2
   3. Leaders   5

CHAPTER II   GENERAL CHARACTERISTICS OF MARXIST-
             LENINIST THEORY OF KNOWLEDGE   13

   4. Sources   13
   5. The Place of Theory of Knowledge in Dialectical
     Materialism   18

CHAPTER III   THE MAIN TENETS OF THE THEORY OF
              KNOWLEDGE OF DIALECTICAL MATERIALISM   29

   6. The 'Leninist Theory of Reflection'   29
   7. The 'Dialectic of Absolute and Relative Truth'   35
   8. 'Practice as Basis of Knowledge and Criterion of Truth'   38
   9. The 'Dialectic of the "Logical" and the "Historical" '   42

CHAPTER IV   BASIC COGNITIVE FUNCTIONS   48

   10. Living Contemplation   49
   11. Sensation   49
   12. Perception   51
   13. Representation   52
   14. Imagination   53
   15. Concept   54
   16. Judgement   60
   17. Reasoning   62

CHAPTER V   BASIC COGNITIVE MODES   67

   18. Generalization   67
   19. Analysis and Synthesis   68

V

20. Abstract and Concrete   69
21. Deduction and Induction   72
22. Hypothesis   73
23. Theory   75
24. Law   76
25. Analogy   76

CHAPTER VI   METHODS AND METHODOLOGIES   79

26. The Classics on Method   79
27. The Classification of Sciences   80
28. General and Special Methods   84
29. The Methodological Significance of Epistemology and
    the Epistemological Significance of Methodology   86

CHAPTER VII   CRITIQUE OF 'BOURGEOIS' THEORIES OF
    KNOWLEDGE   90

30. A Terminological and Philosophical Point of View   93
31. 'Idealism' and 'Metaphysics'   97
32. The 'Epistemological Roots of Idealism and Religion'   102

CHAPTER VIII   SOVIET HISTORIOGRAPHY OF KNOWLEDGE   110

33. Knowledge in Ancient Philosophy   110
34. Modern Philosophy and the Rise of Epistemology   114
35. Contemporary Bourgeois Epistemology   121

CHAPTER IX   EVALUATION   140

36. Positive Elements in Diamat's Theory of Knowledge   140
37. Negative Elements in Diamat's Theory of Knowledge   141
38. Nonsense in Diamat's Theory of Knowledge   143
39. Possibilities of Further Development   145

BIBLIOGRAPHY   146

INDEX OF NAMES   194

INDEX OF SUBJECTS   201

INTRODUCTION

This book offers a complete survey of contemporary Soviet theory of knowledge. It is by no means meant to replace De Vries' excellent treatise on the same subject. Since De Vries depended mainly on the 'classics of Marxism' and the few contemporary Soviet works which were available in German translation, his account is at best an introduction to the contemporary period. In a sense this book is complementary to his: he presents the doctrines of the classics and criticizes them, this book recounts what came after and what is going on now.

Epistemology and theory of knowledge are taken here as equivalent terms, representing the Soviet *gnoseologija* and *teorija poznanija*. No attempt to justify the existence of such a philosophical discipline will be attempted here. Even outside of this question of the legitimacy of epistemology, it is not easy to delimit the domain of its purvey. We have, therefore, taken it in a wider rather than narrow sense. This means that some questions of logic and psychology have been taken up – to the extent that they overlap with the field of philosophical consideration of knowledge.

By contemporary Soviet philosophy we here mean the philosophic activity carried on in Soviet Russia, in the Russian language, from 1947 to 1963. In addition, we have paid relatively little attention to the 'dogmatic bases', which have been competently covered by De Vries, and the 'declassified areas', which are still too few to merit special attention. We have mainly considered here the 'systematic superstructure' of contemporary Soviet philosophy, i.e. that area where discussion is possible and progress can be made.

Our sincere thanks go to Professor J. M. Bocheński, Professor G. L. Kline, Pierre J. Beemans and the members of the Institute for their material and moral assistance in the preparation of this work. Special thanks are due to Rockefeller Foundation whose assistance made our research possible.

In the system used for transcribing the Russian alphabet the following letters are not immediately evident: "š" = "sh" as in "shoe"; "č" = "ch" as in "chew"; "ž" = "g" as in "rouge"; "x" = "ch" as in "loch". The apostrophe stands for the hard and soft signs. Frequently used proper names, like Khrushchov, are given their accepted English equivalents. Abbreviations are explained as introduced (in the text) or on the first page of the bibliography.

CHAPTER I

THE DEVELOPMENT OF SOVIET THEORY OF KNOWLEDGE AND ITS MAIN REPRESENTATIVES

By definition the philosophical treatment of knowledge is an integral part of the philosophy of Marxism-Leninism and one would expect, therefore, that every Soviet philosopher would say at least something on the specific nature of cognition and that, further, there would develop a special group of philosophers – to be called epistemologists – who would devote themselves in a special way to the elaboration of questions dealing with knowledge. That this has not been the case with Soviet philosophy – where the explicit philosophical treatment of knowledge dates from about 1950 and the formation of a group of epistemologists from about 1957 – is due in the main to the peculiar history of this philosophical doctrine as a whole.

1. BEGINNINGS

As far as epistemology is concerned, the period of philosophical activity extending from the Revolution to the decree of 1931[1] was a time of 'house-cleaning' when Lenin's *Materialism and Empirio-Criticism* was established as the official expression of 'Marxist' theory of knowledge and the last vestiges of Plekhanov's 'theory of hieroglyphs' and Bogdanov's empirio-monism were eliminated.[2] For all of its 'dialectical' overtones, the dispute leading up to the decree had very little even indirect bearing on epistemology.[3]

The 1931 decree effectively stifled Soviet epistemology at the point where it should have begun to really develop. Lenin's *Philosophical Notebooks* appeared in article form in 1929 and in book form in 1933; in view of the role which they have played in more recent developments in Soviet theory of knowledge, it is a safe conjecture to assume that this development would already have started in the 30's had the decree not intervened. In the 'quiet period'[4] between 1931 and 1947, if one excepts the *Theory of Reflection* of the Bulgar Todor Pavlov (published in Russian under the pseudonym P. Dosev in 1936)[5], there are no specialized Soviet studies in epistemology and knowledge is only treated in passing in books like B. E. Byxovskij's *Sketch of the Philosophy of Dialectical Materialism*, and the *sbornik, Dialectical and Historical Materialism*.[6] It is true that F. Xasxačix – the principal Soviet author taken into consideration by De Vries[7] – defended his candidate dissertation, 'The Intelligibility of the World and of its Laws', in 1937 but it was not until after his death on the front (1942) that it appeared in book form under the title, *On the Knowability of the World*[8], and became – along with R. Natadze's *Genesis of the Formation of Concepts* (1946) and L. O. Reznikov's *The Problem of the Formation of Concepts in the Light of the History of Language* (1946)[9] – the precursor of a Soviet epistemological renaissance. Stalin's *On Dialectical and Historical Materialism* had no significant influence on the development of Soviet discussion of epistemological questions.

2. CURRENT EVENTS

The development of Soviet epistemology during the current period – from the 1947 discussion to the present[10] – is characterized by its organic dependance on developments in other branches of Soviet philosophy a trait it has possessed from the beginning. With the general upswing in Soviet philosophical activity after the 1947 discussion came an increasing occupation with questions of knowledge. But, in the period 1947–1950 this was little more than a return to where things had been left off in 1931. Thus, the discussion around M. M. Rozental' 's *Marxist Dialectical Method*[11] represented the same point of view that Deborin had espoused in the period before the 1931 decree.[12] And, the discussion around M. A. Markov's article, 'On the Nature of Physical Knowledge'[13], took up again some of the problems of the dispute which had lead to the 1931 decree.[14]

Two events of the year 1950 left a deep mark on contemporary Soviet philosophy and at the same time gave an impetus to the real development of Soviet theory of knowledge. They were the *perestrojka* (reconstruction) in psychology and Stalin's intervention on the question of language.

Although the 'Pavlovian reconstruction'[15] in Soviet psychology principally concerned the psycho-physical problem, its definite influence on Soviet epistemology is undeniable and can be attributed to the fact that the leading philosopher-psychologist in the Soviet Union, S. L. Rubinštejn, had a definite epistemological penchant. The conference was followed by a series of publications where, among other things, the 'reflexological' theory of knowledge of Rubinštejn's opponents predominates. The proceedings of the 'Pavlovian conference' of 1950 are to be found in *The Scientific Session, Devoted to Problems of the Physiological Doctrine of the Academician I. P. Pavlov*[16] and its incidences on Soviet theory of knowledge in *The Doctrine of I. P. Pavlov and Philosophic Questions of Psychology* (1952)[17], N. V. Medvedev: *The Marxist-Leninist Theory of Reflection and the Doctrine of I. P. Pavlov on Higher Nervous Activity* (1954)[18], and *Philosophical Questions of the Doctrine on Higher Nervous Activity* (1954)[19]. Although he was defeated at the conference and forced to make an 'auto-critique'[20], Rubinštejn remained until his death in 1960 the most influential and readable Soviet interpreter of philosophical psychology and his later works bear the same unmistakeably epistemological character – especially *Being and Consciousness* (1957) and *On Thought and Paths of its Investigation* (1958).[21]

Stalin's intervention into the field of linguistics – the essence of which was to remove language from the domain of superstructure – lead to a general widening of perspectives in most of Soviet philosophy[22]. That this was especially true of logic was due – as Soviet philosophers argued at that time – to this science's close affiliation with language.[23] The widening was almost as significant for Soviet epistemology but the effects did not become visible until around 1959 (see below). Stalin's intervention also lead to a heavy emphasis in Soviet philosophy on linguistic aspects represented by *Questions of Dialectical and Historical Materialism in I. V. Stalin's "Marxism and Questions of Linguistics"* (1951–1952, 2 vols.).[24]

In 1954 V. M. Podosetnik challenged M. N. Rutkevič's interpretation of 'practice', the fundamental category of dialectical materialism's theory of knowledge.[25] The dispute lasted over into 1955 and was resolved by an editorial in *Voprosy filosofii* in favor of Podosetnik.[26] Rutkevič – like Rubinštejn in the field of philosophical psychology – has, nevertheless, remained master of the field. His *Practice as Base of Knowledge and Criterion of Truth* (1952)[27] remains the most quoted work on the subject and the thoughts expressed in the article which

3

Podosetnik attacked, 'On the Question of the Role of Practice in the Process of Knowledge'[28], still prevail in contemporary Soviet philosophy. The emphasis on practice has increased with the Twentieth (1956), Twenty-First (1959) and Twenty-Second (1961) Congresses of the CPSU; Rutkevič has been joined by I. T. Jakuševskij, Ju. F. Buxalov and others introduced below while Podosetnik has gone back to a prudent silence.[29]

Also in 1954 appeared I. D. Andreev's *Dialectical Materialism on the Process of Knowledge*[30] which was the first general treatment of epistemology from a Marxist-Leninist point of view. Had it measured up to expectations, 1954 could have marked the birth of a veritable epistemology in the Soviet Union. But, this book – like the same author's *Principles of the Theory of Knowledge* (1959)[31] – seldom rises above the textbook level and Andreev's work has definitely been overshadowed by most of the other Soviet philosophers with whose works we will be dealing.

1957 was marked by a surge in Soviet publications on epistemology which – although the bibliographical data for the period 1961–1963 is not as complete as that for 1947–1960 – seems to be continuing through the present. Whereas the period 1947–1956 saw the publication of 32 books and 174 articles pertinent to epistemology, for the period 1957–1960 we find 60 books and 356 articles. This is an increase from a yearly average of 3 books and 17 articles to a yearly average of 15 books and 89 articles.[32] This increase is even more significant in view of the fact that most of the books of the 1947–1956 period – like B. M. Kedrov's *Engels and Natural Science* (1947)[33], L. P. Gokieli's *On the Problem of Axiomatization in Logic* (1947)[34], and G. A. Kursanov's *Logical Laws of Thought* (1947)[35] – are only marginally pertinent to epistemology while those of 1957 (and subsequent years) include such specifically epistemological treatises as L. Arisjan's *History of the Theory of Knowledge* (1957)[36] and the *sborniki*, *Thought and Language*[37] and *Contemporary Subjective Idealism*[38] (both 1957).

As of 1959 epistemology came into its own in the Soviet Union, the key element being a sort of explosion in the publication of books and articles dealing with 'dialectical logic'. The enormous attention devoted to this subject seems to be best explained as a reaction – after a period of gestation – to the 1950 challenge of K. S. Bakradze and others. In order to refute the contention that dialectical logic is 'Marxist

4

epistemology'[39] a rapidly increasing number of Soviet philosophers set about constructing a logic which would conform to the classics' description of it. The development began in 1959 with the publication of M. N. Alekseev's *Dialectic of the Forms of Thought*[40], and of the *sborniki*, *Lenin and Some Questions of Theory of Knowledge*[41] and *Problems of Dialectical Logic.*[42] In 1960, the richest year for Soviet epistemological publications (24 books, 158 articles), M. N. Alekseev published his *Dialectical Logic*[43] and M. M. Rozental' his *Principles of Dialectical Logic*[44], accompanied by the *sborniki*, *Some Questions of Theory of Knowledge*[45], *Problems of Theory of Knowledge* (Perm')[46], and *Problems of Theory of Knowledge and Logic*[47]. 1961 saw the publication of I. Ja. Čupaxin's *Questions of the Theory of Concept*[48] and P. V. Kopnin's *Dialectic as Logic*[49], one of the most interesting of the whole series. For 1962 B. M. Kedrov and his collaborators prepared *Dialectic and Logic* in two volumes (*Forms of Thought* and *Laws of Thought*)[50] and V. I. Čerkesov published *The Materialist Dialectic as Logic and Theory of Knowledge*[51] with an extensive survey of the history of epistemological (dialectical-logical) problems in the Soviet Union. So far for 1963 we have G. G. Gabriel'jan's *Marxist Logic as Dialectic and Theory of Knowledge*[52], an original attempt to structure dialectical logic along the lines of Hegel's *Science of Logic*, and B. M. Kedrov's *Unity of Dialectic, Logic and Theory of Knowledge.*[53]

In addition to these works specifically on dialectical logic, this same period of 1959–1963 was marked by the publication of many other specialized works on questions of knowledge, most of them *sborniki*. For 1960 alone, we find G. A. Levin's *Questions of Theory of Knowledge in Lenin's "Materialism and Empirio-Criticism"*[54] and the *sborniki*, *The Epistemological Content of Logical Forms and Methods*[55], *World-Outlook and Methodological Problems of Scientific Abstraction*[56], *The Process of Thought and the Laws of Analysis, Synthesis and Generalization*[57], and *Practice as Criterion of Truth in Science.*[58]

3. LEADERS

From this brief survey of the works and problems treated in contemporary Soviet epistemology, it is evident that no one contemporary Soviet philosopher ranks as 'the epistemologist' in the same sense that one can rank M. M. Rozental' as 'the methodologist' of Soviet philosophy.[59] As mentioned above, Andreev's books are too much on the textbook level to merit him this title. As a matter of fact, Rozental' 's four books, *The Marxist Dialectical Method* (1947), *The Development by V. I. Lenin of the Marxist Theory of Knowledge* (1950), *Questions of the Dialectic in 'The Capital' of Marx* (1955), and *Principles of Dialectical Logic* (1960)[60], put him head and shoulders above Andreev as an epistemologist. Although he is mainly to be classed among the dialectical logicians, M. N. Alekseev is the contemporary Soviet thinker who – in our opinion – is doing the most original thinking in the domain of epistemology. His distinction between 'the dialectic of thought' and 'dialectical thinking' could, if it survives the indifference of Mitin and the old guard, be a turning point in the development of contemporary Soviet philosophy as a whole.

However, with the publication of the books on dialectical logic by Rozental', Kedrov, Kopnin and Čerkesov, it is precisely the old guard which is taking over (although Mitin and Konstantinov have not yet ventured a solid contribution). That this development will not lead to a stifling of speculation in the area of dialectical logic and epistemology seems to be indicated by the fact that these old stand-bys of contemporary Soviet philosophy give evidence of being willing to accept innovation and open discussion – in four years of accelerated development in these domains there has not been one serious condemnation.

Despite the fact that there is no contemporary Soviet philosopher who has imposed himself in the field of epistemology, the authors of books on this subject can be subdivided according to specialization and within the sub-groups there are indisputable leaders.

In *general epistemology* there are only F. I. Xasxačix, I. D. Andreev, and F. I. Georgiev. As pointed out above, Xasxačix is rather a predecessor of than a participant in the current developments. Andreev was scrutinized above. And, since his *Knowability of the World and its Laws* (1955)[61], Georgiev has not deployed much activity in the domain of epistemology.

Dialectical logic has provided contemporary Soviet philosophers with the richest opportunities for developing their views on Marxist-Leninist epistemology. The works of Alekseev show the most originality and those of P. V. Kopnin are of some interest. In addition to the old guard

6

– Čerkesov, Čupaxin, Kedrov and Rozental' – A. X. Kasymžanov has a book, *The Problem of the Coincidence of Dialectic, Logic and Theory of Knowledge* (1962)[62], and several articles to his credit.[63]

Psychology has contributed to the development of epistemology in the Soviet Union principally through the works of S. L. Rubinštejn, of which *Being and Consciousness* (1957)[64] has been of particular significance. B. G. Anan'ev's *Theory of Sensations* (1961)[65] contains an introductory chapter which is one of those rare summaries of Soviet epistemology which is clear and concise. A. Spirkin's *The Origin of Consciousness* (1960)[66] is a genetic and rather unsuccessful approach to some epistemological problems. E. A. Asratjan has contributed a series of articles on questions of a mixed – physiological, psychological, epistemological – character.[67]

In non-dialectical *logic*, it is P. S. Popov, the author of *The History of Modern Logic* (1960)[68], who leads the way in the discussion of epistemological problems. To be ranked with him is D. P. Gorskij whose doctoral dissertation, *Problems of Abstraction and the Formation of Concepts* (1961)[69], is a major contribution to the epistemological discussion. Others in this category are E. V. Il'enkov with *The Dialectic of Abstract and Concrete in 'The Capital' of Marx* (1960)[70], V. M. Boguslavskij[71] and mathematical logicians like A. A. Zinov'ev and S. A. Janovskaja who have written on philosophy of logic.[72]

The discussion of the category of *practice* as the foundation stone of Marxist-Leninist epistemology is still lead by M. N. Rutkevič.[73] Others pursuing discussion of this question are A. Spirkin, I. T. Jakuševskij, Ju. F. Buxalov, Ju. G. Gajdukov, and L. M. Arxangel'skij. A newcomer to the field is A. N. Iliadi whose *The Practical Nature of Human Knowledge* (1962)[74] is a refreshing presentation of Rutkevič from the point of view of a theoretician of art. There is also a *sbornik* on the question, entitled *Practice as Criterion of Truth in Science* (1960).[75]

As contributory to the discussion of epistemological problems *methodology* ranks second in contemporary Soviet philosophy only to dialectical logic. M. M. Rozental' is the dean and undisputed leader of Soviet general methodologists.[76] G. A. Podkorytov has also made some contributions to the discussion.[77] In methodology of natural science the development has been less consistent but, nonetheless, important. Pre-eminent in the domain is P. V. Kopnin with *The Hypothesis and*

Knowledge of Reality (1962)[78] and a series of articles.[79] L. B. Baženov's *Basic Questions of the Theory of Hypothesis* (1961)[80] and articles[81] are in the same line as the works of Kopnin but show more influence of readings in recent Western works on the subject. The most eloquent contemporary Soviet philosopher on the classification of sciences is B. M. Kedrov with *Classification of Sciences* (1961)[82], the first of three volumes, and *The Object and Interconnection of the Natural Sciences* (1962).[83]

For a brief period *language* had a pre-eminently epistemological significance in the Soviet Union and, inversely, epistemology took on a linguistic character. This short-lived development was dominated by L. O. Reznikov[84] and L. M. Arxangel'skij.[85]

In the *history of philosophy* and *history of logic* epistemological questions have been most competently discussed by V. F. Asmus in a series of articles on direct knowledge in modern philosophy[86], by K. S. Bakradze – particularly in his *The System and Method of the Philosophy of Hegel*[87], and by B. M. Kedrov with *Engels and Natural Science* (1947)[88] and a flow of articles.[89]

Criticism of contemporary Western philosophy and particularly of all the trends (analytic, semanticist, linguistic analysis, etc.) which Soviet philosophers lump together under the appellation 'neopositivism' is generally epistemological in character.[90] The following are samples of the books published in this domain which have specific implications for the epistemological discussion: A. F. Begiašvili: *The Analytic Method in Contemporary Bourgeois Philosophy* (1960)[91], G. A. Brutjan: *The Theory of Knowledge of General Semantics* (1959)[92], G. A. Kursanov: *The Epistemology of Contemporary Pragmatism* (1958)[93], I. S. Narskij: *Contemporary Positivism* (1961)[94] and a series of articles by the same author[95], S. I. Popov: *Kant and Kantianism* (1961)[96] and a series of articles by the same author, dealing with the same general topic.[97]

REFERENCES

1. On this division of the history of Soviet philosophy into three periods, see J. M. Bocheński: *Der sowjetrussische dialektische Materialismus (Diamat)*. Bern. 1960. pp. 38–39 (henceforeward: Bocheński: *Diamat*) and, by the same author, *Einführung in die sowjetische Philosophie der Gegenwart*. Bonn. 1959. Paragraph 6.
2. Cf. G. A. Wetter: *Dialectical Materialism. A Historical and Systematic Survey of*

Philosophy in the Soviet Union. London. 1958. pp. 154–166. (henceforeward: Wetter: *Diamat*).

3. V. I. Čerkesov claims otherwise in the historical introduction to his *Materialist Dialectic as Logic and Theory of Knowledge* (pp. 12–53) but he can be suspected of trying to prove a point and using a 'Marxist' interpretation of the earlier events in Soviet philosophy. The more objective account in René Ahlberg's '*Dialektische Philosophie*' *und Gesellschaft in der Sowjetunion* (Berlin, 1960) rather supports our contention. An examination of A. M. Deborin's earlier articles, reprinted in *Philosophy and Politics* (Moscow, 1961), shows that his major preoccupation from an epistemological point of view was continuing Lenin's refutation of Bogdanov, Juškevič, *et al.*

4. Cf. Bocheński: *Diamat*. pp. 40–42. With progress in research on Soviet philosophy it is becoming more and more evident that this period is not as quiet as was once thought. Nevertheless, it is completely lacking the dynamic development which characterizes the first and third periods.

5. *Teorija otraženija*. Moskva–Leningrad. 1936.

6. *Očerk filosofii dialektičeskogo materializma*. Moskva–Leningrad. 1930. *Dialektičeskij i istoričeskij materializm*. Č.l. Moskva. 1933.

7. *Die Erkenntnistheorie des dialektischen Materialismus*. München–Salzburg–Köln. 1958.

8. *O poznavaemosti mira*. Moskva. 1946 (2nd ed. Moscow. 1950). For personal data on Xasxačix, see 'Pamjati filosofa-vojna' (Memorial to a Philosopher-Soldier). *VF* 1962, 12, 177.

9. 'Genezis obrazovanija ponjatij'. In *Naučnye trudy*. Tbilisi. 1946. 'Problema obrazovanija ponjatij v svete istorii jazyka'. In *Filosofskie Zapiski. I*. Moskva. 1946.

10. In Soviet epistemology – as in some other domains of contemporary Soviet philosophy, like theory of categories – there are indications that this third period should be divided into at least two subsections. The dividing point would be 1956 or 1957.

11. *Marksistskij dialektičeskij metod*. Moskva. 1947 (2nd ed. Moscow. 1951). Contributions to the discussion: A. Ja. Grekova *VF* 1948, 1, 301–305. G. F. Kir'janov *VF* 1947, 2, 374–375. L. A. Kogan *VF* 1948, 1, 297–301. V. I. Sviderskij *VF* 1947, 2, 304–310. P. S. Trofimov *VF* 1948, 1, 293–296. P. T. Belov *Bol'ševik* 1948, 4.

12. Wetter: *Diamat*. p. 161f.

13. 'O prirode fizičeskogo znanija'. *VF* 1947, 2, 140–176. Contributions to the discussion: D. I. Bloxincev *VF* 1948, 1, 212–214. D. S. Danin *VF* 1948, 1, 217–222. I. K. Kuršev and V. A. Mixajlov *VF* 1948, 1, 207–209. B. G. Kuznecov *VF* 1948, 1, 209–211. A. A. Maksimov *VF* 1948, 3, 105–124. S. A. Petruševskij *VF* 1948, 1, 211–212. L. I. Storčak *VF* 1948, 1, 203–206. Ja. P. Terleckij *VF* 1948, 3, 228–231. S. I. Vavilov *VF* 1947, 2, 138–139. M. G. Veselov and M. V. Vol'kenštejn *VF* 1948, 1, 215–216. See also a letter from some students in *VF* 1948, 1, 224 and the series of editorial comments in *VF* 1948, 1, 225–232; 1948, 2, 227; and 1948, 3, 231–235. For a survey of the whole problem, see Bocheński: *Diamat*, p. 74f. and Wetter: *Diamat*. p. 413f.

14. Cf. Wetter: *Diamat*. 149–154f.

15. *Ibid*. p. 478f.

16. *Naučnaja sessija, posvjaščennaja problemam fiziologičeskogo učenija akademika*

I. P. Pavlova. Stenografičeskij otčet. Moskva. 1950.

17. *Učenie I. P. Pavlova i filosofskie voprosy psixologii.* (edited by S. A. Petruševskij, N. N. Ladygina-Kots, F. N. Šemjakin, and E. V. Šoroxova) Moskva. 1952.
18. *Marksistsko-leninskaja teorija otraženija i učenie I. P. Pavlova o vysšej nervnoj dejatel'nosti.* Moskva. 1954.
19. *Filosofskie voprosy učenija o vysšej nervnoj dejatel'nosti.* Moskva. 1954.
20. Cf. 'Učenie I. P. Pavlova i nekotorye voprosy perestrojki psixologii' (The Doctrine of I. P. Pavlov and some Questions of the Reconstruction of Psychology). *VF* 1952, 3, 197–210.
21. *Bytie i soznanie. O meste psixičeskogo vo vseobščej vzaimosvjazi javlenij material'nogo mira.* Moskva. 1957. *O myšlenii i putjax ego issledovanija.* Moskva. 1958.
22. Cf. Wetter: *Diamat.* p. 196f.
23. Bocheński: *Diamat.* pp. 154–155. Wetter: *Diamat.* pp. 531–533f.
24. *Voprosy dialektičeskogo i istoričeskogo materializma v trude I.V. Stalina "Marksizm i voprosy jazykoznanija".* Moskva. Vyp. 1, 1951. Vyp. 2, 1952. Among the adulatory articles commenting Stalin's innovations, cf. M. D. Kammari *VF* 1950, 2, 9–30. A. S. Koval'čuk *VF* 1950, 3, 371–379. V. K. Kozlov *VF* 1953, 2, 150–157. D. Spasov *VF* 1951, 2, 182–184. B. I. Lozovskij *VF* 1951, 4, 232–238. G. A. Kursanov and S. I. Mixajlov *VF* 1953, 2, 225–229. M. A. Leonov *VF* 1952, 5, 115–131. N. S. Mansurov *VF* 1951, 5, 195–196. The editorial in *VF* 1951, 3, 3–13. A. P. Gagarin *V MGU* 1951, 9, 52. P. F. Judin *V AN SSSR* 1951, 7, 29. The editorial in *Izv. AN SSSR* 1950, 4, 322–359 and *V MGU* 1951, 7, 3. A. V. Topčiev *V AN SSSR* 1950, 7, 8. The purely linguistic point of view was represented in books such as *Protiv vul'garizacii i izvraščenija marksizma v jazykoznanii* (Against Vulgarization and Distortion of Marxism in Linguistics). Moskva. 1951. (edited by V. V. Vinogradov and B. A. Serebrennikov).
25. 'K voprosu o stupenjax processa poznanija istiny' (On the Steps in the Process of the Knowledge of Truth). *VF* 1954, 5, 77–81, which directly attacked Rutkevič's article cited in note 28.
26. In *VF* 1955, 1, 145–149.
27. *Praktika – osnova poznanija i kriterij istiny.* Moskva. 1952.
28. 'K voprosu o roli praktiki v processe poznanija'. *VF* 1954, 3, 34–45.
29. Since this was Podosetnik's only recorded sortie on the question of practice, one is justified in supposing that the whole discussion was artificially provoked for some ulterior motive. This supposition is supported by the fact that Rutkevič neither made and auto-critique nor was deposed.
30. *Dialektičeskij materializm o processe poznanija.* Moskva. 1954.
31. *Osnovy teorii poznanija.* Moskva. 1959.
32. Data based on *Bibliographie der sowjetischen Philosophie.* 1 to 4. Dordrecht–Holland. 1959–1963.
33. *Engel's i estestvoznanie.* Moskva. 1947.
34. *K probleme aksiomatizacii logike.* Tbilisi. 1947.
35. *Logičeskie zakony myšlenija.* Lenizdat. 1947.
36. *Iz istorii teorii poznanija.* Erevan. 1957.
37. *Myšlenie i jazyk.* Moskva. 1957.
38. *Sovremennyj sub"ektivnyj idealizm.* Moskva. 1957.
39. In 'K voprosu o sootnošenii logiki i dialektiki' (On the Relationship of Logic and Dialectic). *VF* 1950, 2, 198–209.

40. *Dialektika form myšlenija.* Moskva. 1959.
41. *V. I. Lenin i nekotorye voprosy teorii poznanija.* Gor'kij. 1959.
42. *Problemy dialektičeskoj logiki.* Moskva. 1959.
43. *Dialektičeskaja logika. Kratkij očerk.* Moskva. 1960.
44. *Principy dialektičeskoj logiki.* Moskva. 1960.
45. *Nekotorye voprosy teorii poznanija.* Irkutsk. 1960.
46. *Voprosy teorii poznanija.* Perm'. 1960.
47. *Voprosy teorii poznanija i logiki.* Moskva. 1960.
48. *Voprosy teorii ponjatija.* Moskva. 1961.
49. *Dialektika kak logika.* Kiev. 1961.
50. *Dialektika i logika. Formy myšlenija.* Moskva. 1962. and *Dialektika i logika. Zakony myšlenija.* Moskva. 1962.
51. *Materialističeskaja dialektika kak logika i teorija poznanija.* Moskva. 1962.
52. *Marksistskaja logika kak dialektika i teorija poznanija.* Erevan. 1963.
53. *Edinstvo dialektiki, logiki i teorii poznanija.* Moskva. 1963.
54. *Voprosy teorii poznanija v proizvedenii V. I. Lenina "Materializm i empiriokriticizm".* Minsk. 1960.
55. *Gnoseologičeskoe soderžanie logičeskix form i metodov.* Kiev. 1960.
56. *Mirovozzrenčeskoe i metodologičeskie problemy naučnoj abstrakcii.* Moskva. 1960. (translated from the Polish).
57. *Process myšlenija i zakonomernosti analiza, sinteza i obobščenija.* Moskva. 1960.
58. *Praktika – kriterij istiny v nauke.* Moskva. 1960.
59. Cf. T. J. Blakeley: *Soviet Scholasticism.* Dordrecht, Holland. 1961.
60. *Marksistskij dialektičeskij metod.* Moskva. 1947. *Razvitie V. I. Leninym marksistskoj teorii poznanija.* Moskva. 1950. *Voprosy dialektiki v "Kapitale" Marksa.* Moskva. 1955. *Principy dialektičeskoj logiki.* Moskva. 1960.
61. *Poznavaemost' mira i ego zakonomernostej.* Moskva. 1955.
62. *Problema sovpadenija dialektiki, logiki i teorii poznanija.* Alma–Ata. 1962.
63. 'K voprosu o sootnošenii logiki, dialektiki i teorii poznanija v učenii I. Kanta' (On the Relationship of Logic, Dialectic and Theory of Knowledge in the Doctrine of Kant). In *Naučnye trudy.* Alma–Ata 1960. 'O myšlenii kak predmete logiki i psixologii' (On Thought as the Object of Logic and Psychology). *VF* 1961, 7, 132–140. His dissertation, presented at the Institute of Philosophy in 1960, is entitled *Razrabotka V. I. Leninym problem sovpadenija dialektiki, logiki i teorii poznanija v "Filosofskix tetradjax"* (The Elaboration by Lenin of Problems of the Coincidence of Dialectic, Logic and Theory of Knowledge in the *Philosophic Notebooks*).
64. Cf. note 21.
65. *Teorija oščuščenij.* Leningrad. 1961. Cf. particularly the introduction, pp. 3–12, and pp. 13–32.
66. *Proisxoždenie soznanija.* Moskva. 1960.
67. Cf. the bibliography.
68. *Istorija logiki novogo vremeni.* Moskva. 1960. Cf. his articles in the bibliography.
69. *Voprosy abstrakcii i obrazovanie ponjatij.* Moskva. 1961.
70. *Dialektika abstraktnogo i konkretnogo v "Kapitale" Marksa.* Moskva. 1960.
71. Cf. the bibliography.
72. E.g., Zinov'ev's 'O razrabotke dialektiki kak logiki' (On the Elaboration of the Dialectic as a Logic). *VF* 1957, 4, 188–190. and Janovskaja's 'Problemy analiza ponjatij nauki i novejšij neopozitivizm' (Problems of the Analysis of the Concepts

of Science and Modern Neopositivism). *VF* 1961, 6, 47–53.

73. Recent contributions by Rutkevič include 'Dialektičeskij xarakter kriterija praktiki' (The Dialectical Character of the Criterion of Practice). *VF* 1959, 9, 43-52. and 'Praktika kak kriterij istinnosti znanij' (Practice as Criterion of the Truth-Value of Knowledge) in the *sbornik* cited in note 58.

74. *Praktičeskaja priroda čelovečeskogo poznanija.* Moskva. 1962.

75. Cf. note 58.

76. Cf. T. J. Blakeley: *Soviet Scholasticism.* Dordrecht, Holland. 1961, and the list of Rozental''s books and articles in the bibliography.

77. The most recent being 'O ponjatii naučnogo metoda' (On the Concept of Scientific Method). *V LGU* 1962, 11, 72–82. and 'Sootnošenie dialektičeskogo metoda s častnonaučnymi metodami' (Relation of the Dialectical Method to the Methods of the Single Sciences). *VF* 1962, 6, 36–47.

78. *Gipoteza i poznanie dejstvitel'nosti.* Kiev. 1962.

79. For example, 'Gipoteza kak forma razvitija nauki' (The Hypothesis as a Form of the Development of Science). In *Naučnye trudy.* Tomsk. 1954, and 'O xaraktere znanija, soderžaščegosja v gipoteze' (On the Character of Knowledge Contained in the Hypothesis). *FN* 1958, 2, 106–120.

80. *Osnovnye voprosy teorii gipotezy.* Moskva. 1961.

81. E.g., 'O gipoteze v estestvoznanii' (On the Hypothesis in Natural Science). *VF* 1962, 9, 154–164.

82. *Klassifikacija nauk.* Moskva. 1961.

83. *Predmet i vzaimosvjaz' estestvennyx nauk.* Moskva. 1962. This is the first volume of a projected ten-volume series, 'Dialectical Materialism and Contemporary Natural Science', under the joint auspices of the Institute of Philosophy and the Scientific Soviet for Philosophic Problems of Natural Science. The project is to be completed in seven or eight years.

84. Cf. his long series of articles in the bibliography.

85. Whose dissertation at the University of the Urals was entitled, *Marksizm-leninizm o edinstve jazyka i myšlenija* (Marxism-Leninism on the Unity of Language and Thought).

86. Cf. *VF* 1955, 5, 43–56; 1957, 6, 59–61; 1959, 11, 128–140; 1962, 9, 112–120.

87. *Sistema i metod filosofii Gegelja.* Tbilisi. 1958.

88. Cf. note 33.

89. Cf. the bibliography.

90. Cf. W. F. Boeselager: 'Recent Soviet Works on Neopositivism'. *Studies in Soviet Thought* III (1963) 230–242 and IV (1964) 81–84.

91. *Metod analiza v sovremennoj buržuaznoj filosofii.* Tbilisi. 1960.

92. *Teorija poznanija obščej semantiki.* Erevan. 1959.

93. *Gnoseologija sovremennogo pragmatizma.* Moskva. 1958.

94. *Sovremennyj pozitivizm.* Moskva. 1961.

95. Cf. the bibliography.

96. *Kant i kantianstvo.* Moskva. 1961.

97. Cf. the bibliography.

CHAPTER II

GENERAL CHARACTERISTICS OF
MARXIST-LENINIST THEORY OF KNOWLEDGE

4. SOURCES

Pre-Soviet Russian philosophy had very little epistemological tradition of its own. "In Russian philosophy – so far as one can judge from its century and a half of development – there are certain specific characteristics which in general relegate theory of knowledge to a secondary place. With the exception of a small group of orthodox Kantians, Russian philosophers have tended in the solution of epistemological problems to *ontologism,* i.e. the recognition that cognition is not the primary and defining principle in man. . . . we may say briefly that Russian ontologism expresses not the priority of 'reality' to knowledge, but the inclusion of knowledge in our relationship to the world, our 'activity' in it."[1] It was with the 1917 Revolution and the consequent shake-up in Russian society that the problem of knowledge came to Russia. It came as a part of 'dialectical materialism', a philosophic aggregate composed of selected passages from the works of Marx, Engels and Lenin.[2]

These three men certainly had a number of things in common. They were all fascinated by the architectonic beauty of the Hegelian dialectic which they took to be a 'mode of being' rather than a 'mode of thought'[3]; they were all convinced that only materialism (viz. anti-Hegelianism) could offer a satisfactory explanation of the world; finally, they were all caught up in the nineteenth-century wave of enthusiasm for 'science' as the means of arriving at a final explanation of the whole of reality. Nevertheless, the basic differences evident in the background and education of each of them make it seem *a priori* quite hazardous to try to build up a theory of knowledge which would be equally representative of the thought of each. Marx was a professionally trained philosopher; Engels learned his philosophy of society from Marx and his philosophy of science through his own readings; Lenin, a lawyer, learned the little philosophy he knew from Plekhanov and his own readings of Hegel, Aristotle, etc. There is, therefore, no question here of trying to reconstruct *ex post factum* the 'classical' theory of knowledge. This is precisely the task which contemporary Soviet philosophy has set itself. Our interest is limited to the elements in the works of Marx, Engels and Lenin which have been selected for this task by the Soviet philosophers themselves.

Karl Marx wrote no work which can be properly characterized as epistemological. Outside of the numerous excerpts from *The Capital*, with which contemporary Soviet writers on theory of knowledge embellish their articles, the sole epistemological comment by Marx which remains in force in contemporary Soviet thought is the second thesis on Feuerbach: "The question as to whether human thought attains objective reality is not a theoretical but a *practical* question. Man must prove the truth, i.e. reality and power and actuality, of his thought in practice. The conflict on the reality or irreality of a thought which is separated from practice is a purely scholastic question."[4] However, certain derivations from Marx' theory of alienation – which is seldom mentioned by Soviet philosophers today – continue to influence the spirit of Soviet epistemology. The basic alienations are listed by Marx as: *an sich – für sich* (in Self – for Self), *Bewußtsein – Selbstbewußtsein* (consciousness – selfconsciousness), and *Objekt – Subjekt* (object – subject) whereby "the human essence ... in opposition to abstract thought objectifies itself"[5], which is to be overcome by a socio-economic revolution which will make it so that "man becomes the supreme being for men".[6] On the strictly epistemological plane, Marx attempted to invert Hegel. Whereas Hegel – according to Marx – had put the predicate (e.g. the State) in the place of the subject (e.g. man) thus deducing the real from the abstract and substantializing the abstract (the idea) as the real, Marx wanted to put man (back) as center of reality and relegate all abstractions to the realm of derivatives.[7]

This inversion – already hazardous in view of the immensity of the Hegelian synthesis – makes Marx' thought difficult to interpret. Adding to this inherent difficulty is the fact that Marx' heritage was interpreted out by an Engels, who was untrained in philosophy and more interested in science and philosophy of science than in a metaphysics of man, by a Lenin who was very busy most of his relatively brief life and who saw Marx through his rather eclectic readings of Hegel, Aristotle, etc., and

14

by Soviet philosophers who are bound to an official interpretation of this already limited tradition.

Friedrich Engels wrote three works which touch on questions of theory of knowledge. From *Anti-Dühring* (1878)[8], Soviet philosophy has extracted two fundamental thoughts. First, human thought, properly speaking, is not that of one man but rather the individual thoughts of many billions of past, present and future humans. Just as, for 'Marxist historicism', it is the group rather than the individual which makes history, so in 'Marxist epistemology' it is the totality of human thought, the sum-total of the thought of mankind, which is the object under investigation. Engels, in his polemic with Dühring, adds that 'sovereignty' is a characteristic not of the individual act of knowing but of the absolute knowledge of the totality of humanity. In reference to individual acts of knowing, then, truth and error are dialectically polar opposites which have absolute validity only in a limited domain. Second, there are three types of sciences, distinguished by the number of 'absolute truths' which they can provide: the sciences on inanimate nature do provide a few incontrovertible 'absolute truths'; the sciences on animate nature are already much poorer in this regard; finally, the sciences on history provide almost no 'absolute truths' excepting a few banalities.[9]

In *Ludwig Feuerbach* (1888)[10] are to be found four further theses. Engels states the 'basic question of all philosophy': which is primary, thought or being, spirit or matter? The 'second side' or 'aspect' of this 'basic question' is: can we know the world accurately? Further, Engels defines the 'dialectic' as the general laws of the movement of the external world and of thought. The 'two series' (laws of the world and laws of thought) are 'factually identical' but differ 'in expression' the second being amenable to conscious application by the human knower. Philosophy has been eliminated from nature and history; alone as object of philosophy remains logic and dialectic as science of the laws of the thought-process.

Engels' *Dialectics of Nature*[11] falls into the class of 'non-books': it is the carcass of a work which he began around 1873 but never finished. It was first published in Moscow in 1925. Among the theses to be found in its disjointed components, the following are of significance for contemporary Soviet theory of knowledge: The science on thought is

15

the science on the history of thought. The 'subjective dialectic' is the reflection of the 'motion through opposites' of the 'objective dialectic'. 'Dialectical logic' is higher than formal logic since it derives judgements one from the other instead of just juxtaposing them. Just as 'infinite matter' is composed of finite things, so 'absolute knowledge' is composed of the activities of finite minds. The infinite (the 'law') is known in the finite.

It is Lenin, however, who must be considered the actual founder of the Marxist-Leninist theory of knowledge. His *Materialism and Empirio-Criticism* (1909) is the only 'classic' work which is completely devoted to theory of knowledge. The book is a polemic against Mach and Avenarius and against their Russian disciples: A. A. Bogdanov, V. A. Bazarov, N. V. Valentinov, and others. As such, it is far more a case-book of what Joravsky calls "the frightful style of quote and club"[12] than of well thought-out and clearly presented philosophic arguments. In the introduction Lenin puts selected quotations from the works of Mach and Avenarius in parallel with those of Berkeley, showing – according to Lenin – that empiriocriticism is little more than a latter-day version of 'subjective idealism'. Lenin's central theme is that, although the 'idealists' – with their 'matter has disappeared; therefore, only thought remains' – are currently having a field-day in the natural sciences, they are in reality only an infinitesimal minority, and the vast majority of scientists are, with 'dialectically gradual necessity', coming around 'spontaneously' to the materialist view, whence they will eventually attain the only true theory of knowledge for modern science, that of dialectical materialism. In the first chapter Lenin refutes the Machist contention that the world is made up of 'elements' (i.e. sense-data) with the following common-sensical argument: there are sensations; sensations are either of self or of other things; if sensations were of self, there would be no communication and no world; therefore, sensations are of other things; whence it follows that there are things external to us. Chapter Two defends Engels against Černov's contention that Engels held for the subjectivity of sense-knowledge. According to Lenin, any good dialectical materialist – therefore, *a fortiori*, Engels – holds that knowledge is the reflection of the external world; practice is the criterion of its truth; absolute truth is composed of relative truths. In the third chapter, Lenin attacks the 'Machist' interpretation of a

16

series of categories; causality, space and time, freedom and necessity, etc., but his most significant thesis is: the Russian Machist contention that Engels' definition of philosophy is circular misses the point; matter and spirit can only be described one in reference to the other and not defined because they are the most general terms of philosophic discourse – they are the *summa genera* which fall, therefore, under no other *genus*. Chapter Four is the prototype of Soviet philosophy's 'assimilation and condemnation' technique. Lenin assimilates all his opponents – empirio-symbolism, empirio-monism, immanentism, Kantianism, Berkeleyianism, Humism, etc. – to 'Machism' and to empirio-criticism and considers them condemned for the same reason, i.e. for not admitting the existence of an external, objective reality. A more gentle condemnation is reserved for Plekhanov's 'hieroglyphs' which Lenin regrets as giving the 'idealists' a toe-hold in their attempt to destroy dialectical materialism. Chapter Five presents Lenin's central thesis on the inevitable dialectical-materialization of natural science. In the sixth chapter Lenin fires a parting shot at the empirio-critical distortion of historical materialism, due – according to Lenin – to an identification of 'social being' with 'social thought'.

Like Engels' *Dialectics of Nature*, Lenin's *Philosophical Notebooks*[13] is a non-book. B. M. Kedrov has this to say about it: "... all the materials of the Leninist *Philosophical Notebooks* can be provisionally distributed into the following groups, which are of unequal significance: (1) quotations, (2) extracts from quotations, (3) evaluational remarks, (4) interrogative remarks, (5) interpretative remarks, (6) aphoristic remarks, (7) fragmentary generalizations, (8) planification notes, (9) fragments with a generalizing character."[14] Most of these sections were written around 1915. They were first published in the *Leninist Miscellanies* of 1929–1930, and in book form in 1933. The work contains the following epistemological theses: Logical laws are 'empirical' in the sense that they are the result of the million-fold repetition of certain 'practical figures' which, therefore, obtain the value of axioms. Concepts are flexible, not 'sophistically' but 'dialectically'. Truth is a process, not only of knowing reality but also of transforming it. The 'logical' and the 'historical' must, by and large, coincide. Logic, dialectic and theory of knowledge are the same (three words are not needed). Knowledge has the form of a series of spirally ascending circles, incessant approximations to absolute truth. The history of philosophy is the

17

history of knowledge. Theory of knowledge and dialectics should be built up from: (1) the history of the separate sciences, (2) the history of the mental development of the child, (3) the history of the mental development of animals, (4) the study of language, (5) psychology, (6) the physiology of the sense organs.

There are many factors which contribute to the heterogeneous character of Marxist-Leninist philosophy. Among them, and of particular significance for contemporary Soviet theory of knowledge is the delay in publication both of the *Dialectics of Nature* and of the *Philosophical Notebooks*. Lenin constituted himself the official interpreter of the theory of knowledge of dialectical materialism but the *Dialectics of Nature* was unknown to him, at least at the time of his writing of *Materialism and Empirio-Criticism*. This means that – as of 1925 – Soviet philosophy disposed of two major sources on theory of knowledge: Lenin's more or less synthetic presentation in *Materialism and Empirio-Criticism* where he explicitated not only his own thought but also an interpretation of that of Engels; and Engels' *Dialectics of Nature*, uninterpreted by Lenin. The views of Soviet philosophers on theory of knowledge were already forming when the *Philosophical Notebooks* appeared in 1933 – a period when Soviet philosophy was already in the grip of Stalinist 'hero-worship' *(kul't ličnosti)*.

5. THE PLACE OF THEORY OF KNOWLEDGE IN DIALECTICAL MATERIALISM

The philosophy of Marxism-Leninism is composed of dialectical materialism and historical materialism. The latter was established – at least as concerns its basic principles – by Marx and Engels. The former is a latter-day construct, distilled out of the works of Marx, Engels and Lenin, which is gradually being amplified and completed by contemporary Soviet philosophers.[15] The standard textbook presentation of dialectical materialism has the following major sections: Matter and its existential forms; Matter and consciousness; The regular bonds of the phenomena of reality; The laws of the dialectic; The dialectic of the process of knowledge.[16]

Knowledge, then, appears twice. By and large the distinction between the two is that in the first (Matter and consciousness) knowledge is viewed as a 'property' of matter – like motion, space and time, while in the second (The dialectic of the process of knowledge) knowing is viewed as the function of an agent, sense-knowledge and 'rational' knowledge are distinguished, and the question of practice crowns the whole dialectical-materialist edifice.

This ambiguity of optic is due – at least in part – to a confusion which one passage from Lenin's *Philosophical Notebooks* introduced into Soviet philosophy and, in the second place, to the failure of contemporary Soviet philosophers to satisfactorily determine – on dialectical-materialist principles – the exact relationship between mental and physical events.

The first of these confusions revolves around the exact sense of the Russian word '*sovpadenie*' which Lenin used in defining the relationship between 'dialectic', logic and theory of knowledge. The 'problem of *sovpadenie*' as it appears in Soviet philosophy today can be formulated as follows: is there one philosophical science – called 'materialist dialectic' or 'dialectical materialism' – which has as its proper object the totality of dialectical reality; or does dialectical materialism contain three distinct parts each of which has its own proper object, to wit dialectic – as the science on the dialectical nature of reality (matter), logic – as the science on the forms of thought, and theory of knowledge – as the science on the processes and validity of thought? From the prestige point of view: does dialectical materialism retain the traditional distinction in philosophy between ontology, logic and epistemology? or is it a new and 'revolutionary' philosophy which has no need of such a division?

One way – the most obvious it seems – of solving this problem would be to carefully observe the activities of those contemporary Soviet philosophers who occupy themselves with these and related questions. One would then be able to say that, as a matter of fact, the three sets of questions are developed in different ways, with different terminologies, with distinct conceptual apparatuses and, generally, by different men; or that the same men use the same techniques, terminology and conceptual apparatus – that, therefore, there is only one philosophical science on these questions. Soviet philosophers, however, take the exegetic path.

Engels set the stage for the *sovpadenie*-problem when he said: "As soon as each special science is required to make clear its position in the totality of things and of knowledge as a whole, a special science dealing with the totality is superfluous. What still independently remains of all earlier philosophy is the study of thought and its laws – formal logic and dialectics. Everything else is absorbed in the positive science of nature and history."[17] Lenin explicitated this positivist affirmation in a rather Hegelian form. "In *Capital* is applied to one science the logic, dialectic and theory of knowledge of materialism (there is no need for three words: it is one and the same thing) . . ."[18] But the real crux of the problem – to judge by contemporary Soviet writings on the subject – is the following passage from Lenin's *Philosophical Notebooks*: ". . . logic coincides with *(sovpadaet s)* the theory of knowledge."[19] Now, the Russian word *'sovpadat''* is a linguistic calque on the Latin *'coincidere' (so-v-padat' = co-in-cidere)* and its root-meaning is, there-fore, 'coincide'. But, in ordinary usage *sovpadat'* also means 'to be identical with'. Therefore, Lenin's statement that logic *sovpadaet s* theory of knowledge can be interpreted in two ways: 'logic coincides with theory of knowledge' or 'logic is identical with theory of knowledge'. This confusion is all the more strange because Lenin himself – at least in *Materialism and Empirio-Criticism* – was perfectly aware of the ambiguity of *sovpadat'*, precisely in the context of theory of knowledge. He wrote: "This is either an idealist lie or the subterfuge of the agnostic, Comrade Bazarov, for sense-perception *is not* the reality existing outside of us, it is only the *image* of that reality. Are you trying to make capital of the ambiguous Russian word *sovpadat'*? Are you trying to lead the unsophisticated reader to believe that *sovpadat'* here means 'to be identical', and not 'to correspond'? That means basing one's falsification of Engels *à la Mach* on a perversion of the meaning of a quotation and nothing more." (p. 110, Engl.)[20] Fifty years later, Lenin's philosophical heirs are still trying to decide who is the 'Machian idealist' in the solution of the question of the interrelations of dialectic, logic and theory of knowledge: those who interpret the *sovpadenie* as an identity or those who give it the meaning of coincidence.[21]

Those contemporary Soviet philosophers who hold to the identity-interpretation can be called the 'classicists' because they tend to hold conservative, dogmatically bound, opinions on most of the other questions discussed in contemporary Soviet philosophy. The classicists are in a very strong position because of Lenin's statement that there is

20

no need for three words. On the other hand, they are in a very weak philosophical position since they have not been able up to now to find a satisfactory philosophical explanation of the fact that the three sciences are actually distinguished in contemporary Soviet philosophical practice. Typical of this line of thought is the following passage from the *History of Philosophy:* "Analysis of the basic traits of dialectical materialism in the works of Marx and Engels shows that the materialist dialectic – to use the terms of the old philosophic systems – is not only an ontology (doctrine on being) but also an epistemology (theory of knowledge), and the logic of Marxism. In dialectical materialism is found the unity, coincidence, of the dialectic, logic and the theory of knowledge, the importance of which was especially stressed by V. I. Lenin in the *Philosophical Notebooks.*" [22] In the other official presentations of dialectical materialism the opinion is uniform.[23] The *Philosophic Encyclopedia* says: "The materialist dialectic is at the same time the theory of knowledge and the logic of Marxism, since the laws of the dialectic are the laws of being and knowledge." [24] In other words, according to the classicist position, there is one dialectical-materialist philosophical science: the using of three different words to designate it is merely an unfortunate remnant of the "old philosophic systems".

The other interpretation of the *sovpadenie* – as coincidence of dialectic, logic and theory of knowledge – has been increasingly espoused by the 'modernist' wing of contemporary Soviet philosophy, by those who in word and deed are moving more and more in the direction of a rationalization of dialectical materialism and of its theory of knowledge. One will note in the following passage from *On the 'Philosophical Notebooks' of V. I. Lenin,* however, that the authors are quite cautious in their wording lest their opponents condemn them by showing that they have departed from the letter of Lenin's pronouncements: "However, the affirmation of the unity (identity, coincidence) of the dialectic, theory of knowledge and logic, which is explained on the basis of the general laws of the dialectic, should not be taken as a denial of a specific process of knowledge or thought. Its specific character appears in special problems of theory of knowledge and logic and justifies the right to existence of theory of knowledge and dialectical logic as parts of Marxist philosophy, which are inseparably bound up with the dialectic and identical to it as to their laws and categories." [25] (p. 260) Whereas the classicists affirm an absolute 'overlapping' of dialectic, logic and theory of knowledge, the modernists hold that the three sciences overlap as to some essentials (laws and categories) but differ as to others (e.g. mode of procedure, field of application). The coincidence consists in the fact that all three 'Marxist' sciences – dialectic, logic and theory of knowledge – operate on the same basis, i.e. on the laws of the dialectic. Schematically, the two positions can be represented as follows:

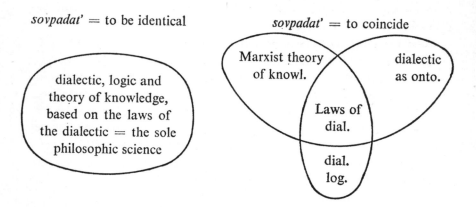

sovpadat' = to be identical

dialectic, logic and theory of knowledge, based on the laws of the dialectic = the sole philosophic science

sovpadat' = to coincide

Marxist theory of knowl.

dialectic as onto.

Laws of dial.

dial. log.

This whole discussion had a rather academic and abstruse character until the facts of life – in this case the development of the applications of mathematical logic in Soviet industry – forced the dialectical-materialists to clarify the whole question of logic, its types and its relationship to philosophy. Coupled with this situation – and contributing significantly to it – was the alacrity with which Soviet philosophers followed up Stalin's 'de-classification' of linguistics with a similar operation in logic.[26] By 1950 it had become evident that some precision would have to be given to dialectical materialism's underdeveloped area – 'dialectical logic'.

The existence and excellence of dialectical logic had been definitely and repeatedly affirmed by the classics – especially by Engels and Lenin[27] – but they had left unanswered a whole series of questions. The answering of these questions was important for the development of dialectical materialism but it was of utmost importance if dialectical materialism were to receive anything more than a nod from the rest of

22

the philosophic world which is strongly influenced by mathematical logic and by the enormous progress which formal logic has made in the last two or three decades. Soviet philosophers made an all-out effort in 1950 and 1951 to definitively establish the limits between formal and dialectical logic.[28] That they did not fully succeed is due – at least in part – to the great complexity of the problem.

All the participants in the discussion had to agree on one proposition: there is a dialectical logic because Engels and Lenin said so. With this taken for granted, there are four ways to dialectical-materialistically solve the problem.

(a) If the *sovpadenie* means 'coincidence' and logic is dialectical logic, then the place of formal logic must be explained. Solution (of V. I. Čerkesov, A. D. Aleksandrov, V. P. Rožin, and others): formal logic is a 'special case' or 'lower calculus' within dialectical logic. Dialectical logic is the philosophic science on the universal relations which exist in reality. Formal logic is the philosophic science on the purely formal aspects of these relations; therefore, it is subsumed to dialectical logic as part to whole. This description is in line with Engels' statement that formal logic is to dialectical logic as lower mathematics is to higher mathematics. This is the view which triumphed in the discussion since it was officially approved in the editorial which was supposedly the end of the discussion.[29]

(b) If the *sovpadenie* means 'identity' and logic is dialectical logic, then formal logic ceases to exist; for only a 'dialectical' logic can be identical to the Marxist dialectic and to the Marxist theory of knowledge. According to this view of I. I. Os'makov and others formal logic has had its day; the only logic of any significance in contemporary philosophy is dialectical logic. Mathematical logic, which pretends to be the successor of the old formal logic, is nothing more than 'idealist obscurantism'. This current of opinion was already moribund at the time of the discussion: it has since died out completely – without even the *coup de grâce* of an official condemnation.

(c) If the *sovpadenie* means 'coincidence' and logic is formal logic, then it is necessary to explain how dialectical logic is more than just a word. Solution: dialectical logic is 'Marxist epistemology'. This view – seemingly the most tenable from the empirical point of view – was precisely the most violently attacked in the 'official decision' which was

23

to have closed the discussion. Held – with nuances – by K. S. Bakradze, N. I. Kondakov and others, this interpretation maintains that logic is formal logic, i.e. the philosophic science dealing with the 'forms' of thought; dialectical logic, which also deals with thought, is the philosophic science on the 'content' of thought. In other words, dialectical logic deals rather with how that which the knower knows corresponds to the known – it is 'Marxist epistemology'.

(d) If the *sovpadenie* means 'identity' and logic is formal logic, then it remains to be shown how formal logic is dialectical so that it can coincide with the dialectic and theory of knowledge. This position did not figure significantly in the discussion under review but it has emerged since 1960 as one of the goals of the flow of literature on dialectical logic.[30]

That the question of dialectical logic was anything but settled by the discussion is evidenced by the fact that Bakradze and Kondakov came back to the charge in 1956[31] and also by the fact that a significant number of contemporary Soviet philosophers have accepted the challenge and are devoting themselves to developing dialectical logic in great detail.[32]

Soviet epistemology's positioning within dialectical materialism also depends on the solution given to the problem of the relationship of psychology and physiology which depends, in turn, on the explanation – on the systematic level – given to the 'mind – body' problem. Treatment of this question in Soviet philosophy has been, to say the least, hit and miss. For several years in the period beginning around Lenin's death (1924), various attempts were made at the construction of a philosophical psychology of dialectical materialism, based on experimental theories like the reflexology of Bechterev and the reactology of Kornilov.[33] A serious effort in the direction of a philosophic theory of psychology, based on dialectical materialism, did not make its appearance until the period around the publication of S. L. Rubinštejn's *Principles of General Psychology* (1940).[34] These efforts were cut short by the Joint Session of the Academy of Sciences of the USSR and the Academy of Medical Sciences (1950) which condemned Rubinštejn as an 'idealist' and decreed the 're-Pavlovization' of Soviet psychology.[35] That the subsequent efforts at a 're-materialisation' of contemporary Soviet philosophical psychology have not yet achieved any positive results can be seen from a comparison of the conflicting opinions presented at the 1950 conference with current Soviet writings on psychology and its relationship to dialectical-materialist theory of knowledge.

Contemporary Soviet philosophy claims to be a 'monistic materialism', a claim which we will examine in detail in its place. But, the advocacy of monism does present the following quandary to a philosopher who would try to explain 'mental events': either the mental events are identical with the physical events and it is pointless to speak of a psychology distinct from physiology, or mental events are distinct from physical events; if the distinction is only quantitative, the same difficulty appears of distinguishing a psychology from a physiology (because psychology would still be dealing with the same physical events but which have become 'mental' because 'bigger' in one respect or another); if the distinction is fundamentally qualitative, then there is reason to ask what 'monism' means here.

The participants in the 1950 discussion (and the authors of some books and a series of articles which followed in the *Voprosy filosofii*[36]) did defend points of view which – taking into account differences of vocabulary depending on whether the speaker was mainly psychologist or mainly physiologist – correspond to the above dilemma. These points of view may be summarised as follows:

(1) Psychic phenomena (mental events) are higher neural phenomena (physical events) was the point of view prevailing up to the opening of the conference. Its opponents pointed out that, if this be so, there would be no psychology, or only a physiology called psychology. Since the conference such views have tended to vanish until now they are of mainly historical interest.

(2) The psychic and physical are two 'sides' *(storony)* or aspects of material nature which is one. Thus, physical events would cause two qualitatively distinct groups of effects: mental events and other physical events. For example, the sensitization of the cortical nerve ends would cause physical effects in the brain and, at the same time, mental effects in the 'psyché' (which is not a 'soul' but the 'subjective aspect' of neural reaction). From this point of view, the object of physiology would be the investigation of the physical events – both causes and effects – and that of psychology would be the analysis of the laws of the mental events caused by neural activity.

25

(3) The third point of view is, in fact, not a solution but a dogmatic affirmation: the psychic is the 'subjective portion' of the physical. The problem is not solved but avoided.

Contemporary Soviet literature on psychology and theory of knowledge as related to one another gives evidence that the problem has not been solved even to the satisfaction of the least demanding of contemporary Soviet philosophers. In *On the 'Philosophical Notebooks' of V. I. Lenin* we read: "Psychology, based on the physiology of higher neural activity, studies psychic processes which arise as a result of the activity of the milieu on the central nervous system. The theory of reflection of dialectical materialism is the philosophic basis for the materialistic study of these processes. In their turn, the data of psychology are necessary material for the elaboration of the theory of knowledge. Psychology is, to a great extent, an experimental science. ... Theory of knowledge, not being an experimental science, uses certain results of the experimental data obtained by psychology."[37] In a similar vein, A. X. Kasymžanov makes the following distinctions: logic is the theory of 'knowing thought' *(poznajuščego myšlenija)*; theory of knowledge is the theory of the process of knowledge as the reflection of the 'objective dialectic of things' *('logika' veščej)*; psychology is the theory of thought, studied in the system of relations (which are) determined by the real situation, acting on the individual.[38] Thus, the lack of a serious and defendable distinction between psychology and physiology has forced contemporary Soviet philosophers to temporize by giving a purely functional description of the distinction between psychology and theory of knowledge. Most philosophers could grant that describing psychology as a mainly empirical science and theory of knowledge as a mainly philosophical one is a pedagogically interesting distinction; but it has little philosophic relevance until one knows if the empirical data with which psychology deals are the same as those dealt with by physiology.

These two central issues – the effort to develop a 'dialectical' logic and the search for a satisfactory dialectical-materialist philosophical psychology – set the tone in contemporary Soviet theory of knowledge and contribute to its basic ambivalence. On the one hand, there is an almost mystical way of speaking and of approaching questions, generated by the attempts at founding a 'non-formal' logic *(soderžatel'naja logika)*.

26

On the other, there is a definite tendency toward 'functional' definitions of epistemological categories, stemming from the unresolved antinomy of 'mental' and 'physical'.

REFERENCES

1. V. V. Zenkovsky: *A History of Russian Philosophy.* London. 1953. 2 vols. Here: Vol. 1, p. 5.
2. For general surveys, see Bocheński: *Diamat;* Wetter: *Diamat;* H. B. Acton: *The Illusion of the Epoch. Marxism-Leninism as a Philosophical Creed.* London. 1955.
3. The best survey in English of Hegel's philosophy is J. N. Findlay: *Hegel. A Re-examination.* London. 1958.
4. First published as appendix to Engels' *Ludwig Feuerbach* (Stuttgart. 1888), pp. 69–72. Already in the notes to his doctoral dissertation Marx said: "Allein die *Praxis* der Philosophie ist selbst *theoretisch . . .*" Indem die Philosophie als Wille sich gegen die erscheinende Welt herauskehrt, ist das System zu einer abstrakten Totalität herabgesetzt, das heißt, es ist zu einer Seite der Welt geworden, der eine andere gegenübersteht. Sein Verhältnis zur Welt ist ein Reflexionsverhältnis. Begeistert mit dem Trieb, sich zu verwirklichen, tritt es in Spannung gegen anderes." (cf. Karl Marx: *Die Frühschriften.* Herausgegeben von Siegfried Landshut. Stuttgart. 1953. pp. 15–16).
5. Marx: *op. cit.* p. 261.
6. *Ibid.* p. 216.
7. *Ibid.* p. 32f.
8. *Herrn Eugen Dührings Umwälzung der Wissenschaft.* Leipzig. 1878. (MEGA Sonderausgabe: Moscow. 1935). English: *Herr Eugen Dühring's Revolution in Science (Anti-Dühring).* Chicago. 1935.
9. Engels: *op. cit.* (English) p. 86f.
10. *Ludwig Feuerbach und der Ausgang der klassischen deutschen Philosophie.* (Articles published in *Neue Zeit.* 1886). Stuttgart. 1888. English in: K. Marx, F. Engels: *Selected Works,* I–II. Moscow–London. 1950–1951.
11. *Dialektik der Natur* (MEGA Sonderausgabe). Moscow. 1935. English: London. 1934. and Moscow–London. 1954–1955.
12. David Joravsky: *Soviet Marxism and Natural Science 1917–1932.* London. 1961. p. 36.
13. *Filosofskie tetrady.* Moskva. 1933. English: V. I. Lenin: *Collected Works.* Moscow. 1960ff. Vol. 39.
14. B. M. Kedrov: 'O leninskix tetradjax po filosofii' (On the Leninist Notebooks on Philosophy). *VF* 1947, 2, 55–83. Here: p. 73.
15. To follow the current evolution, consult the works in the series, *Sovietica,* and the quarterly, *Studies in Soviet Thought,* both published by the Institute of East-European Studies of the University of Fribourg (Switzerland).
16. Cf. *Osnovy marksistskoj filosofii* (Principles of Marxist Philosophy). Moskva. 1958 (Henceforeward: *Osnovy*). *Dialektičeskij materializm* (Edited by A. D. Makarov, A. V. Vostrikov and E. N. Česnokov). Moskva. 1960. I. D. Andreev: *Dialektičeskij materializm.* Moskva. 1960. *Dialektičeskij materializm* (Edited by D. I. Danilenko). Moskva. 1961.
17. Engels: *Anti-Dühring* (English) p. 23.

18. V. I. Lenin: *Sočinenija* (Complete Works). 4th ed. Moskva. 1941ff. (Henceforeward: Lenin: *Soč.* followed by volume and page). Here: t. 38, p. 15.
19. Lenin: *Filosofskie tetrady*. Moskva. 1947. p. 150.
20. Lenin: *Materializm i empiriokriticizm.* (*Soč.* t. 14). English: *Materialism and Empirio-Criticism.* Moscow–London. 1952. Here: English, p. 110.
21. "Among Soviet philosophers there are two points of view on the interpretation of Lenin's statements. Some say that Lenin had in mind the *identity* of dialectic, logic and theory of knowledge. Others maintain that Lenin had in mind the *unity* of dialectic, logic and theory of knowledge." (*Filosofskaja enciklopedija* (Philosophical Encyclopedia). Moskva. 1960ff (Henceforeward: *FE*). Here: vol. 1, p. 485 note).
22. *Istorija filosofii* (The History of Philosophy). Moskva. 1957ff. Here: vol. 3, p. 247.
23. *Osnovy* p. 303f. Cf. also *FE* vol. 1, p. 485f.
24. *FE* vol. 1, p. 477.
25. *O "Filosofskix tetradjax" V. I. Lenina* (On the *Philosophic Notebooks* of Lenin). Moskva. 1959. p. 260.
26. Cf. Chapter I, p. 3.
27. Engels: *Anti-Dühring* p. 151. *Dialectics of Nature* pp. 58, 282. Lenin: *Soč.* 23, 72.
28. Cf. Chapter I, pp. 4–5.
29. Briefly, "The Marxist point of view boils down to the following: formal logic is the science of the elementary laws and forms of correct thought . . . Formal logic is elementary. . . . There are not two formal logics; the old, metaphysical, and the new, dialectical, . . . Marxist dialectical logic coincides with *(sovpadaet s)* the dialectic and theory of knowledge of Marxism; it is, in essence, identical with them." 'K itogam obsuždenija voprosov logiki' (Conclusion of the Discussion on Questions of Logic). *VF* 1951, 6, 143–149. Here: p. 146.
30. Cf. Chapter I, pp. 6–7.
31. Cf. K. S. Bakradze: 'Protiv nenaučnoj i nedobrožedatel'noj kritiki' (Against Unscientific and Evil-Minded Criticism). *VF* 1956, 2, 218–224 and N. I. Kondakov: 'O formal'noj logike' (On Formal Logic). *VF* 1956, 2, 224–228.
32. Cf. Chapter I, pp. 6–7.
33. Cf. G. A. Wetter: *Philosophie und Naturwissenschaft in der Sowjetunion*. Hamburg. 1958. pp. 96–112.
34. *Osnovy obščej psixologii*. Moskva. 1940.
35. Cf. Chapter I, Reference 16. Cf. also *Filosofskie voprosy fiziologii vysšej nervnoj dejatel'nosti i psixologii* (Philosophical Questions of the Physiology of Higher Nervous Activity and of Psychology). Moskva. 1963.
36. Cf. Wetter: *loc.cit.* and our Chapter I, pp. 2–3.
Cf. also Bocheński: *Diamat* pp. 68–69.
37. *O "Filosofskix tetradjax" V. I. Lenina* p. 257.
38. 'O myšlenii kak predmete logiki i psixologii' (On Thought as the Object of Logic and Psychology). *VF* 1961, 7, 132–140. For a résumé of the discussion, cf. Ja. V. Bol'šunov, V. G. Safrošin: 'Ob osveščenii problemy sootnošenija material'nogo i psixičeskogo v sovetskoj filosofskoj literature' (On the Clarification of the Problem of the Relationship of the Material and Psychic in Soviet Philosophical Literature). *FN* 1962, 6, 101–105.

CHAPTER III

THE MAIN TENETS OF THE THEORY OF KNOWLEDGE OF DIALECTICAL MATERIALISM

The theory of knowledge of contemporary dialectical materialism is marked off from that of any other contemporary philosophy by a series of doctrinal tenets which are drawn directly from the classics. Among these the most characteristic are: the 'Leninist theory of reflection', the 'dialectic of absolute and relative truth', 'practice as basis of knowledge and criterion of truth', and the 'dialectic of the logical and historical'.

6. THE 'LENINIST THEORY OF REFLECTION'

The thesis that thought is a 'reflection, copy, photograph' of reality is dialectical materialism's fundamental characterization of knowledge, with which all other statements of contemporary Soviet philosophy's stand on theory of knowledge have to accord. In addition to the preservation of the purity of the classical tradition, contemporary Soviet theory of knowledge seems to have two other reasons for preserving intact this sometimes bothersome statement of the problem. First, there is the belief that this explanation is the best means of preserving the materialist monist and epistemologically transcendentist character which contemporary Soviet philosophers attribute to dialectical materialism. In other words, the reflection theory of knowledge is supposed to permit a reduction of spirit to matter, thereby avoiding both dualist materialism and any form of spiritualism – all of which, according to the classics and to contemporary Soviet philosophy, lead to the recognition of a supernatural being. Second, there is the utility of the reflection theory of knowledge for the refutation in a dialectical-materialistic way of the many forms of 'idealism' with which contemporary Soviet philosophy has to come to grips. The reduction of the spiritual to the material eliminates 'idealism's' duality of matter and spirit. The same reduction renders inoperative the 'idealist' claim of the primacy of spirit over matter. Finally, the 'idealist' distinction between the ontological and the logical becomes untenable if it is shown that what is generally called spirit is part and parcel of the homogeneous development of self-moving matter and not an independent existant.

For a long time Soviet philosophers were content to affirm and comment Lenin's statements on the reflective nature of thought[1]; it was considered the final and extremely brilliant solution to the problem of the place of knowledge in dialectical materialism. This was 'epistem-ological' reflection. At the same time, they were affirming and commenting Pavlov's theory of reflexes as the scientific demonstration of the validity of the 'Leninist theory of reflection' and of the classical thesis on the brain as the organ of thought. This was 'physiological' reflection. In order to reconcile these two disparate types of reflection, contemporary Soviet philosophers have been forced to find an inter-pretation of material reality which would serve – so to speak – as the underpinning for these two species of reflection. The result is the 'Leninist thesis on reflection as a general property of all matter'.[2]

As the 'general property of all matter' reflection (otraženie, a calque on the Latin 'reflectere') is defined in contemporary Soviet philosophy as interactivity (vzaimodejstvie)[3] of things. The character of this inter-activity is determined by the character of the action itself, by the character of the agent, and by the character of the recipient. Thus, the interactivity implied in the contact of two billiard balls is conditioned by (a) the structure and properties of the ball set in motion by the cue (roundness, smoothness, resiliency, etc.); (b) by those of the ball struck by the first; (c) by the nature of the action (force imparted by the cue, trajectory, 'english', etc.). Or, another example, the melting of wax is conditioned by the intensity of the flame, the directness of its action and the melting-point of the wax in question. In a material reality which is necessarily developing and evolving, interactivity increases in complexity as matter evolves to higher states.

Reflection at the level of inorganic matter takes the form of what science calls 'change of state'. In the above example of the billiard balls the force and direction of the rolling ball influence the force and direction assumed by the stationary ball – when struck by the first – in function of the make-up and position of both the first and the second. Already at this level – according to contemporary dialectical materialism – 'reflection' implies a certain minimal 'internal re-organisation', i.e. at the instant of impact between the two billiard balls there is an internal reorganisation of both the first and the second. It is this internal reorganisation in function of external influences which is the proper of 'reflection'.[4]

Reflection at the organic level takes the form of sensibility *(čuvstvitel'nost')*[5] and is distinguished from inorganic reflection by the fact that matter has attained a higher degree of complexity: it is organised into 'cells'. The organic cell can react to stimuli not only by external change of place but also and above all by an internal, structural adaptation which corresponds not only to the change in milieu (stimulus) but also to the immediate biotic needs of the cell itself. The internal reorganisation of the billiard balls is a temporary displacement of molecules which lasts only the time necessary for the transfer of kinetic energy from one ball to the other: it is purely 'mechanical'. The internal reorganization of the cell is structural: this means that the cell can reorganize itself whereas the billiard ball is reorganized from without. Structural also means that the cell tends to retain reorganizations which contribute to the satisfaction of its immediate biotic needs. In other words, reflection at the cell-level is already a rudimentary form of adaptation. This ability of the organic cell is based on the fact that it contains the beginnings of specialization of parts into functional groups – the predecessors of tissues and organs at the animal level.

The appearance of 'living substance' as the next step in the evolution of matter occasions the formation of even more complex biological forms of reflection. The simplest of these is irritability *(razdražimost')*, in respect of which sensibility is only a 'chemical predecessor' *(ximičeskij predšestvennik)*. Irritability is defined as "the ability of all that is living to respond to external activity by accelerating or decelerating the metabolism, by changing the rate of growth, by a spatial displacement, etc., as a result of which there is an adaptation of the organism to the changed milieu."[6] Thus, the living matter which has its cells formed into tissues and organs is capable of a more active and far-reaching adaptation and this is its mode of reflection.

Excitability *(vozbudimost')*, the next level of biological reflection, is the property of more perfected living bodies. The more 'plastic' tissues, i.e. those which best perceive external stimuli, evolve into intermediaries *(posredniki)* between the milieu (external stimuli) and the other, less sensitive, parts of the body.[7] As a consequence, there is an increase in the speed of transmission of the stimuli to all parts of the body which, in turn, permits a perfecting of the organism's reaction and adaptation to the milieu. Whereas irritability is a blind reaction of the organism as a whole to a change in milieu, excitability is a channeled reaction of an organism whose components are already distinguished into less excitable and more excitable.

The reflex *(refleksa)* is the highest and most complex form of biological reflection. Living matter which has reflexes has a central nervous system. Those tissues which were specialized in the transmission of excitability have developed into sense-organs *(organy čuvstv)* and are connected by nerves with the brain which is the center of the central nervous system. Reflexes are conditioned or unconditioned. The unconditioned reflex is the animal's reaction to the immediate presence of a biotically significant factor or thing. The conditioned reflex is the animal's reaction to an abiotic factor or thing in the absence of the biotic factor or thing which had previously been present in conjunction with it (Pavlov's dog, but also the lion's connection of 'licked salt-lick' with 'salt-licking-deer').[8] The conditioned reflexes of the animal make up what contemporary Soviet philosophy calls the 'first signal system' *(pervaja signal'naja sistema)* [9]: the abiotic factor or thing serves as a 'signal' of the biotic factor or thing. But the conditioned reflex has a double character: it is both physiological and psychical. "The special significance of the conditioned reflex, among the other forms of reflection which are present in matter according to its varying complexity, consists in the following: first, the conditioned reflex is a mode of the activity of the highest section of the central nervous system of the animal, of his brain; second, the conditioned reflex is not a purely physiological process but is, at the same time, a *psychic phenomenon (psixičeskim javleniem)*. It is the simplest psychic phenomenon."[10] This is sensation.

Specifically human reflection is the work of the 'second signal system' *(vtoraja signal'naja sistema)*.[11] The second signal system is the ultimate stage in the evolution of matter's general property of reflection. Because of his highly developed central nervous system man has not only 'signals' but also 'signals of signals', i.e. words.[12] The word is a stimulus like any other stimulus but it also conveys meaning: it signifies the meaning of the thing for the human organism: it signifies the 'signal':

it is the 'natural matter' *(prirodnaja materija)* of thought.[13] Man's 'higher neural activity' *(vysšaja nervnaja dejatel'nost')* forms the 'consciousness' *(soznanie)*[14] whose main characteristic is knowledge *(poznanie)*. Knowledge is of two types: sense-knowledge *(čuvstvennoe poznanie)* and intellectual knowledge *(logičeskoe* or *racional'noe poznanie)*.[15] The first is the first signal system and is embodied in 'images' *(obrazy)*; the other is the second signal system and is embodied in 'concepts' *(ponjatii)*.

These are the underpinnings with which contemporary Soviet philosophers have attempted to shore up the 'Leninist theory of reflection', which breaks down into three component affirmations: thought is a reflection of being; the subjective dialectic reflects the objective dialectic; the laws of being are the laws of thought.

'Thought is a reflection of being' is the expression of the fundamental transcendentist epistemological position of Lenin and of contemporary Soviet philosophy. 'The laws of being are the laws of thought' expresses the materialist monist point of view which dialectical materialism claims for itself. 'The subjective dialectic reflects the objective dialectic' forms the link between these two: in reference to the first it specifies the two terms of the cognitive relation; in reference to the second it is to provide the required fundamental unity.

The relationship of reflection between the subjective and objective dialectic, then, is the pivotal point of contemporary Soviet theory of knowledge.

The 'objective dialectic' is reality as 'dialectically constituted (structured) matter'. And it is this which is reflected in the 'subjective' dialectic, thought. Immediately two problems are posed; the first on the adequacy of the reflection; the second on the precise meaning of 'dialectical' in reference to the subjective dialectic. The first question is the theme of the next section.

A priori it seems that thought, the 'subjective dialectic', is 'dialectical' in two ways. First of all, both the knower and the act of knowing are part of the real world (objective dialectic); hence, the act of knowing must accord with the basic laws of the dialectic. In other words, human thinking is an epi-phenomenon of matter as are all the other forms of reflection: as such, it necessarily conforms to the laws of matter. This means that there is a fundamental 'resonance' between the knower and the known: the knowability of all things is founded in the knower's belonging to the same dialectical reality as the known. In the second place – and this seems to have been the primitive meaning of Lenin – the subjective dialectic is dialectical because the reality it reflects is dialectically constructed matter. Here we are dealing not with thinking, a process which is dialectical because it is the activity of a dialectically real being, but with thought, the end-product of this process: images in the case of sense-knowledge and concepts in the case of rational knowledge. Since these end-products of thinking are reflections of reality they must be reflections both of reality's materiality and of its dialectical character. Thus, in my knowing of the house there is the dialectical process of knowing which is due to my belonging to the real world and there is the dialectical character of the concept 'house' which is due to its being a reflection of the real house which is dialectically structured.

For a long time – in fact, until the recent flow of publications on dialectical logic[16] – contemporary Soviet philosophers payed little, if any, attention to the dialectical nature of the knowing subject since this – as it seems – smacks too much of the 'subjective creativity' of certain forms of 'idealism'.[17] But, already in the *Osnovy* we read: "The contradictions in knowledge, which reflect the contradictions of the objective world and the contradictory character of the process of its reflection, should not be confused with formal-logical contradictions which are the result of inconsequences and confusions of the thought of one or another man."[18] (p. 307) M. M. Rozental' presents the case even more forcefully: "The subject is himself part of nature ... and, since the most general laws of the objective world appear everywhere, they are also the laws of the cognitive activity of the subject. In other words, the identification of these laws of being and knowledge (with each other) results from the unity of object and subject."[19] However, it is M. N. Alekseev who has presented the most convincing argument to date. According to Alekseev, one must distinguish in the 'subjective dialectic' two aspects: the dialectic of thought *(dialektika myšlenija)* and dialectical thought *(dialektičeskoe myšlenie)*. The 'dialectic of thought' is independent of the knower, i.e. it is present in all thought by the very fact that thought is a reflection of dialectical reality. To illustrate this point Alekseev states that, for example, any thought contains a development from confusion toward clarity; every thought contains a contradiction between the subject and predicate of the 'judgement' used to express it, etc. On the other hand, 'dialectical thought' is thinking with awareness of the objective dialectic or – as Alekseev says – the 'dialectic of the object'. Dialectical thought is of two types: spontaneous *(stixinij)* and conscious *(soznatel'nij)*. Spontaneous dialectical thought is unsystematized and non-reflective grasping of the objective dialectic – and Aristotle is given as an example.[20] Conscious dialectical thought is proper to the knower who already knows the most general laws of the object (the 'basic laws of the dialectic') and need only determine their specific 'incarnation' here and now in the object under study.[21]

The question as to the adequacy of the subjective dialectic's reflection of the objective dialectic is the question of truth.

7. THE 'DIALECTIC OF ABSOLUTE AND RELATIVE TRUTH'

For the sake of simplicity and clarity we have up to now taken the word 'dialectical' in its fundamental meaning, i.e. as 'in accordance with the basic laws of the dialectic'. In order to correctly understand dialectical materialism's affirmations on truth, we must widen the description to include movement as a property of all reality (matter). According to contemporary Soviet philosophy the universal presence of 'unity and conflict of opposites', 'transition from quantitative changes to qualitative changes' and 'negation of negation' is the explanation of movement as the universal (and inalienable) attribute of matter.[22] Henceforward, 'dialectical' will be taken as meaning 'in dialectical motion' or 'in movement according to the three basic laws of the dialectic'.

According to dialectical materialism, truth is a correspondence. "Truth in the widest sense of the word is, according to dialectical materialism, the correspondence of our knowledge to objective reality, the correct reflection of the objective world in scientific concepts. Such a general definition of truth obviously follows directly from the materialist theory of knowledge."[23] Truth, then, is the correspondence of the subjective dialectic (our knowledge) to the objective dialectic (objective reality). But, if the subjective dialectic is a reflection of the objective dialectic, then it either reflects it as it is or 'reflection' is used

35

here only in a metaphorical sense. The latter is inadmissible in a dialectical materialism which wishes itself to be an epistemological transcendentism. On the other hand, to admit that knowledge is a reflection in the strict sense of the term, i.e. that there is complete isomorphy between the subjective and objective dialectics, would invalidate two essential aspects of contemporary dialectical materialism: its theory of knowledge and its doctrine on truth.

Dialectical materialism's theory of knowledge would be invalidated by an interpretation of reflection as strict isomorphy because theory of knowledge is itself knowledge. Now, if the objective dialectic means the constant evolutionary movement of reality and if the subjective dialectic is an isomorphic reflection thereof, the evolution of which is in strict parallel to that of the objective dialectic, then theory of knowledge is also in isomorphic evolution. The most that would then be left for theory of knowledge would be an account of the history of knowing – which is exactly the definition which Lenin gave of logic.[24] Even if this difficulty be ignored or explained away – which it must be since contemporary Soviet philosophers are firm in their belief that 'Marxist philosophy' is a complete philosophic system, therefore necessarily including a theory of knowledge – there remains the problem of explaining how dialectical materialism can have a theory of truth. For, if the subjective dialectic is a strictly isomorphic reflection of the objective dialectic, then it must reflect 'what is there' and nothing else and, if so, there can be no error. But, a theory of truth is senseless and superfluous in a theory of knowledge which does not admit the possibility of error. To circumvent these two difficulties contemporary Soviet philosophers have effected a 'de-mechanization' of the Leninist theory of reflection. It is now maintained (a) that as matter reaches higher stages of evolution and reflection becomes increasingly complex, knowledge becomes highly abstract and there arises a possibility of inaccuracy in the subjective dialectic's reflection of the objective dialectic[25]; (b) that the reflection *in itself*, objectively considered, is adequate and accurate, but that there is a 'subjective aspect', i.e. the accuracy of the reflection is limited by the capacities of the individual knower.[26]

Truth can, therefore, be 'objective' or 'subjective'. Objective truth is a term applied by dialectical materialism to two different aspects of knowledge. In the wide sense, to say that objective truth exists is to assert that human knowledge is sovereignly capable of giving a correct reflection of reality; there are no limits to man's knowledge; there are no unknowable things, only things which are not yet known.[27] It is important to note that human knowledge here means the totality of what mankind knew, knows and will know – faithful to Engels' statements on the matter in *Anti-Dühring*.[28] In the more limited sense, objective truth is used to refer to that actually known cognitive content which is a correct reflection of reality.[29] Subjective truth is the reflection of things as effected by the 'concrete individual' with all of his limitations. However, strictly speaking, there is no question of subjective truth in dialectical materialism. Subjective knowledge is the knowledge of the individual; the individual knows objective truth when his reflection correctly and adequately corresponds to the objective dialectic; otherwise, he is in error. Therefore, all truth is objective. The more discerning of contemporary Soviet philosophers now speak rather of the 'objective and subjective limits of knowledge', as in the following passages: "The subjectivity of knowledge is conditioned by the fact that its bearer is always a single man. The limitation of the subject inevitably leaves its mark on knowledge and leads to its limitation."[30] "The limitedness of knowledge cannot be attributed solely to its subjectivity. In it is reflected the other fact that at a given moment objective reality is limited in function of its historically determined character..."[31] On the one hand, knowledge of truth is limited by the capacities of the knower; on the other, it is restricted to that stage in the development of the objective dialectic which has already been reached.

Truth, according to dialectical materialism is not only a correspondence but also a process[2] – it is dynamically continuous and it is cumulative. Truth is a dynamically continuous process because the subjective dialectic as a reflection of the ever-moving and ever-evolving objective dialectic must itself move and evolve in order to remain a correct reflection of the objective dialectic, i.e., in order to provide objective truth in the sense of (b) above.[33] Truth as a process is also cumulative. This means that there is a progression of knowledge in the course of which partial (relative) truths are amassed, constituting greater and greater approximations to absolute truth.

The *Osnovy* describe absolute and relative truth as follows: "Objective truth in its full and complete form is called *absolute truth*.

Absolute truth is knowledge which is not able to be refuted by the further course of the development of science and practice. . . . *Relative truth* is knowledge which is a basically true reflection of reality, but it is not full: it is limited and (valid) only under certain conditions and relations. In the further development of science this knowledge is corrected, completed, deepened and made concrete."[4] Absolute truth, then, is objective truth as complete: this means Engels' "the individual thoughts of many billions of past, present and future humans".[35] It is the sum-total of all possible human knowledge. Because reality – including man – is in eternal movement and evolution, this sum-total is an ideal limit which may be progressively approached but never completely attained.[36] But, this is only part of the dialectical-materialist doctrine on absolute truth. "Absolute truth is not just the limit toward which our knowledge strives but which it in reality never reaches. In all areas of scientific knowledge there are absolutely true statements *(absoljutno vernye položenija)* which cannot be refuted by the further course of the development of science."[37] In other words, each individual act of knowledge contains relative truth: relative truth is objective truth as subjected in the individual knower to the so-called 'subjective' limitations. Absolute truth is the accumulation of all the relative truths – past, present and future. But, among the relative truths there are some which are 'absolute', i.e. which have an absolute validity. Among these portions of the 'ideal limit' which are already in the possession of the individual, the most important, of course, are the 'basic laws of the dialectic'.[38]

It is 'practice' which serves to distinguish objective truth from error and relative truth from absolute truth.

8. 'PRACTICE AS BASIS OF KNOWLEDGE AND CRITERION OF TRUTH'

Criteriology is the heart of any theory of knowledge. In other words, an epistemological doctrine stands or falls to the extent that it succeeds or fails in satisfactorily defining a criterion, i.e. a means of distinguishing valid knowledge from invalid error. It is peculiar to the theory of knowledge of dialectical materialism that its criterion, practice *(praktika)*[39], is also held to be the 'basis of knowledge'. Practice, then, – which is intimately bound up with the 'historical' (cf. the next section) – is the all-embracing context and *sine qua non* of knowledge.

The *Osnovy* describes practice as follows: "Knowledge arises on the basis of and for the satisfaction of the needs of man's practical activity. *Practice* is the sensible-material activity of people which changes the objects, phenomena and processes of reality. Practice, as the basis of knowledge, is the interactivity of the subject (man) and the object (the material object), the direct result of which is the transformation of the object."[40] Practice is, first of all, a human activity; it is the doing of man and not of animals. Second, practice is social, i.e., it implies inter-subjectivity. Third, practice is sensible-material. This means that practice involves the presence of material things which are used at the level of sense-knowledge. Fourth, practice is transformatory: it implies a manipulation and modification by man of the material things presented to him. Finally, practice is always consciously directed: accidental manipulations of material things are excluded.[41]

Practice as the basis of knowledge has two distinct, albeit com-plementary, meanings in contemporary Soviet theory of knowledge. In the broad sense, the practice which is the basis of knowledge is the sum of the practical activities which mankind – all men – has successfully effected up to now. It is the sum-total of the experiences of mankind.[42] More particularly, the practice which serves as basis of knowledge is the specific 'problem-situation' with which an individual is faced as a result of being engaged in the performance of some task.[43] The two meanings of practice as basis of knowledge are held to be complementary in the sense that valid knowing comes to be only in the presence of a 'problem-situation' and this, in turn, can be successfully resolved only on the basis of mankind's previously accumulated 'practical' ex-periences. In other words, in order that the subjective dialectic reflect the objective dialectic it is not sufficient that the knower be simply in the presence of the objective dialectic. The knower must be in the process of a consciously directed transformation of the objective dialectic (material reality) before the cognitive image or concept can come to be. Here we find a strict interpretation of *nihil in intellectu nisi prius in sensibus:* for dialectical materialism not only does all knowledge stem in one way or another from sense-knowledge but also every cognitive act must be, as it were, 'set off' by immediate contact with a sensible object. And there is even more: every cognitive act corresponds to an

39

engagement of the knower with the known. In other words, every cognitive relation is based on and parallel to a real relation: the subjective dialectic reflects the objective dialectic – and the circle closes. But, one may object, what about the laws of logic? and logical operations? and purely formalistic logical calculi? According to contemporary Soviet philosophy – doggedly faithful to Lenin on this point – practical activity leads consciousness to the repetition of various logical figures, millions of times until they get the value of axioms.[44]

For dialectical materialism practice is also the 'criterion of truth'. One of the most striking features of contemporary Soviet philosophy – up to the very recent past – was the almost unanimous insistence of the Soviet philosophers that a philosophical thesis, like the 'Leninist theory of reflection' could be 'proved' to be correct because Khrushchov's latest decree on the ways and means of disposing of excess dung had improved matters in the kolhoz barns.[45] Paradoxically enough this seemingly vulgar propagandistic use of contemporary Soviet philosophy seems to be consonant even with its most elaborated and academic interpretation. Among the few contemporary Soviet philosophers who give a serious philosophical consideration to the problem of practice as the criterion of truth, M. N. Rutkevič has developed the most coherent dialectical-materialist doctrine on the subject.[46] According to Rutkevič, knowledge is based on an antecedent series of practical experiences. As a reflection of these series of experiences, knowledge is true – even before it is 'verified' by subsequent practice. Confirmation (verification) is, therefore, a process which implies both antecedent and subsequent practice, although the latter is decisive as criterion of truth. The criterion of practice is relative when it confirms the relative truth of incomplete, subjectively conditioned knowledge. It is absolute when the totality of practical experience pertinent to a given domain confirms the absolute truth of the whole set of propositions which make up knowledge in this domain. The highest domain is philosophy. The whole history of mankind provides the practical confirmation of Marxist-Leninist philosophy.

There is, then, a strict parallel. Relative practice confirms relative truth; 'relative' meaning, in both instances, limited by the capacities of the knower and restricted to the stage of evolution attained by the objective dialectic. Absolute practice confirms absolute truth. And, just as absolute truth is the sum-total of all possible human knowledge, so absolute practice is the sum-total of all possible human experiences of a practical-transformatory type. Absolute practice and absolute truth in this sense are ideal limits which the individual practitioner and knower can only approximate but never reach. But, just as there are absolute truths which are here and now in the possession of the individual knower, so too there are practical activities which have an absolute validity. The absolute truths are enshrined in 'Marxist-Leninist philosophy'; the absolutely valid practical activities are those which contribute to the successful 'construction of Communism in the USSR'. The subjective dialectic (Marxism-Leninism) is a reflection of the objective dialectic (the nature of reality as revealed in the 'practice of Communist construction'). Since both the subjective and objective dialectics are integral wholes (no element of either has validity except in the context of the whole of both dialectics), any theoretical element can be demonstrated by any practical element (like Khrushchov's effective decree on dung) and, inversely, any practical activity can be justified by any theoretical statement. This is the epistemological root of the 'dialectical unity of theory and practice'.

This view on the place of practice is the classical position: it says in effect – faithful to Lenin[47] – that practice is a third step in the process of knowledge. Both sense-reflection and intellectual reflection are enveloped in the vast range of human practical experience, which is, therefore, the basic cognitive category and the highest stage in the process of knowledge. Rutkevič attacked this position in 1954, maintaining that the criterion of knowledge had to be something outside of knowledge itself: therefore, if practice were the third step in knowledge, it could only be the criterion of already had knowledge – it could not be the basis of knowledge.[48] V. M. Podosetnik defended the classical position in a subsequent article where he brought the whole battery of classical quotes against Rutkevič.[49] Podosetnik's basic argument runs as follows: practice is both basis of knowledge and criterion of truth; but, as criterion of truth it consists in a 'confirmation in action' *(proverka na praktika)* and, since this is neither sense-knowledge nor intellectual reasoning, it must be a third and distinct step in knowledge. Rutkevič's reply accused Podosetnik of confusing practice as 'an extension of knowledge' with practice as 'a distinct stage in the cognitive process'.

41

The opinions expressed on this question by other contemporary Soviet philosophers seemed to give Rutkevič a majority.[50] But, in the official decree which ended the discussion it was Podosetnik who was approved: Rutkevič was condemned for having raised a question 'already solved by the classics'.[51]

In addition to 'proof by practice' contemporary dialectical materialism does admit another type of proof, the logical. I. D. Andreev, author of *Principles of the Theory of Knowledge*, explains it as follows: "A scientific theory is also considered proved if its veracity is established by a logical proof *(logičeskim dokazatel'stvom)* which is the establishment of the truth of one judgement through others which have earlier been established and tested by social practice."[52] But, since the subjective dialectic reflects the objective dialectic, "logical proof is the establishment of the veracity of certain judgements using other, true, judgements and can be effected only if the bonds between the concepts and judgements in the process of proof correctly reflect the real bonds between the things and phenomena expressed in these concepts and judgements."[53] Ultimately, then, the derivation of all theory through practical confirmation is true of logic itself: ". . . logic as a science on thought has as its content not purely extra-empirical and *a priori* dogmas but statements taken from objective reality, verified by the centuries of experience of mankind; its laws, forms and categories are reflections of the laws, objectively present to reality itself; whence it is no surprise that the conclusions, drawn as a result of the application of the laws and categories of logic to true statements, are true, i.e. correspond to reality and are verified by life and practice."[54]

Practical, human activity is, therefore, the 'historical' which underlies the 'logical' in knowledge.

9. THE 'DIALECTIC OF THE "LOGICAL" AND THE "HISTORICAL"'

The objective dialectic is in constant evolution: it has not only a present and future but also and above all a past. The past of the objective dialectic appears in contemporary Soviet theory of knowledge as the 'historical'. The history of the objective dialectic is summed up in the subjective dialectic in the form of the 'logical'. The following passage is a relatively clear explanation of what the contemporary Soviet philosopher means by the 'historical' and the 'logical' and the dialectical relationship existing between them: "Under the logical in thought dialectical materialism understands the determined system of thought in which is reproduced the process of the development of nature and society. In the concept 'logical' are found all the forms and means of rational knowledge taken in their interrelation and consequential development. The historical is the real course of history itself. The historical also reflects the history of the very process of knowledge. The logical is inseparably bound up with the historical and in a definite dialectical relationship to it. The logical expresses the historical in a theoretically generalized form as the sum or conclusion of history. And, to the extent that the logical reflects the basic traits of the historical process of development, to this extent it coincides with the historical." [55]

The *historical* is the objective dialectic along with all that has happened in it and to it in its eternal existence (matter has always existed). This is especially the case with that part of the historical occupied by the higher forms of matter like man and the society he has formed. But, it is equally true of all matter. Every object in the real world has undergone a series of changes and influences each of which has necessarily left its mark on the 'reflective' matter of which the object is made. Thus, each and every object has its own history and, what is more, each object carries this history with it at all times. In addition, all matter – the whole material universe – is in constant evolution and always has been. The history of this evolution is reflected in the make-up of present-day reality. Therefore, the historical is equivalent to the objective dialectic. [56]

The *logical* is the subjective dialectic as reflecting, in abbreviated form, the history of the objective dialectic. [57] Thus, the 'logical' is not equi-extensional with the subjective dialectic. The subjective dialectic is the reflection of the objective dialectic: it reflects things and relations between them; it reflects processes and relations between them; it also reflects the history of things and processes. It is this last which constitutes the 'logical'. The 'logical' is that portion of the subjective dialectic which reflects – in a summarized, generalized, abbreviated form – the historical development of the objective dialectic. Thus, whereas the subjective dialectic as a whole reflects the objective dialectic in its entirety – the unimportant and secondary as well as the primary and

43

essential, the logical is a resumé of the essential in the evolution of the objective dialectic.

In the relationship of the logical to the historical there is a 'unity and conflict of opposites', i.e. it is 'dialectical'. For the 'logical' sums up all that is essential in the 'historical': they are identical. But, the historical contains a wealth of detail which the logical does not reproduce: they are distinct. Because it is richer, fuller, more complete, the historical is primary and the logical is derived.[58] All that the logical has is drawn from the historical. Logical laws are abbreviations of repeated historical experiences.[59] Formal logic deals with axioms which have been abstracted from repeatedly successful practical experiences. Dialectical logic is superior to formal logic because it deals not only with the logical but also with the historical, i.e. the real in all its detail.[60] The validity of the laws and categories of logic depends on and is demonstrated by the historical, i.e. by practice as immediate, sensible, transformatory contact with the reality of the objective dialectic.[61] For the same reasons, formal logic deals with truth only as a correspondence: dialectical logic deals with truth which is both a correspondence (the logical corresponding to that which is essential in the objective dialectic) and a process (the subjective dialectic reflecting the objective dialectic's process of evolution in all its detail). Finally, it is obvious that the historical represents absolute truth. The 'logical' alone can only provide relative truths since it abstracts, by definition, from a whole host of details without which a faithful reflection of the objective dialectic is not possible.[62]

In addition to the 'dialectic of the logical and the historical' contemporary Soviet theory of knowledge makes use of a series of other 'dialectical pairs': abstract and concrete, analysis and synthesis, particular and general, etc. These will be taken up in the next chapter along with the other constituents of contemporary Soviet theory of knowledge.

REFERENCES

1. "The world is matter moving in conformity to law, and our knowledge, being the highest product of nature, is in a position only to *reflect* this conformity to law." (*Materialism and Empirio-Criticism*, p. 170). "Matter is a philosophical category denoting the objective reality which is given to man by his sensations,

and which is copied, photographed and reflected by our sensations, while existing independently of them." (*Ibid.*, p. 127). "Natural science leaves no room for doubt that its assertion that the earth existed prior to man is a truth. This is entirely compatible with the materialist theory of knowledge: the existence of the thing reflected independent of the reflector (the independence of the external world from the mind) is a fundamental tenet of materialism. The assertion made by science that the earth existed prior to man is an objective truth." (*Ibid.*, pp. 120–121).

2. "Basing himself on the thesis of the unity of the world and the interconnection of its phenomena, Lenin drew the conclusion that *all* matter must have the property – essentially related to sensation – of reflection which exists at the very foundation of the edifice of matter, i.e. is present in its very simplest forms. This property is not sensation; it is only 'related' *(rodstvenno)* to sensation." (*Istorija filosofii*, vol. 5, p. 101). Cf. Lenin: *Materialism and Empirio-Criticism*, p. 38.

3. "The simplest form of reflection, present in all matter, is a reaction *(reagirovanie)* of certain material objects to the action of others such that the characteristics of the external action are so to speak reproduced and imprinted in the material objects. The best known form of this reflection in anorganic nature is the reflection of objects in a mirror." (*Osnovy*, p. 175). More analytic treatments are to be found in P. K. Anoxin: 'Operežajuščee otraženie dejstvitel'nosti' (The Outstripping Reflection of Reality). *VF* 1962, 7, 97–111. and V. S. Tjuxtin: 'O suščnosti otraženija' (On the Essence of Reflection). *VF* 1962, 5, 59–71. The *Filosofskaja enciklopedija* defines *vzaimodejstvie* as follows: "a universal form of the bonds of bodies or phenomena, realized in their mutual transformations. Two or more interacting bodies or phenomena constitute a system in which is accomplished the process of the transformation of motion . . ." (p. 250).

4. "Reflection as the general property of matter of all spheres of interactivity in the material world consists, first, in the fact that external activities condition even the internal nature of things and phenomena both putting aside in itself the results in each phenomenon of the activity on it and as 'representations' *(predstavleny)*, reflecting all the objects which are in interaction with it; and, second, any activity of one phenomenon on another is refracted by the internal properties of the phenomenon on which the activity is exerted." (S. L. Rubinštejn: *Principy i puti razvitija psixologii* (Principles and Paths of the Development of Psychology). Moskva. 1959. p. 11).

5. Cf. *Osnovy*, p. 175.

6. *Osnovy*, p. 176. Cf. also Rubinštejn: *op.cit.* p. 12. and I. D. Andreev: *Osnovy teorii poznaniia* (Principles of the Theory of Knowledge) Moskva 1959. Henceforeward: Andreev: *Osnovy*. Here: p. 94.

7. *Osnovy: loc.cit.*

8. *Osnovy*, p. 178. Cf. also *Dialektičeskij materializm* (Vysšaja partijnaja škola pri CK KPSS). Moskva. 1960. Henceforeward: VPŠ: *Diamat*. Here: p. 117.

9. *Osnovy*, p. 179. Cf. also VPŠ: *Diamat*, p. 122. For a physiological point of view, see M. A. Logvin in *FN* 1962, 5, 42–49, E. A. in *VF* 1962, 8, 66–77, Graščenko *et al.* in *VF* 1962, 8, 36–49.

10. *Osnovy*, p. 178.

11. *Ibid.*, p. 179.

12. VPŠ: *Diamat*, p. 125.

13. *Osnovy*, p. 190.
14. *Ibid.*, p. 179.
15. Andreev: *Osnovy*, p. 175 and *Osnovy*, p. 303.
16. Cf. Chapter I, pp. 6–7.
17. Cf., e.g., P. S. Popov: 'Predmet formal'noj logiki i dialektika' (The Object of Formal Logic and the Dialectic). *VF* 1951, 1, 210–218.
18. *Osnovy*, p. 307. Cf. N. Lobkowicz: *Das Widerspruchsprinzip in der neueren sowjetischen Philosophie.* Dordrecht, Holland. 1960. p. 22.
19. M. M. Rozental': *Principy dialektičeskoj logiki* (Principles of Dialectical Logic). Moskva. 1960. p. 114.
20. Cf. K. G. Ballestrem: 'Soviet Historiography of Philosophy'. *Studies in Soviet Thought* III (1963) 107–120.
21. Cf. M. N. Alekseev: *Dialektika form myšlenija* (Dialectic of the Forms of Thought). Moskva. 1959.
22. *Osnovy*, p. 229.
23. VPŠ: *Diamat*, p. 341.
24. Cf. *Philosophical Notebooks*, pp. 92–93. Cf. also Engels in K. Marks, F. Engel's: *Sočinenija*, t. 14, p. 337.
25. VPŠ: *Diamat*, pp. 301–302. Andreev: *Osnovy*, pp. 246–247.
26. Andreev: *Osnovy*, p. 245.
27. *Istorija filosofii*, vol. 5, p. 105. VPŠ: *Diamat*, pp. 341–342. *Osnovy*, p. 339.
28. Engels: *Anti-Dühring* (English) p. 86.
29. I. D. Andreev: *Dialektičeskij materializm*. Moskva. 1960. p. 452.
30. *O "Filosofskix tetradjax" V. I. Lenina* (On the *Philosophic Notebooks* of Lenin). Moskva. 1959. Henceforeward: *OFT*. Here: p. 207.
31. *Ibid.*, p. 209.
32. *Osnovy*, p. 339.
33. Rozental' even says: "Development is an existential form of thought, of knowledge." (*Principy dialektičeskoj logiki*. Moskva. 1960. p. 120, in italics).
34. *Osnovy*, p. 340.
35. Engels: *Anti-Dühring* (English), p. 85.
36. "The Process of human knowledge can never be ended since objectively existing matter, nature, is eternal in time, unlimited in space and in constant change and development. Knowledge is the reflection of the endless and constantly changing objective world; hence, it is itself an unending and always developing process." (VPŠ: *Diamat*, p. 347).
37. *Osnovy*, p. 340. Andreev: *op.cit.*, p. 456.
38. Cf., e.g., VPŠ: *Diamat*, p. 350. and Andreev: *Osnovy*, p. 263. In *VF* 1948, 1, 294, P. S. Trofimov cites the law of the conservation of energy as an example of an absolute truth.
39. *Praktika* has more the meaning of 'practical activity' or 'implementation' in English. We use 'practice' for convenience.
40. *Osnovy*, p. 333.
41. Cf. I. T. Jakuševskij: 'O dialektiko-materialističeskom ponimanii praktiki' (On the Dialectical-Materialist Conception of Practice). *FN* 1958, 4, 113–121.
42. Cf. M. N. Rutkevič: 'Dialektičeskij xarakter kriterija praktiki' (The Dialectical Character of the Criterion Practice). *VF* 1959, 9, 45.
43. S. L. Rubinštejn: *op.cit.*, p. 97.
44. "... the practical activity of man had to bring the consciousness of man to the

million-fold repetition of different logical figures *in order* that these figures come to have the character *of axioms.*" (Lenin: *Filosofskie tetrady.* Moskva. 1947, p. 164).

45. Extreme cases of this type have become much rarer since Stalin's death. Because Khrushchov has written no philosophical works thus far, contemporary Soviet philosophers can be content with vague references to his speeches on corn-raising and chemical (fertilizer) production.

46. Cf. Bibliography, on page 182.

47. *Filosofskie tetrady.* Moskva. 1947. pp. 146–147. More recently, P. P. Čupin has universalized practice on the basis of this quotation. (s. *FN* 1962, 1, 80–87).

48. Rutkevič *VF* 1954, 3, 34–45. Cf. Chapter I, pp. 3–4.

49. Podosetnik *VF* 1954, 5, 77–81.

50. For Rutkevič's reply and the report of other opinions, see G. S. in *VF* 1955, 1, 139–144.

51. *VF* 1955, 1, 144–149.

52. Andreev: *Osnovy*, p. 317.

53. *Ibid.*, p. 318.

54. *Ibid.*, p. 322.

55. VPŠ: *Diamat*, pp. 339–340. Cf. *Osnovy*, p. 324.

56. *OFT*, pp. 269–270. *Osnovy*, p. 323.

57. Andreev: *Osnovy*, p. 218.

58. *Osnovy*, p. 323.

59. Lenin: *Soč.* t. 38, p. 309.

60. "Just as formal logic is oriented toward the investigation of means and rules of the correct combination of concepts and judgements and the ordered derivation of some thoughts from others, so dialectical logic tries to more adequately express *(vyrazit')* in concepts and other forms of thought the content of really changing things and processes." (M. M. Rozental': *op.cit.*, p. 88).

61. *Ibid.*, pp. 88–89.

62. *Ibid.*, p. 190.

CHAPTER IV

BASIC COGNITIVE FUNCTIONS

In the actual practice of philosophical discussion of epistemology, contemporary Soviet philosophers do not limit themselves to these four basic tenets. In general, it can be said that their discussion follows the common lines of classical psychologistic logic with departures due to the four, specifically Marxist-Leninist, tenets. This is to say that the originality of the dialectical-materialist theory of knowledge is pretty well exhausted by the theory of reflection, the theory of truth, the category of practice, and the 'dialectic of the logical and historical'. What remains to be seen is how Soviet philosophers conceive the basic cognitive functions (this chapter) and the basic cognitive modes (Ch. V). Since most of these are carry-overs from traditional philosophies, we shall limit ourselves to an account of what changes they have undergone in the transfer – principally as a result of being integrated into the currently developing dialectical logic. These changes determine the peculiarly dialectical-materialist doctrine on methods and methodology (Ch. VI). Finally, we shall examine Soviet philosophy's use of its own epistemological doctrines for criticism of contemporary Western (bourgeois) philosophy (Ch. VII) and for the construction of an account of knowledge in the history of philosophy (Ch. VIII).

By cognitive functions we mean here those structural parts or – dynamically seen – constitutive phases which are necessarily implied in human knowledge, according to the theory of knowledge of contemporary Soviet philosophy.

These functions are listed by contemporary Soviet theoreticians of knowledge as follows: living contemplation *(živoe sozercanie)*, sensation *(oščuščenie)*, perception *(vosprijatie)*, representation *(predstavlenie)*, imagination *(voobraženie)*, concept *(ponjatie)*, judgement *(suždenie)*, reasoning *(umozaključenie)*. If one excepts the first element (which, as we will see, is most likely a pleonastic insert), it seems that we have here nothing more nor less than the venerable psychologistic tradition of Descartes, Locke, etc. – an impression which is not weakened by a more careful examination of the definitions and descriptions offered in contemporary Soviet writings on theory of knowledge.

10. LIVING CONTEMPLATION

This item figures in the list of dialectical-materialist epistemological elements because of a remark Lenin made in his *Philosophical Notebooks:* "From living contemplation to abstract thought *and from it to practice* – such is the dialectical path of the knowledge of truth and of objective reality."[1] In view of the fact that serious studies on the subject are completely lacking, one would be tempted to say that this sentence – at least as concerns the part on living contemplation – is an *obiter dictum*. Up to now at least contemporary Soviet philosophers have been content to treat it as such. Thus, Andreev says: "In the final analysis, knowledge always begins with immediate living contemplation *(s ne-posredstvennogo živogo sozercanija)*" and adds, by way of definition: "with the observation of things and phenomena of the material world, i.e. with direct interactivity of man with the object under study by means of the sense organs".[2] Other texts from contemporary Soviet philosophy confirm this identification of living contemplation with sense-knowledge. For example: "Sense-knowledge, or living contemplation, is the first stage of knowledge . . ."[3] This explains why contemporary Soviet theoreticians of knowledge use the term without considering it necessary to make any special analysis outside of that already contained in their treatises on sense-knowledge. It seems that the conservation of this cognitive element – or at least of a term distinct from 'sensation' – is due to the importance which Lenin's words (quoted above) have assumed in the context of the contemporary Soviet philosophic treatment of practice.[4]

11. SENSATION

In the dialectical-materialist theory of knowledge, sensation is the genetically first and generically most important form of pre-logical knowing, the other two being perception and representation. Just as there is a difference of opinion in contemporary Soviet philosophy as to whether there are two or three distinct levels of cognitive activity –

49

the question on whether practice is a distinct cognitive level[5], so there is a discussion among contemporary Soviet theoreticians of knowledge as to whether there are two or three distinct forms of knowledge on the sense-level. B. G. Anan'ev, in his *Theory of Sensation*, gives an account of the two schools of opinion. He says: "One approach to the structural analysis of sensible reflection is the qualitative distinction of its basic forms: sensation, perception and representation".[6] Among the advocates of the tri-partite distinction, Anan'ev names: F. I. Xasxačix in *Matter and Consciousness*[7], I. D. Andreev in *Dialectical Materialism on the Process of Knowledge*[8], T. I. Ojzerman in *The Basic Stages in the Process of Knowledge*[9], and F. F. Kal'sin in *The Basic Questions of the Theory of Knowledge*.[10] The two-form point of view is defended, albeit in different ways and for conflicting reasons, by M. A. Leonov in *Essays on Dialectical Materialism*[11], Ju. G. Gajdukov in *The Knowability of the World and its Laws*[12], T. Pavlov in *The Theory of Reflection*[13], and A. Kiselinčev in *The Marxist-Leninist Theory of Reflection and the Doctrine of I. Pavlov*.[14] Strangely enough Leonov, after explaining that representation is not a form of sense-knowledge because it is indirect while the very nature of sense-knowledge is to be direct contact with reality, adds that sensation is a 'component' of perception. In a similar line of thought, Gajdukov calls sensation a 'moment' of perception. The tri-partite view is that which predominates in contemporary Soviet theory of knowledge: there are, then, three qualitatively distinct forms of sense-knowledge and sensation is the first, both as to time and as to importance.

Anan'ev defines sensation as follows: "Ontologically, sensation is a complex reflectorial act, a signal and the means of man's orientation in his milieu. .... Epistemologically, if it is question of the sensations of *man* as the subject of knowledge, they are direct-sensory *knowings (neposredstvenno-čuvstvennymi znanijami)*."[15] This description succinctly presents the two characteristics which contemporary Soviet theory of knowledge attributes to sensation. Sensation is, first of all, a reflection which man (or animal) as part of the objective dialectic and, therefore, matter possesses. It is the first signal system. This is the 'passive reception' aspect of dialectical-materialist sensation. The properties of the 'thing', of the objective dialectic, are reflected by the knower in the form of neural readjustments. But, sensation is also the activity of the knower whose 'subjective' particularities determine *how* the objective dialectic is reflected in the sense-image. Sensations are the result of this combined activity of knower and material known. "Sensations are subjective as to the form of their manifestation but objective as to their content since the objects of the objective world which is independent of human consciousness are reflected in them."[16]

Sensation is the 'historical' in reference to rational thought which is the 'logical'. It is sensation which is in direct reflectorial contact with the objective dialectic. In fact, sensation is properly a part of the objective dialectic. It is distinguished from the rest of the objective dialectic by the fact that it is sensation which supplies the immediate material with which logical thought operates. The similarity with the Kantian way of presenting sensation is striking; with the difference that dialectical materialism categorically affirms the existence of the 'thing-in-it-self'.[17] It is in sensation that the dialectical transition from matter to consciousness is effected: neural activity ceases to be purely neural and takes on a cognitive function.

Sensation is accomplished through the sense-organs which dialectical materialism holds – along with the tradition – to be five, although some of the more physiologically-minded contemporary Soviet philosophers distinguish innumerable sub-species.[18]

12. PERCEPTION

"The reflection by man and animal – in the form of holistic sense-images – of objects as a result of their direct activity on the organs of sense" is the definition of perception given by the *Philosophic Encyclopedia*.[19] The distinction between sensation and perception lies, for dialectical materialism, in the fact that the first is made up of discrete images each of which stems from the activity of one type of sense-organ, while the second presents a single image which is a synthesis of the information gathered by a number of sense-organs. Just as there is no agreement among contemporary Soviet theoreticians of knowledge on the number of types of sense-knowledge, so there is some confusion on the difference between sensation and perception. There are seemingly contradictory characterizations in two of Andreev's most recent works. In his *Dialectical Materialism* he says: "Perception is not the mechanical sum of sensations; it is a holistic image of objects with all their properties, qualities and aspects, reflected in sensations."[20] Which gives the impression that he agrees with the characterization we quoted above from the *Philosophic Encyclopedia*. But, in his *Principles of the Theory of Knowledge*, he says: "Corresponding to man's sense organs, there are the following forms of perception: visual, auditory, olfactory, gustatory, tactile and motive *(dvigatel'nye)*."[21] This passage would lead one to conclude that perceptions are holistic only in reference to the results of each separate sense-organ. This is not in harmony with the generally accepted explanation, which runs as follows: "While sensations give us only images of single traits and properties of objects, perceptions give us images of the objects as wholes. In perception different sensations are not isolated one from another but organically connected and united into a holistic image."[22] Perception marks the appearance of the 'image' *(obraz)* and is more strongly touched by the subjective factor than are sensations. There is already some degree of synthesis: it is the sense-knowing, the reflection, of the object as a whole and not just of some of its properties.[23]

13. REPRESENTATION[24]

The last stage in sense-knowledge is the representation. It is already more and less than the sense-image of traditional psychologistic logic. It is less in the sense that it lacks some of the sense-data-content which the perceptive image has: it is more in the sense that it pre-figures conceptual knowledge by being abstract to a certain degree. "In representations, as distinguished from sensations and perceptions, the objects and phenomena of the external world are reflected not with all the multifarious individual peculiarities but without a series of details *(bez rjada detalej)*; in representations certain *general*, *typical* traits of similar objects and phenomena are brought to the fore."[25] Thus, despite the fact that it is pre-logical for dialectical materialism's theory of knowledge, the representation already has a certain level of abstraction. We will consider this topic more in detail when we come to the question of abstraction.[26]

52

14. IMAGINATION

Imagination, as an element of contemporary Soviet theory of knowledge, has not received much attention from contemporary Soviet philosophers: it has been more the prey of experimental psychologists. The *Philosophic Encyclopedia* defines imagination as "the psychic activity of establishing representations and mental situations which were never – as such – directly experienced in reality by man. The activity of the imagination is based on man's sensible experience. ... The deviation from reality, which is characteristic of imagination, results from a more or less complex transformation of this material in the consciousness."[27] Already in the representation, the element of subjectivity is quite high since there is a rejection of a "series of details" and the constatation of similarities and typical properties. The imagination is much more unrestrained in this regard: it can compose images at discretion. But, this freedom exists only in reference to the image formed and not in reference to the images used in the formation of the imaginative image. The *Osnovy* hasten to add that the imagination is a synthesis of representations which, in turn, are founded on perceptions and sensations. These are reflections of the objective dialectic. Whence it follows that the imagination, too, is based on reflections of objective reality.[28]

Sense-knowledge, then, is – according to contemporary Soviet theory of knowledge – still a part of the objective dialectic: it is the first signal system. But, as it is definitely cognitive, there is a dialectic of the 'objective content' and the 'subjective mode' of its realization.

That sense-knowledge is knowledge *par excellence* for dialectical materialism is evident from the fact that its basic epistemological category, practice, is *sensible*-transformatory activity. The ultimate court of appeal for all knowledge – including that of logical laws – is the immediate contact of the first signal system with the objective dialectic. Finally, not only is sense-knowledge practical knowledge but it is also knowledge which is constantly being perfected through the development of practical activities: "The higher the level of the development of science and social practice, the more refined are human sensations because the process of the deepening of human knowledge and the process of the perfecting of social production demand from man more exact and refined knowledge in touch, smell, hearing and taste, and force him to constantly train and perfect all the organs of sense." [29]

The treatment of sense-knowledge in contemporary Soviet treatises on knowledge constitutes a prelude to what dialectical materialism considers the object of theory of knowledge in the proper sense of the term. The 'logical' elements of human cognition are the concept, judgement and reasoning.

15. CONCEPT

Intellectual knowledge is, for contemporary dialectical materialism, non-concrete (abstract), indirect and essential. It is non-concrete because it abstracts its forms from 'concrete' knowledge, i.e. from sense-knowledge. It is indirect because all the information which comes to reason comes from the senses. It is essential because, in contradistinction to sense-knowledge which only attains the superficial and non-essential aspects of reality, intellectual knowledge pierces the appearances to reach the essence.

Intellectual knowledge has the character of 'immaterial reflection'. Immaterial means that "consciousness, thought, does not possess the physical properties which material bodies do." [30] The 'reflection' involved here is that of the 'second signal system': it consists of 'signals of signals', being a further development of the first signal system which is sensation. "This form of reflection (logical *T. B.*) of the world is also impossible without sensation. But, thought as distinguished from sensations, perceptions and representations, does not have a concrete-sensible character and reflects not only single things and phenomena but principally the *general* in things and phenomena, their internal essences and the bonds and laws proper to them." [31] Thought, then, as an immaterial reflection is based on sense-knowledge but it is more abstract and general than the representation.

Intellectual knowledge is indirect. In contemporary Soviet theory of knowledge this means that intellectual knowledge is mediated by practice, and this in two ways. First of all sense-knowledge (the practical, the historical) is basic; intellectual knowledge is derived. All that intellectual knowledge contains is a reflection of sense-contents. Sense-knowledge is

54

immediate, practical, contact with the objective dialectic; intellectual knowledge is an abstract and schematic reflection of the objective dialectic.[32] Secondly, practice is responsible for the 'leap' *(skačok)* from sense-knowledge to intellectual knowledge. "The transition from sense-knowledge to intellectual knowledge is a transition from one quality in knowledge to another, which is much higher, and takes place as a leap on the basis of practice, in the course of which are collected sense-data which are then generalized in man's thought."[33] Practice serves, then, both as a 'collector of sense-data', on which are based the generalizations of intellectual knowledge, and as impetus to the qualitative leap from the mere agglomeration of sense-information to the new quality which is intellectual knowledge.

Contemporary Soviet theory of knowledge defines the concept as "that form of thought in which are reflected the most general, essential and necessary properties, characteristics and qualities of real things and phenomena."[34] It has to be delimited from the representation, on the one hand, and from the judgement, on the other. The first problem has left contemporary Soviet philosophers almost completely indifferent. The second, on the contrary, has become the center of a long and voluble discussion which seems destined to continue as long as dialectical materialism retains its present form.

Andreev dismisses the question of the distinction between the concept and representation as follows: "There is a similarity between concepts and representations because both reflect the characteristics of the properties and qualities of the objects of the material world. But, as distinct from representations, concepts do not reflect all the characteristics of the objects but only the more important and essential."[35] He does not seem to be alone in his indifference to the problem of difference of degree of abstraction since serious studies on the question are completely lacking in contemporary Soviet writings on theory of knowledge.

The problem of defining the relationship between the concept and the judgement is another story. The three different solutions given to this problem in contemporary Soviet theory of knowledge are very typical of the difficulty which contemporary Soviet philosophy in general is having in reconciling the disparate elements which it has inherited through the classics from previous philosophic systems. All of the classics held their notions of logic from a combination of three sources: the psychologistic tradition, that which is enshrined in the majority of the world's logic textbooks[36]; Kant; and Hegel. Their subsequent philosophic development took two radically divergent lines – at least as pertains to knowledge. First, they were fighting off Kant's separation of knowledge and the thing-in-itself, using as their main weapon the Hegelian dialectic – here taken as the inter-penetration and inter-communication of all existants. At the same time – lest their insistence on the dialectic as the achievement of monist materialism erase the distinction between knower and known – they reintroduced a little Kant by affirming that the concept was not just a reflective aspect of the universal dialectic but also the result of a preliminary analysis of the sense-information. Thus, on the one hand, the all-pervasive and all-reflecting concept absorbed all other forms of knowing and, on the other, the concept could only result from an analysis of the sense-information, which implies the antecedence of a 'judgement'.

But, a more immediate source of the divergent explanations of the character and connection of concepts and judgements in contemporary Soviet theory of knowledge is to be found in the discussion of 1950 on the nature of logic and on its place in philosophy[37], and in the subsequent efforts to distinguish formal and dialectical logic by the construction of a viable dialectical logic.[38] As a logic, dialectical logic must talk – according to contemporary Soviet philosophers – about the 'forms of thought', i.e. concept, judgement and reasoning. But, as a logic distinct from and higher than formal logic (under which contemporary Soviet philosophy understands textbook logic), dialectical logic must say something other and more profound than what is already said by formal logic. Whence the development of a series of opinions on the character and place of the concept in the two species of logic.

P. V. Kopnin represents a point of view which can be properly termed Hegelian: the concept is a specific form of judgement which reflects that which is universal and essential in things. It is formed by repeated practice which includes not only comparison but also analysis, synthesis, abstraction, concretization, etc. This view is that of the majority of contemporary Soviet theoreticians of knowledge who are in the traditional dialectical-materialist line – especially those who have embarked on a serious effort to construct a dialectical logic.[39] The basic

56

line of argument of this tendency is that, if the concept reflects the most general, essential and necessary properties of objects – a definition which no contemporary dialectical-materialist can deny – then there are only two possibilities: either the concept represents an antecedent analysis and subsequent synthesis of these general properties of the known as presented in the sense-image and it, therefore, is a judgement or series thereof, or the concept is preceded by an analysis and synthesis on the sense-level which, for Kopnin and the others, would be a form of 'Kantianism', i.e. the positing of logical processes on the pre-logical level of sense-knowledge. Kopnin says: "The concept (is) the reflection of the universal and essential in the object. On this level the concept is a specific type of judgement, a specific form of knowledge, laying claim to truth."[40] In other words, of the alternatives 'concept = judgement' or 'judgement on the sense-level preludes the concept', Kopnin, Rozental' and other 'dialectical-logicians' have chosen the first.

Choice of the second member of the alternative is usually the result of a half-hearted effort to make 'dialectical' logic grow out of a partial transformation of traditional textbook logic. Succinctly put, this point of view runs as follows: "The process of formation of concepts requires not only analysis of the interrelations of things and the abstraction of their general properties, but also synthesis, the reunion of these already analyzed basic, essential properties of the objects into one whole."[41] The principal proponent of this point of view is I. D. Andreev. "As a form of thought judgement is closely bound up with the concept. This tie appears, first, in the fact that concepts are inevitably found in the structure of every judgement. Second, not one concept can be formed without the aid of judgements. Third, the content of the concept . . . can be revealed only through judgements because to reveal the content of a concept means to give a definition of this concept, i.e. to enumerate the essential characteristics of the object reflected in the concept in question; and this can be done only with the aid of judgements."[42] This and similar passages could be construed as meaning very simply that judgements are useful in the explicitation of the 'content' of the concept – a statement as accurate as it is secondary. But, the fact that Andreev and cohorts do put more generalization (contemporary Soviet theory of knowledge's term for formation of general concepts) in the representation, i.e. in sense-knowledge, than is habitual even in dialectical materialism, indicates a definite propensity toward the extrapolation of logical categories and operations onto the sense-level. "It is to be noted that these devices of knowledge (analysis, synthesis, abstraction, generalization *T. B.*) exist to some degree even at the level of sense-knowledge."[43] Or again: "The epistemological importance of the representation is also determined by its direct ties with the other forms of sense-knowledge (sensations and perceptions) as well as with *imagination*, i.e. with man's ability to perceive and produce ideal images *(ideal'nye obrazy)* which are generalized reflections of the world around us."[44]

The remainder of contemporary Soviet philosophers – especially those working in formal logic and not paying too much attention to dialectical logic – hold that the concept is, as Kopnin puts it "any sense *(značenie)* of a term. Here, the concept is a member or part of a judgement (subject and predicate)."[45]

A cognate difficulty in the elaboration of a workable meaning for the dialectical concept of dialectical logic is the matter of the 'plasticity' of concepts. Both Engels and Lenin spoke of the 'fluidity' *(gibkost')* of concepts. Contemporary Soviet theoreticians of knowledge – prefering the term 'plasticity' *(plastičnost')* – have seized on this classical characterization of the concept as being decisive in any attempt to make a clear distinction between dialectical logic and formal logic. The basic question may be formulated as follows: if the subjective dialectic is a reflection of the objective dialectic and this latter is in eternal, contradictory movement and change – two statements which, as we have seen, no dialectical-materialist can deny – then the subjective dialectic must reflect the eternal, contradictory movement and change of the objective dialectic. But, precisely, the ontology of dialectical materialism maintains that the essence of the objective dialectic lies in the fact that the objects of the real world are not rigidly isolated from one another, that a thing can pass over into another thing – even into its 'opposite' or 'contradictory'. This implies that concepts, as reflections of objects in the real world, must pass over one into the other in harmony with the movement and change of the objects they reflect. But, it also means that the forms of thought – concept, judgement and reasoning – are dialectically related one to the other: they can pass one into the other. In other words, not only the 'content' of thought – i.e. the objective dialectic as reflected by the subjective dialectic – is dialectically 'plastic' but the same is also true of the forms of thought.

The dialectical logicians accept both of these consequences: both the form and the content of the subjective dialectic, specifically of the concept, are in dialectical evolution and both are involved in a constant series of interchangings. As Rozental' puts it: "Concepts are mobile because they are reflections of reality . . ."[46] And, even more clearly: "Concepts reflect the objective world in its contradictory, dialectical development and reveal the contradictions in the very essence of things and processes. . . . Since concepts reflect things in their dialectical development and change, they themselves cannot be fixed and rigid. Concepts – like the things whose reflection they are – dialectically change, are in constant movement and pass one into the other."[47]

However, the majority opinion on this question in contemporary Soviet theory of knowledge – philosophically defended by Ščedrovickij, Gorskij and others – is that, irrespective of what the content of a mental event may be or be doing, the logical forms of thought are the stable framework of every mental process. According to them, to try to maintain that the forms of thought reflect the real contradictions of the objective dialectic would mean to abandon any possibility of distinguishing logical validity from inconsequence. This would mean the end of logic as a universally valid criterion of correct thought and would mark the end of rational thought in general. In other words, logical laws are, by definition, non-contradictory. Therefore, the plasticity of the concept – which this school of opinion accepts as dialectical-materialist, because 'classical' – refers only to the first of the two consequences mentioned above. The content of a concept may be enriched by the further progress of science. A concept may even disappear because its content, made more precise, is found to be better expressed by another concept – in this sense it 'passes over' into another concept (phlogiston is a frequently used example). This is the only sense in which concepts reflect the 'dialectic of things'.[48]

The upshot of this difference of opinion among contemporary Soviet theoreticians of knowledge – which has not to date been the subject of a direct confrontation – is that the partisans of the plasticity of both the form and content of the concept believe that they have thereby vindicated the existence of a 'dialectical' logic. Those who deny any dialectical character to the forms of thought are automatically espousing the *sovpadenie*-coincidence point of view, defining logic as the science on the forms of thought and leaving to dialectical logic the area untouched by formal logic, i.e. the relationship between logical forms and cognitive contents, the question of truth, which brings us to the next cognitive function in the epistemological arsenal of contemporary Soviet philosophy.

16. JUDGEMENT

Contemporary Soviet characterizations of this form of thought will obviously follow pretty closely the descriptions of the concept. There is, however, the following difference: there seem to be only two major points of view. The members of the group we called Hegelian above tend to join hands with the Kantians to form a united front of dialectical logicians against the other, more traditional, logicians. This is especially clear when it comes to the truth-functional description of the judgement.

In their *Logic* of 1956 Tavanec and Gorskij list the judgement as "the thought *(mysl')* which is either true or false."[49] Gorskij's *Logic* of 1958 defines the judgement as follows: "The *judgement* is a thought *(mysl')* in which something is affirmed or denied about things in reality, and which is objectively either true or false and necessarily one of the two."[50] Typical of the dialectical logicians' view is the following definition from P. V. Kopnin's *Dialectic as Logic:* "The judgement is any relatively complete thought *(otnositel'no zakončennaja mysl')* which reflects things and phenomena of the material world (and) their properties, bonds and relations."[51] The first point of view holds the concept to be primary and the judgement to be derived from (composed of) concepts. The second defines judgement in such a way that it is indistinguishable from the concept.

As a consequence, wheras the logicians hold truth to be proper only to the judgement, the dialectical logicians extend truth to the concept and, by analogy, to all other forms of thought – even those on the level of sense-knowledge. Andreev's explanation shows how – for the dialectical logicians – this conception of the truth-value character of the concept goes hand in hand with the extreme interpretation of the plasticity of concepts as an indeterminacy of both the form and the content of the concept. "If it were true that concepts did not contain truth or falsity, then they would be eternal, given once and for all, and there could not be any argument on how to define a concept. But, one and the same concept is defined by scholars at different times in different ways, depending on the level and depth of our knowledge of the things reflected in the concepts."[52] And he goes on to affirm that truth is also a property of other forms of thought, because they also are reflections of the objective dialectic. "Consequently, the positing and solving of the question on the veracity of concepts is as necessary as it is in the case of the veracity of sensations, perceptions and representations – of all human knowledge – because concepts are forms in which are reflected the properties and relations of things of the real world, while the objective criterion of the veracity of all this knowledge is social practice."[53]

The end-effect of the attribution of truth and falsity to any and all cognitive acts is the elimination of any distinction between formal correctness and informal (contentful) correspondence, between logical validity and epistemological truth. Logic is absorbed by theory of knowledge and *vice versa*. The *sovpadenie*-identity wing of contemporary Soviet theory of knowledge has thus closed the circle of the historicization of logic and has implicitly confirmed Bakradze's statement that logic is formal and dialectical logic can only be – if anything – a theory of knowledge.[54] It is precisely while taking exception to Bakradze's position that V. I. Čerkesov affirms: "On the basis of the arguments developed in the preceding paragraph, it can be considered proved *(možno sčitat' dokazannym)* that there does not exist a formal correctness *(formal'noj pravil'nosti)* which would be completely independent of the character of its content in the sense of truth or falsity."[55]

M. N. Alekseev does not fit into either of these groups.[56] We mentioned above his general distinction in the subjective dialectic of two aspects: the dialectic of thought *(dialektiku myšlenija)* which is independent of the knower and present in all thought by the very fact that thought is a reflection of dialectical reality; and dialectical thought *(dialektičeskoe myšlenie)* which is thinking with awareness of the dialectical character of the objective dialectic. Alekseev has extended this analysis to the concept and the judgement. Thus, just as there is the dialectic of the concept *(dialektika ponjatija)* and the dialectical concept *(dialektičeskoe ponjatie)*, so there is the dialectic of the judgement *(dialektika suždenija)* and the dialectical judgement *(dialektičeskoe suždenie)*. The 'dialectic of judgement' indicates that every judgement – even that used in ordinary formal logic – contains a reflection of the contradictions of the objective dialectic. To use the terminology of Rozental' *et al.*, it is the dialectical content of the judgement as a reflection of the real, contradictory world. Alekseev exemplifies this as follows: "a rose is a rose" and "a rose is a plant"; in as far as the rose is a rose, it is identical to itself; in as far as the rose is a plant, it is distinct from itself. In the dialectic of the judgement, therefore, is contained the unity (rose is rose) and conflict (rose is plant) of opposites, the first law of the dialectic. Turning to the 'dialectical judgement', Alekseev concentrates his attention on the extensional characteristics of the concepts used in the judgement. Whereas in formal logic the concept and judgement are related as part to whole, in dialectical logic the (dialectical) judgement is one thought *(ponjatie)* distributed into subject (singular) and predicate (general). The concept is a dissimulated judgement and the judgement is a distributed concept. Thus, to take the above example: the one thought, rose, appears as singular in the subject (the first occurence of 'rose' in '*rose* is rose' designates 'this (which) is a rose') and as general in the predicate (the second occurence of 'rose' in 'rose is *rose*' designates the 'class of roses' or 'rose in general'). Thus, the concept 'rose' is a dissimulated judgement ('this is a rose') and the judgement, 'rose is rose', is a distributed concept ('rose' as singular in the subject and general in the predicate).

17. REASONING[57]

In general, what the contemporary Soviet theoretician of knowledge says about the concept and judgement and their mutual relationship will determine his view on the nature and function of reasoning. As a matter of fact, however, most contemporary Soviet philosophers – even the dialectical logicians – are not very voluble on this form of thought. They seem to feel that enough has been said when the concept and judgement are clearly defined and related. The standard definition of reasoning is: "Reasoning is the conceptual method *(priem myšlenija)* by which from something known we attain new, inferred knowledge."[58]

One exception to this rule is V. I. Čerkesov who, having rejected any distinction between dialectical logic and formal logic, feels obliged to show that 'dialectical reasoning' is distinct from and superior to the classical syllogism of traditional logic. Čerkesov chooses Khrushchov's peaceful coexistence as exemplifying a form of the 'dialectical syllogism'. The formalization is as follows:

> If there exist A_b and $\bar{A}_b$, then V is possible.
>
> In present circumstances A_o and $\bar{A}_o$ exist.
>
> Therefore, in present circumstances V is possible.

$$A_b = \text{'forces of peace'}$$
$$\bar{A}_b = \text{'forces of war'}$$
$$V = \text{'peaceful coexistence of governments with different social structures'}$$
$$A_o = \text{'situation of the forces of peace'}$$
$$\bar{A}_o = \text{'situation of the forces of war'}$$

Interpreting the symbols in all three statements, we get the following formulation of the 'inference to peaceful coexistence':

If there exist forces of peace and forces of war, then the peaceful coexistence of governments with different social structures is possible.

In present circumstances the forces of peace and the forces of war exist.

Therefore, in present circumstances the peaceful coexistence of governments with different social structures is possible.

By way of explanation, Čerkesov adds that faced with a formal structure like this the formal logician would use the law of identity. But the dialectical logician uses the 'dialectical relationship of universal and particular': 'A_b and $\bar{A}_b$' forms a 'unity of contraries' from either of which V can be inferred.[59]

Another exception to the rule of dialectical-materialist silence on the reasoning-process is M. N. Alekseev's extension of the theory on dialectic of thought and dialectical thought to include a dialectic of reasoning *(dialektika umozaključenija)* and dialectical reasoning *(dialektičeskoe umozaključenie)*. The dialectic of reasoning is analogous to the dialectic of the concept and the dialectic of the judgement in that it designates the dialectical character of any reasoning as a reflection of the dialectical character of the objective dialectic. According to Alekseev, dialectical reasoning is based on a 'dialectically conscious'

63

analysis of the middle term of the syllogism. Thus, in the 'modes' *(v modusax)* the middle term has singular, particular and general notes, i.e. it functions as a concept. In the 'figures' *(v figurax)* it sometimes has singular notes and other times it has general notes, i.e. it functions as a judgement. Finally, in the 'types' *(v vidax)* the middle term has the function of the singular, of the particular and of the general, i.e. it is a reasoning.[60]

These few examples show that dialectical materialism's theoreticians of knowledge are still in search of a peculiarly 'dialectical syllogism'.

In résumé, the basic presentation of the cognitive elements of contemporary Soviet theory of knowledge is rooted in the tradition of psychologistic logic as it is presented in most non-mathematical-logical textbooks. Deviations from this norm are due to efforts to produce a distinctly dialectical-materialist dialectical logic. Up to now, the over-all result of this effort has been an undeniable reduction of dialectical logic to a type of theory of knowledge which is as related to formal logic as the Scholastic *logica maior* was to *logica minor*.

REFERENCES

1. Lenin: *Filosofskie tetrady*, pp. 146–147.
2. Andreev: *Osnovy*, p. 130.
3. VPŠ: *Diamat*, p. 310.
4. Cf. Chapter III, pp. 38–42.
5. *Ibid., loc. cit.*
6. *Teorija oščuščenija*, pp. 75–76. Cf. pp. 76–79 for the whole survey.
7. *Materija i soznanie*. Moskva. 1951.
8. *Dialektičeskij materializm o processe poznanija*. Moskva. 1954.
9. *Osnovnye stupeni processa poznanija*. Moskva. 1957.
10. *Osnovnye voprosy teorii poznanija*. Gor'kij. 1957.
11. *Očerk dialektičeskogo materializma*. Moskva. 1948.
12. 'Poznavaemost' mira i ego zakonomernostej'. In *O dialektičeskom materializme*. Moskva. 1952.
13. *Teorija otraženija*. Moskva–Leningrad. 1936.
14. *Marksistsko-leninskaja teorija otraženija i učenie I. P. Pavlova o vysšej nervnoj dejatel'nosti*. Moskva. 1956.
15. Anan'ev: *op.cit.* p. 75.
16. VPŠ: *Diamat*, p. 113. Cf. also A. M. Koršunov: 'Obraz i znak' (Image and Sign). *V MGU* 1962, 1, 60–70.
17. "*The association of sensations is determined by the direct, joint activity of external objects on diverse analyzers. (p. 433)* ... Therefore, there is no doubt that the conditioned reflex or temporal bond in its most general form forms the material

basis of the association of sensations. (p. 434) . . . The inclusion of oral-auditory sensations in any association of various sensations means the necessary inclusion of the temporal bonds of the second signal system in the system of temporal bonds of the first signal system. (p. 440) . . . From what was said above, it follows that: (1) the interactivity of analyzers takes place conditioned-reflectively *(uslovno-reflektorno)*, changing with changes of external circumstances; (2) this interactivity proceeds according to the law of the mutual induction of neural processes and of their motion in the cerebral core; (3) in the association of sensations during the process of conditioned-reflective interactivity of the analyzers there is a change in the level of sensibility and, consequently, there is a preparedness for new reactions of the principal analyzer in the given association. (p. 445) . . . The intermodal association of sensations expresses the integrality of man's sensible reflection of objective reality and of the unity of the material world. (p. 446)". (Anan'ev: *op.cit.*)

18. Cf. *Ibid.* pp. 88–89. Andreev adds a sixth in *Osnovy* p. 142.
19. *Filosofskaja enciklopedija*, vol. 1, p. 292.
20. Andreev: *Diamat*, p. 429.
21. Andreev: *Osnovy*, p. 142.
22. VPŠ: *Diamat*, p. 313.
23. *Osnovy*, p. 168. Cf. F. I. Georgiev: 'Problema čuvstvennogo i racional'nogo v poznanii' (The Problem of the Sensible and the Rational in Knowledge). *VF* 1955, 1, p. 32.
24. Since the *predstavlenie* corresponds neither to the traditional 'image' nor to the *phantasma* of the Scholastics, we choose to translate it as 'representation'.
25. *Osnovy*, p. 173. Cf. Georgiev: *op.cit.*, p. 35.
26. Cf. Chapter V, p. 69 f.
27. *Filosofskaja enciklopedija*, vol. 1, p. 285.
28. *Osnovy*, p. 172.
29. Andreev: *Osnovy*, p. 138.
30. *Osnovy*, p. 160.
31. *Ibid.*, p. 173. In *O roli abstrakcii v poznanii* (On the Role of Abstraction in Knowledge). Erevan. 1957. G. A. Gevorkjan says: "The representation *describes (opisyvaet);* the concept *explains (ob'jasnjaet)*." (p. 127).
32. Cf. V. I. Čerkesov: *Materialističeskaja dialektika kak logika i teorija poznanija.* Moskva. 1962. p. 264ff. M. M. Rozental': *Principy dialektičeskoj logiki.* Moskva. 1960. p. 176ff.
33. VPŠ: *Diamat*, p. 326. Cf. also Georgiev: *op.cit.* p. 36.
34. Andreev: *Osnovy*, p. 154.
35. *Loc.cit.*
36. E. g. B. Erdmann: *Logik.* Erster Band. Halle 1907. and A. Höfler: *Logik.* Wien–Leipzig. 1922. Cf. J. M. Bocheński: *Formale Logik.* Freiburg–München. 1962. pp. 568–571 for further titles.
37. Cf. Chapter II, p. 22 f.
38. *Loc. cit.*
39. Cf. M. M. Rozental': *op.cit.*, p. 204f.
40. P. V. Kopnin: *Dialektika kak logika* (Dialectic as Logic). Kiev. 1961. p. 269.
41. VPŠ: *Diamat*, p. 338.
42. Andreev: *Osnovy*, p. 173.
43. *Ibid.*, p. 162.

44. *Ibid.*, p. 143.
45. Kopnin: *loc.cit.*
46. Rozental': *op.cit.*, p. 239.
47. VPŠ: *Diamat*, p. 330. "Solving, from the position of dialectical materialism, the question on the relation between the spiritual and the material, Marx and Engels formulated the basic thesis of their theory of knowledge: any content of our sensations, representations, concepts, is a reflection of objective reality. Not only the content of representations but also the logical forms and categories in which the process of knowledge takes place are correspondent reflections of the external world. Whence it is clear that the principles of the dialectical-materialist interpretation of objective reality are at the same time the principles of scientific investigation of it. In this sense, dialectical materialism marks the end of the opposition of ontology and epistemology which characterized many pre-Marxist philosophic systems." (*Istorija filosofii*, vol. 3, p. 238).
48. Cf. G. P. Ščedrovickij: 'O nekotoryx momentax v razvitii ponjatii' (On some Moments in the Development of Concepts). *VF* 1958, 6, 55–64 and D. P. Gorskij: 'O vidax naučnyx abstrakcij i sposobax ix obosnovanija' (On Types of Scientific Abstractions and Modes of their Establishment). *VF* 1961, 9, 65–78. The dialectical logicians violently attack both this moderate point of view and that – more extreme, in their eyes – of Bakradze as "separation of theory and practice" because there is a separation of the form and content of thought. Cf. Rozental': *op. cit.*, p. 91.
49. *Logika.* Moskva. 1956. p. 72.
50. *Logika.* Moskva. 1958. p. 86.
51. Kopnin: *op.cit.*, p. 235.
52. Andreev: *Osnovy*, p. 291.
53. *Ibid.*, p. 293.
54. K. S. Bakradze: *VF* 1956, 2, 218–224.
55. Čerkesov: *op.cit.*, p. 98.
56. Cf. his works in bibliography; especially, *Dialektika form myšlenija* (1959); *Dialektičeskaja logika* (1960); and the articles in *FN* 1959, 3, 69–79. and *Izvestija AN Armjanskoj SSR* 1959, 3.
57. *Umozaključenie* can also mean 'conclusion' or 'inference'. We use 'reasoning' because what contemporary Soviet philosophers usually mean by *umozaključenie* is the cognitive process which is formalized in the syllogism.
58. Gorskij: *op.cit.*, p. 124. Rozental': *op.cit.*, p. 357. Kopnin: *op.cit.*, p. 328.
59. Cf. Čerkesov: *op.cit.*, pp. 466–472.
60. Cf. M. N. Alekseev: *FN* 1959, 3, 69–79.

CHAPTER V

BASIC COGNITIVE MODES

By cognitive modes we mean here those processes or dynamic relationships in which the cognitive elements dealt with in the previous section are included.

Because the subjective dialectic is a reflection of the objective dialectic, there are – in principle – as many cognitive modes as there are modes of being. In this case, there would be a cognitive pair corresponding to every ontological pair – i.e. to every categorial pair (e.g. cause and effect, form and content, etc.). In practice, however, contemporary Soviet theoreticians of knowledge limit themselves to the following basic cognitive functions: generalization *(obobščenie)*, analysis and synthesis *(analiz i sintez)*, abstract and concrete *(abstraktnoe i konkretnoe)*, deduction and induction *(dedukcija i indukcija)*, hypothesis *(gipoteza)*, theory *(teorija)*, law *(zakon)* and analogy *(analogija)*.

18. GENERALIZATION

The formation of general concepts (not only 'universals' but also any concept designating more than a single thing), or generalization, is distinguished from abstraction in contemporary Soviet theory of knowledge by the fact that generalization can also take place on the sense-level whereas abstraction is limited by most contemporary Soviet philosophers to the logical level. As mentioned above, it is not easy to determine the exact difference between sense-generalization and conceptual generalization in the minds of contemporary Soviet authors. The *Osnovy* describe sense-generalization as follows: "in representations certain *general, typical* traits of similar objects and phenomena are brought to the fore."[1] This is distinguished from conceptual generalization by the fact that "thought reflects not only singular things and phenomena but mainly the *general (obščee)* in things and phenomena, their internal essences, the bonds and laws which are proper to them."[2] This seems to mean that the sense-generalization is a type of comparative statistical average of the physical characteristics of several similar things while the conceptual generalization attains that which is essential. S. L. Rubinštejn is clearer, if not more explicit: "We distinguish two forms of generalization: primary, empirical generalization through comparison and distinction of the general in two or more distinct phenomena or situations, and the higher form of scientific generalization based on the selection of the essential aspects of phenomena and their interconnections."[3]

As an example of sense-generalization, A. A. Vetrov offers the following: we can form a general representation (i.e. a sense-image) of 'sheep-dog' or 'bulldog', but we cannot form a general representation of 'dog' because 'dog' is epistemologically based on 'sheep-dog' and 'bulldog', etc. It, therefore, can only be generalized as a concept, i.e. on the logical level. The reason for this, according to Vetrov, is that the essential characteristic of the concept is 'distributivity of notes' which is impossible at the sense-level.[4]

Thus, sense-generalization isolates some superficially general properties while conceptual generalization permits an isolation of that which is essential to the object under study. At both levels generalization requires an analysis of the phenomenon into its conceptual parts.

19. ANALYSIS AND SYNTHESIS

According to contemporary Soviet theory of knowledge, analysis is "the conceptual distribution of the object into its constituent parts in order to discover the simplest elements of that which is complex"[5] and synthesis "gives knowledge on the object as a totality. But this knowledge (1) is attained on the basis of a previous analysis and (2) combines in thought only that which is objectively combined in reality."[6]

For the dialectical-materialist theory of knowledge these two operations form a dialectical whole; either of them, without the other, leads to a 'vulgar materialist' (if analysis is taken without synthesis) or 'metaphysical idealist' (if synthesis is taken without analysis) separation of theory and practice.

In principle, analysis and synthesis are conceptual operations and, therefore, only pertinent to intellectual knowledge or – in Soviet terminology – to the 'logical' level. But, as we have seen in the previous section, sense-generalization requires some analysis and synthesis already at the level of sense-knowledge which is, by definition, pre-logical. There are two general ways in which contemporary Soviet theoreticians of knowledge attempt to justify this extrapolation of logical operations into the domain of sense-knowledge. The logicians *(sovpadenie*-coincidence wing of contemporary Soviet philosophy) explain that although the reality reflected in the subjective dialectic is 'discrete', i.e. the objective dialectic is 'distributed' in the form of singular existant things, they are connected to one another by 'real' relations. Among these real relations are those of similarity – of varying degrees. It is the superficial similarities which the senses collate in the process of forming the representation from sensation and perception. Therefore, the generalization, analysis and synthesis found at the sense-level are not extrapolated logical operations: they are more or less automatic results of the combination of several perceptions in one representation.[7] The dialectical logicians have a more synthetic approach: they maintain that there is a dialectical unity of the singular and universal both in the objective dialectic and in the subjective dialectic. Put in the terms of the medieval discussion on 'universals', the dialectical logicians propose a *universale in re* and a *singulare in conceptu*.[8] This is explained in the context of the 'dialectic of abstract and concrete'.

20. ABSTRACT AND CONCRETE

Abstraction as a process *(abstrakcija*[9] or *abstragirovanie)* "is one of the moments of the process of knowledge, which consists in a mental turning away *(otvlečenie)* from a series of non-essential properties and bonds of the studied object and a selection of its basic properties, bonds and relations."[10] There are then two basic steps or aspects to abstraction: the exclusion of all that is superficial, non-essential, accidental, and the hitting upon what is essential to the object under study. The first of these coincides with sense-generalization; the second is proper to abstraction. D. P. Gorskij, the most voluble contemporary Soviet theoretician of knowledge on the subject of abstraction, adds that one must carefully distinguish the abstraction of formal logic from that of dialectical logic. In the former all abstracted properties and relations

69

are formalized on a single epistemological plane; in the latter the nature of reality is conserved by means of a dialectical abstraction which preserves the hierarchical distribution of properties and relations as they actually are in the objective dialectic. The former is extensional and that of dialectical logic intensional. But, the process of abstraction itself is not very extensively treated in contemporary Soviet theory of knowledge.[11] It is rather the categories 'abstract' and 'concrete' which are discussed.

The 'abstract' and the 'concrete' are a categorial pair to which along with 'singular' and 'general', contemporary Soviet philosophy gives great epistemological importance. Andreev explains this situation as follows: "A clear manifestation of the dialectical character of the process of knowledge, of the inseparable unity of all of its aspects and stages and especially of the organic unity of the sensible and rational stages of knowledge, is the dialectic of the singular and general and of the concrete and abstract in knowledge. Embodying the unity and conflict of contraries, these categories occupy a very prominent place in the conceptual process. This is to be explained by the fact that these contraries are objectively contained in the objects, phenomena and processes themselves and are reflected in the process of knowledge in our concepts, representations, judgements, etc."[12] The 'abstract and concrete' are not just categories which the mind uses in the analysis and comprehension of reality. They are to be found as well in the objective dialectic as in the subjective. Just as the subjective dialectic contains concepts which designate the singular and 'concretized', so the objective dialectic contains, in addition to concrete and singular things, general (therefore, abstract) properties, laws, etc. In particular, the abstract is intellectual knowledge which, although it gives a true reflection of reality, cannot give a complete picture because it is not in direct contact with the objective dialectic. The concrete is sense-knowledge which, as we indicated above, is knowledge *par excellence* for dialectical materialism. It is in direct contact with the objective dialectic and, therefore, gives a complete and full picture of it. The abstract, then, is a one-sided reflection which only approximates reality by reflecting certain, general aspects of it; the concrete is the full picture of the objective dialectic – it subsumes the singular and general and, therefore, also contains the abstract in 'concretized' form. This conception has

70

given rise in dialectical materialism to a peculiar cognitive mode – a method of thought – known as the 'ascent from abstract to concrete' *(vosxoždenie ot abstraktnogo k konkretnomu)* which contemporary Soviet philosophers describe as follows: knowledge begins with the sensible-concrete, i.e. with direct sense-contact with the objective dialectic. This knowledge is already concrete, but only 'abstractly concrete' since the representation already generalizes to a certain extent. Intellectual or logical knowledge is abstract, meaning that there is a concentration on certain aspects of the thing in question to the detriment of others. The 'ascent from abstract to concrete' is a 're-knowing' of the thing in question, adding to the abstract image all the wealth of concrete detail. The result is the 'concrete' which is full, profound, all-round knowledge of the object.[13]

Intimately bound up with the 'dialectic of the abstract and concrete' is the 'dialectic of the general and singular'. Contemporary Soviet philosophy does not know a problem of universals as was known in medieval philosophy and as is current in contemporary Anglo-American philosophy. The 'universal', together with the 'singular' and the 'particular', is a category which reflects something in the objective dialectic. "The category 'universal' is a reflection of the real universal, i.e. of the objective unity of the multifarious phenomena of nature and society in the consciousness of man. The objective universal is reflected in thought in the form of a system of concepts and definitions. The abstract universal, selected by comparison from the mass of singular and particular phenomena, plays a significant but limited role in knowledge. In itself the abstract universal is not in a position to reflect basic universality because the universal exists outside of consciousness not as simple similarity or as abstract identity of phenomena but as living, concrete bonds of distinct and opposed things, phenomena and processes, as law, necessity, etc."[14] Thus, there are singulars and universals in reality, in the objective dialectic; there are singulars and universals in thought, in the subjective dialectic. The 'real' singulars are the distinct things which exist in reality and go to make up the objective dialectic. The 'real' universals are the actual relations which unite the distinct things into one whole, called the objective dialectic. The universal in thought, in the subjective dialectic, is the 'abstract universal'; it presents a one-sided view of the thing in question, i.e. it abstracts one or another of the real relations which go to make up the real universal. The singular in thought is two-fold. On the one hand, it is the simple reflection in the subjective dialectic of the singular thing. On the other hand, when the singular in thought is the result of an 'ascent from abstract to concrete', it is the concrete, i.e. the full and profound reflection of the singular in all its generality. Since the generality or the universality of the singular consists in its real relations to the other components of the objective dialectic, the concrete is the reflection of the thing with all its properties, relations, etc.[15]

21. DEDUCTION AND INDUCTION

With the exception of the works of an increasing number of mathematical logicians, most Soviet treatises on induction and deduction remain on the level of nineteenth century science. The following definitions are representative of the point of view current in contemporary Soviet writings. "In the process of knowledge man observes single cases and then generalizes them, forming general statements *(položenie)*. This is the inductive process. He extends the obtained generalizations to new phenomena, facts and cases. This is deduction."[16] Thus, induction and deduction are the two phases in the so-called hypothetical-deductive method. Further: "(in) induction ... the process of reasoning goes from particular to general, from single facts to general conclusions. Deduction (is) reasoning from the general to particular, distributing the general statement into its single cases."[17]

Again – as in the case of abstraction and the universal – contemporary dialectical materialism is interested not so much by the epistemological and logical problems (the aspects which most interest non-Soviet philosophers) of induction and deduction as cognitive processes, but by the interrelationship of the two in the context of the reflection of the objective dialectic by the subjective dialectic. There is necessarily a dialectical unity of induction with deduction and *vice versa*. Deduction without induction leads to 'idealistic a-priorism' and to formalism. Induction without deduction is 'metaphysical empiricism'. The place of induction and deduction in the process of knowledge is closely bound up – for Soviet philosophers – with the abstract and concrete and general and singular. Induction begins with the 'concrete-sensible' and

72

proceeds to the 'abstract-general', i.e. it is the mental operation involved in the first step in the dialectical relations between the 'abstract and concrete' and 'general and singular'. From the 'abstract-general' deduction moves to the 'concrete' – neither the 'sense-concrete' nor the 'abstract concrete', but the 'dialectical concrete', i.e. the real in all its fullness as related to all other components of the objective dialectic. Thus, a true deduction must (a) be based on an antecedent induction, (b) follow the 'ascent from abstract to concrete'. The 'metaphysician' – among other shortcomings – performs only a pseudo-deduction, i.e. one which remains on the level of the 'abstract-concrete' and is out of contact with reality.[18] Induction moves from practical sense-contact with the historical, the objective dialectic, to the abstract and incomplete logical. By 'ascent from the abstract to the concrete', deduction moves from the abstract and incomplete logical to the complete 'dialectical concrete' which reflects the 'historical reality (actuality)' of the objective dialectic.

22. HYPOTHESIS

The treatment of the hypothesis as a cognitive mode in the dialectical-materialist context is a relatively recent phenomenon. And, as in the case of the treatment of induction and deduction, contemporary Soviet philosophy remains on the level of nineteenth century philosophy of scientific method. Since we will be considering in detail the contemporary Soviet views on scientific method, we will limit ourselves here to a description of how contemporary Soviet theoreticians of knowledge integrate the main notions of scientific procedure into the context of dialectical materialism's theory of knowledge.

P. V. Kopnin is the most eloquent contemporary Soviet philosopher on the hypothesis and its cognitive function. In an article, published in 1954, he describes the hypothesis as follows. The hypothesis is a form of transition from the collection of facts to laws wherein knowledge moves from the singular to the general, from appearance to essence, from secondary essentiality to primary essence. In other words, the hypothesis – like all knowledge – begins with the sensible-concrete and forms an abstract-general. Kopnin goes on to show how the hypothesis differs from any knowledge which moves from the objective dialectic

73

to the subjective dialectic. The hypothesis proceeds by (a) the collection of data, (b) the formation of propositions expressing the bonds between the things and processes expressed in the data, (c) the verification of deductions from (b) through new observations. The hypothesis implies both sense-knowledge and intellectual knowledge. It talks not only about causal relations but about all types of 'bonds' which exist in the objective dialectic. As a reflection of reality, the hypothesis also contains the dialectic of relative and absolute truth. Like the scientific theory, the hypothesis is a complex form of reflection in which induction, deduction and tradition come into play. The propositions on bonds which are formed in the hypothesis are based on analogy ("between many cases"); induction, based on previous analysis and synthesis, complements analogy by providing systematization of the data. The deduction involved in the hypothesis consists in the extrapolation and/or inference of conclusions which are then verified. A working hypothesis is a guess which is based on a minimum of sound data; a 'real hypothesis' is based on "already established scientific knowledge". The hypothesis should be simple but it can be complex if the reality which it reflects is complex. The value of the hypothesis depends on (a) the quantity of basic data at hand, (b) the extension of the hypothesis, (c) the essentiality of the bonds involved. The hypothesis, verified by practice, becomes a scientific theory (see below).[19] In a later article, Kopnin adds a few formal characteristics to his description of the hypothesis. The hypothesis is a complex of judgements in which the probable judgements (i.e. the hypothetical elements) are necessarily based on the established (i.e. proved) judgements. The hypothesis has a "central principle" which is what is to be proved. The premises of the hypothesis are necessarily provable. In building a hypothesis the scientist (a) poses a question, (b) makes a first surmise, (c) checks the surmise against the data. The hypothesis is not fantastic (i.e. the work of freely creative imagination) because scientific imagination is limited by the reality with which it works. The hypothesis is a means of approaching absolute truth through relative truth.[20] L. B. Baženov lists the following conditions which must be fulfilled by a legitimate scientific hypothesis. It must be based on facts and take into account all the material pertinent to the domain in question. It must not contradict established scientific theories unless it can show them to be insufficient or false. It cannot be unverifiable in principle. It should apply to many cases; at least to more than those directly involved in the experiments from which the hypothesis is built. The hypothesis should be as simple as possible: the simpler is truer because the explanation is forced back to such basic laws as the materiality of the world, the laws of the dialectic, etc.[21] In the *Philosophic Encyclopedia* Baženov distinguishes two types of hypothesis: the descriptive *(opisatel'nyj)* hypothesis is a presupposition on one or another form of bond between observed phenomena; the explanatory *(ob'jasnitel'nyj)* hypothesis is a presupposition of bonds between observed phenomena and the internal base which produces them.[22]

In brief, the hypothesis embodies all the basic dialectical-materialist cognitive categories: it is a reflection of the objective dialectic; like imagination it is objective because based on elements (judgements) which are objective reflections of reality. It is based on practice, i.e. on sense-contact, and verified in practical (experimental) activity. It is a relative truth, a special stage on the road toward absolute truth. Finally, the hypothesis dialectically combines the logical and historical, the abstract and concrete, the singular and general, and deduction and induction.

23. THEORY

"The hypothesis is transformed into a scientifically established theory when and only when, thanks to the development of science and social practice and to the accumulation of new facts and established scientific statements, there appears the possibility of establishing the veracity of this hypothesis either directly through human practice or (indirectly) by infering it as consequence from other true statements."[23] Briefly, a theory is a hypothesis without the hypothetical element. Therefore, it shares in all the dialectical-materialist epistemological categories possessed by the hypothesis.

That which Kopnin calls the 'central principle' of the hypothesis becomes in the theory or 'established hypothesis' what contemporary Soviet philosophers call the 'idea' *(ideja)*. 'Idea' is here used in the sense of the German *Leitidee*. Kopnin defines it as follows: "The idea reflects that law which is at the basis of a scientific theory. A scientific

75

theory may contain a great number of laws and concepts ... but among them there is a law such that it expresses the most general, most all-inclusive and most marked uniformity *(zakonomernost')* which is fundamental to all the other laws."[24]

24. LAW

For contemporary dialectical materialism the law is the proper object of knowledge. All of the elements and processes in Soviet theory of knowledge draw their value from the fact that they are thought to permit the discovery of laws. The law is defined as "a definite and necessary connection between things, phenomena or processes, which flows from their inner nature, from their essence."[25] There are laws of being and laws of thought. The laws of being, or laws of the objective dialectic, are of two types. The 'basic laws of the dialectic' constitute the 'essence' of all reality. The more particular laws of being are the 'essences' of particular things and processes. They are what is necessary, general, stable, identical, etc. in the phenomena which make up the objective dialectic.[26] The laws of thought are the reflection and expression of the laws of being, i.e. of the laws which constitute the objective dialectic. "The laws of science are reflections of the objective laws of nature and society."[27]

25. ANALOGY

Only recently has contemporary Soviet philosophy begun to consider the role of analogy in knowledge. For the moment, the Soviet accounts remain at the level of J. S. Mill's canons. Reasoning by analogy is defined by Andreev as "a reasoning in which from the similarity of several characteristics of two or more objects or phenomena a conclusion is drawn on the similarity of the other characteristics of these objects or phenomena."[28] In a recent study, A. A. Starčenko puts reasoning by analogy, along with deduction and induction, as one of the basic forms of reasoning. He calls it 'traductive' *(traduktivnyj)* and gives the following description: *A* has qualities *a, b, c, d, e; B* has the ostensive qualities *a, b, c, d;* therefore, *B* has *e*.[29]

Our presentation of the constituents of contemporary Soviet theory of knowledge in this chapter is incomplete in one regard. We have restricted our attention to those elements and aspects thereof which are properly dialectical-materialist, i.e. which follow from the ontological premisses of the metaphysical and cosmological doctrines of contemporary Soviet philosophy. There is another influence at work in contemporary Soviet theory of knowledge. It is the strain of 'scientism' which was already inherent in the 'classical' heritage and which has been reinforced by contemporary Soviet philosophy's contact and conflict with methodology of science in more recent times. This is the subject-matter of the next chapter.

REFERENCES

1. *Osnovy*, p. 173. Cf. also A. M. Koršunov's attack (*FN* 1962, 2, 83–90) on Andreev's and Rutkevič's *Dialektičeskij materializm* (Moskva. 1959) because they limited sense-generalization to the representation. According to Koršunov, the dialectic of singular and general is already in sensation (the distinction of some properties of the thing from the others) and perception (holistic unity of distinct sensations).
2. *Osnovy, loc.cit.*
3. S. L. Rubinštejn: *Principy i puti razvitija psixologii.* Moskva. 1959. p. 89.
4. In *VF* 1958, 1, 39–46.
5. *Osnovy*, p. 330.
6. *Ibid.*, p. 331.
7. B. G. Anan'ev: *Teorija oščuščenija.* Leningrad. 1961. p. 31.
8. Cf. *Filosofskaja enciklopedija* vol. 1, pp. 301–302
9. *Abstrakcija* has the same double use as the English 'abstraction', i.e. indicating a process or its result.
10. *Filosofskaja enciklopedija*, vol. 1, pp. 12–13.
11. D. M. Kedrov distinguishes five sorts or levels in 'O sootnošenil form dviženija materii v prirode' (On the Inter-relation of the Forms of the Motion of Matter in Nature). *VF* 1959, 4, p. 52. Of late mathematical abstraction is much in vogue: cf. G. I. Ruzavin: 'O xaraktere matematičeskoj abstrakcii' (On the Character of Mathematical Abstraction). *VF* 1960, 9, 143–154.
12. Andreev: *Osnovy*, p. 202.
13. Cf. the article by A. A. Zinov'ev in *Filosofskaja enciklopedija* vol. 1, pp. 295–298. See, also E. V. Il'enkov: *Dialektika abstraktnogo i konkretnogo v "Kapitale" Marksa.* Moskva. 1960. and M. M. Rozental': *Voprosy dialektiki v "Kapitale" Marksa.* Moskva. 1955. In *VF* 1962, 3, p. 89, V. S. Kazakovcev suggests a *vosxoždenie ot konkretnogo čerez abstraktnoe k konkretnomu.*
14. *Filosofskaja enciklopedija*, vol. 1, pp. 301–302.
15. Cf. the works cited in note 13 (above). P. P. Čupin (*FN* 1962, 1, 80–87) maintains that practice is the most universal of universals because its universality (a) precedes that of thought, (b) is richer than that of thought, (c) is direct. For a verbose but clear treatment of all aspects of abstraction, see G. A. Gevorkjan: *O roli abstrakcii v poznanii.* Erevan. 1957.

16. *Osnovy*, p. 328.
17. *Ibid.*, p. 327.
18. Cf. Andreev: *Osnovy*, p. 179ff. *Osnovy*, p. 327ff. and V. S. Švyrev in *VF* 1961, 3, 74–85.
19. *VF* 1954, 4, 48–59.
20. *FN* 1958, 2, 106–120.
21. Cf. *Osnovnye voprosy teorii gipotezy* (Basic Questions of the Theory of Hypothesis). Moskva. 1961. and his article: 'O gipoteze v estestvoznanii' (On the Hypothesis in Natural Science). *VF* 1962, 9, 154–164.
22. *Filosofskaja enciklopedija*, vol. 1, p. 371.
23. Andreev: *Osnovy*, p. 187.
24. 'Ideja i ee rol' v poznanii' (The Idea and its Role in Knowledge). *VF* 1959, 9, 53–64.
25. *Osnovy*, p. 202.
26. Cf. *Osnovy*, pp. 202–208 and *Filosofskaja enciklopedija*, vol. 1, pp. 301–302.
27. *Osnovy*, p. 208. Strangely enough, the authors use *zakon* instead of the usual *zakonomernost'*. Cf. also I. D. Andreev: 'Materialističeskaja dialektika kak teorija poznanija i dialektičeskaja logika' (The Materialist Dialectic as Theory of Knowledge and Dialectical Logic). In *Voprosy teorii poznanija i logiki*. Moskva. 1960. p. 81.
28. Andreev: *Osnovy*, p. 180.
29. *Rol' analogii v poznanii* (On the Role of Analogy in Knowledge). Moskva. 1961. p. 7.

CHAPTER VI

METHODS AND METHODOLOGIES

The study of scientific methods and the development of methodology as a scientific discipline is one of the fruits of the contemporary advances in formal logic. The cultural isolation of the Soviet Union under Stalin led to an almost complete ignorance on the part of Soviet philosophers of the progress made in the non-Communist world in these and related domains.[1] On the other hand, ignorance of what is being done in these fields in the Soviet Union is almost as profound on the part of Western researchers. We have elsewhere taken up the question of the value of Soviet reflections on methodology in the light of principles generally accepted in Western science.[2] Here we will restrict ourselves to those aspects of Soviet speculation on method and methodology which have an epistemological significance.

26. THE CLASSICS ON METHOD

That ruminations on method and methodology do not abound in the works of the classics of Marxism-Leninism is to be expected since the era in which they were written was given over to another type of philosophic activity. Nevertheless, their works – especially Engels' *Dialectics of Nature* – do contain random notes and a few *ex professo* passages on such questions.[3] In drawing its methodological inspiration from these meager beginnings Soviet philosophy has, from the outset, been plagued by a basic ambiguity.

On the one hand, there is Engels' openly positivistic and anti-philosophical tendency to eliminate all philosophy in favor of the 'positive' sciences and logic. According to Engels the appearance of each positive science in the course of history has served to restrict the domain of application of philosophy. When the natural and historical sciences have reached a sufficient degree of development philosophy will be reduced to the study of thought, viz. logic.[4] Therefore, when Engels turns in his works to questions of a methodological nature, the main emphasis is on the classification of the natural sciences. He is seeking 'unified science' from below.

On the other hand, Marx and Lenin when they speak of the 'dialectical method' have in mind a method which, although it is applicable both to theory and practice, is primarily philosophical as is particularly evident in Lenin's *Materialism and Empirio-Criticism*. The universal dialectical method is first and foremost the general method of knowledge; it is *a fortiori* and by reduction the method of the natural (positive) sciences. In contradistinction to Engels this is 'unified science' from above.

Contemporary Soviet philosophy's speculations on method and methodology are developments along both of these lines coupled with an effort to harmonize them. The effort at harmonization has led, on the one hand, to a great concentration – exemplified in the work of B. M. Kedrov – on the question of the classification of the empirical sciences and, on the other, to the speculations of M. M. Rozental' *et al.* on the nature of the 'Marxist dialectical method' and on its applicability to the investigatory work of the natural sciences.

27. THE CLASSIFICATION OF SCIENCES

Although the classification of sciences is decidedly a methodological question and is accepted by Soviet philosophers as such, the principles of division which are held to be applicable are of a decidedly non-methodological character. These principles are easily traceable to their dialectical-materialist origin.

Corresponding to the definition of Marxism-Leninism as the 'science on the general laws of nature, society and thought', the sciences are divided into natural, social and philosophic.[5] But even this basic division is not a hard and fast delimitation – this would be 'metaphysics' – but an approximation subject to the vicissitudes of dialectical development and made to conform to the requirements of 'materialist objectivity', as is explained below.

Significant here, too, is Marxism-Leninism's doctrine on base and superstructure. Science belongs to superstructure and, as such, is a reflection of the material-productive base. Concretely, this means that the material object of a science is more significant for its characterization than are any considerations of the methods employed[6] and goes a long way toward explaining the seemingly congenital inability of contemporary Soviet philosophers to discuss methodological questions in abstraction from ontological and psychological considerations.[7]

But, the fundamental considerations in Soviet classification of sciences derive directly from the dialectic, on the one hand, and from dialectical materialism, on the other. The 'dialectic' here has the fundamentally historicist sense that everything is involved in a process of constant development and differentiation. A first and primary consequence of the dialectic for the classification of sciences is that not only the object of the science – which, as indicated above, is decisive for its characterization – is in constant evolution but even the knowledge itself of the object is in constant evolution.[8] The objective dialectic's evolution is reflected in the 'scientific' sub-section of the subjective dialectic. For the classification of sciences this means: (a) the object of any given science is in constant evolution, whence the science in question is significantly different from its historical predecessors. For example, physics today differs from physics of the time of Newton not only because more is known about the object thereof but also because the object itself has evolved. (b) the science itself as a *corpus* of knowledge – a sub-section of the subjective dialectic – undergoes a constant evolution. Thus, in physics there has been a constant accumulation of new knowledge since Newton's time, the result of which is an increase in the depth and accuracy of man's knowledge of the physical universe.

This dialectical point of view explains the two salient characteristics of contemporary Soviet classification of sciences: the hierarchical subordination of sciences and the proliferation of intermediary scientific disciplines. According to contemporary Soviet philosophers who write on the classification of sciences, the old method of classifying sciences by 'coordination' (e.g. juxtaposition of physics, chemistry and biology) has been superseded by the Marxist-Leninist principle of 'subordination' which uses a 'correct historical view of the evolution of science' as the basis for the arrangement of sciences in relation to each other.[9] Sciences are dialectically inter-related in the same way that their respective objects in the real world are dialectically related in the course of evolution. In order to correctly classify sciences it is necessary, for example, in addition to distinguishing from one another such sciences

81

as physics, chemistry and biology, also to point out the reciprocal influences between them in the course of the evolution of scientific knowledge.

The proliferation of intermediary scientific disciplines follows as a result of taking into account the evolutive movement of both the objects of sciences and of the sciences themselves. In the evolution of the objects there are 'transitional phases' in the process of 'transition from quantitative changes to qualitative changes' which, although they may fall under the purvey of no existant scientific discipline, are legitimate objects of scientific investigation. In the evolution of the sciences themselves there are borderline cases where it is necessary – at least temporarily – to establish a science the object of which seems to conflict with those of other, already established, sciences.[10]

To this basic dialectical orientation of contemporary Soviet classification of sciences must be added the influence of dialectical materialism's 'materialist' component. Materialism here means that objectivity which requires that a science and the methods it uses conform to the character of the object with which it has to deal. This is meant not only in the sense that a science is determined by the character of its object but also with the strict proviso that every science has to see its object as embodying a previous historical evolution and as being the bearer of a contemporaneous continuation of this evolution.[11] At least one Soviet author – although he seems to be a voice crying in the wilderness of the non-metropolitan hinterland (he works in Perm') – has written on 'Materialism as a Method of Knowledge and of Practical Activity'[12] where it is maintained that materialism is as much a 'method' as is the dialectic: it requires that 'one take objective reality as it is'. This is, however, not the commonly accepted doctrine.

B. M. Kedrov, the leading proponent of the Marxist-Leninist classification of sciences, published in 1961 the first volume of his *opus maior, The Classification of Sciences*.[13] There one finds a detailed presentation of the current state of affairs in Soviet classification of sciences. After enunciating the basic principles which we have mentioned above, Kedrov begins by describing the history of the classification of sciences. In the beginning there was no classification of sciences because philosophy absorbed all fields of knowledge. In the period from the fifteenth to the nineteenth century, classification of sciences was made

82

on purely analytic, accidental and *a priori* grounds and the positivist spirit denied any rights at all to philosophy. Now, the appearance of the classics of Marxism-Leninism has solved the problem by integrating all the sciences; the differentiation of sciences is here a necessary prerequisite for their integration according to the inner bonds which unite things. The classification used in the second period was unsatisfactory because it was strictly of the 'coordination' type, i.e. each science was strictly and hermetically distinguished from every other science. This 'metaphysical' method of classification falsified the situation by not taking into account the dialectical relations and transitions between sciences. It was the classics of Marxism-Leninism – above all Engels – who showed that the classification of sciences which best corresponds to the real state of affairs has to be based on the principle of subordination which takes into account the 'real' bonds between the sciences and between their respective objects.

Pre-Marxist-Leninist classification of sciences contained, according to Kedrov, many valuable elements which were incorporated by the classics into the Marxist-Leninist doctrine on the subject. Among these positive elements which have been retained Kedrov lists: procedure from the simple to the complex; distinction of sciences into sensible-empirical and abstract-theoretical, concrete and abstract, theoretical and practical; the use in analysis of the general and particular, subjective and objective (method and object), etc. In his reform of the classification of sciences Engels even retained the positive aspects of the principle of coordination by dialectically combining it with the Marxist-Leninist principle of subordination. Among the 'metaphysical' characteristics which Engels eliminated from the classification of sciences, the principal were its Europocentrism, its ignorance of the materialism-idealism conflict in the history of thought, its lack of genetic approach, its encyclopedic character, and its concentration on the evolution of thought rather than on that of the object.

Overshadowing all these contributions to the classification of sciences is Engels' discovery and development of the basically dialectical-materialist principle of classification according to the forms of motion. According to Kedrov, this discovery by Engels has put classification of sciences on a firm scientific basis. The principle of classification according to the forms of motion can be best explained as follows.

83

For dialectical materialism all is matter. All matter is not only in space and time but also and necessarily in motion. There is, for diamat, no matter without motion just as there is no motion without matter. Carrying the description further, Engels and his successors – led in this respect by Kedrov – affirm that for every form of matter there exists a corresponding type of motion just as for every kind of motion there is a form of matter which serves as its 'carrier'. Since knowledge proceeds from appearance to essence and from 'essence of the first degree' to 'essence of the second degree', and so on, the various forms of matter are identified through the intermediary of their peculiar types of motion. Each science, therefore, deals with a particular type of motion.[14] The classification of sciences which best fits the factual situation will then be that which is based on the ordering of sciences according to the types of motion with which they deal.

According to Kedrov, Engels' success in this matter was due to his use of the 'Marxist dialectical method'.[15] Since what Kedrov designates here as 'Marxist dialectical method' only faintly resembles what is commonly indicated by Soviet use of the term we will now have a glance at what methodology means for Soviet philosophers who are less involved with the natural sciences.

28. General and special methods

Methodology as that branch of logic which investigates the 'how' of scientific procedure can be divided into two major sections: general methodology which deals with problems and elements common to all or a great number of methods, and the various special methodologies which deal with the methods employed in a single science or in a group of related sciences. Contemporary Soviet philosophy makes a similar distinction with certain differences.

In the arsenal of contemporary Soviet philosophy general methodology is confined to speculation on the character and applicability of the so-called 'Marxist dialectical method'. As we have tried to demonstrate elsewhere[16] the Marxist dialectical method is not a method in the ordinary sense of the word. It is presented as the 'analog of reality', 'the reflection of the laws of the real world', etc. To this more or less ontological characterization of the Marxist dialectical method is usually added a series of psychologistic recommendations: know the past of the object considered!; see the object in space and time!; select the essentials of the object!; look to the new!; take the object as a part of its system!; be practical!, etc.[17]

This conception of method offers little difficulty as long as one continues to talk of it as a *philosophic* method universally applicable to problems of ontology, epistemology and logic. For, as long as the philosophy in question is – like Marxism-Leninism – based on the same ontological and psychological premisses as is the method, there is little risk of conflict between them and it is quite likely that there will be a flattering degree of agreement between them. For example, when Rozental', Kopnin *et al.* speak of using the 'dialectical method' to solve the problem of *sovpadenie* – once the dialectic, epistemology and logic have been 'dialectically' defined – one can accuse them of using a circular argument but not of using an inapplicable method.

Serious difficulties arise when efforts are made to extrapolate the Marxist dialectical method to the non-philosophic sciences. As we saw above, the natural science wing in contemporary Soviet methodology is on relatively safe ground when discussing the classification of the sciences. But, Kedrov, Fataliev, Orlov, *et al.* run into difficulty when they try to show how what they are doing in the philosophy of natural science derives from the application of the Marxist dialectical method. Similarly, the philosophical methodologists are unable to show a single instance of a fruitful application of the Marxist dialectical method outside of the strictly delimited domain of Marxist-Leninist philosophy.

The reason for the failure of both sides to find the correct solution seems to be that there is no such solution. The Marxist dialectical method is based – as said above – on ontological and psychological pre-suppositions which simply are not those of the natural sciences. It is obvious, at least, that the procedure of natural science tries to be as free as possible from psychological premisses. And, although it cannot get along without some ontological premisses, there is a definite effort to restrict these to the simplest and most obvious. On both counts, then, dialectical materialism and its method are ruled out.

It is in the domain of special methodology, however, that the weakness of the Marxist dialectical method becomes most evident. It isn't that Soviet thinkers have not contributed to such fields as mathematics, cybernetics and model-theory; it is just that the philosophers' claims that the Marxist dialectical method contributed essentially to the work in these domains rings hollow in the face of the evidence at hand. For instance, when M. S. Akperov says that mathematics progresses through relative truths to absolute truths he seems to think that he thereby has contributed to the discussion on the foundations of mathematics.[18] And, N. A. Kiseleva's article on mathematical abstraction as a reflection of the objective world[19] gains little in clarity from the copious references to the essential influence which social conditions have on mathematics. On one of the more difficult questions of contemporary science – the nature and significance of models – V. A. Štoff has had quite a bit to say and much of it is high calibre philosophical analysis.[20] But the characterization of representational models as 'subjective' because created and abstract, and as 'objective' because related to objects and their properties is neither specifically dialectical nor particularly enlightening. The reader experiences the same unenlightened indifference on being told that complementarity can be interpreted as the composition of models which reflect the contradictions of reality.[21] The description offered above of contemporary Soviet ideas on the scientific hypothesis are sufficient to show that the Marxist dialectical method has not only not permitted a 'Marxist-Leninist breakthrough' but has even kept Marxism-Leninism far below the level reached by the rest of science.[22]

29. THE METHODOLOGICAL SIGNIFICANCE OF EPISTEMOLOGY AND THE EPISTEMOLOGICAL SIGNIFICANCE OF METHODOLOGY

This brief examination of contemporary Soviet doctrine on method shows that the long Stalinist isolation of Soviet science from the mainstream of world-thought has left Marxism-Leninism without a methodology worthy of the name. The gap has been filled with an ontological-psychological *Ersatz* which, while it does perform some of the functions of a methodology, is more in the nature of an epistemology. It is more involved with the relationship between things and thought than with the ways things are treated by thought.

In our discussion of the problem of the *sovpadenie* the three main components of Marxist-Leninist philosophy – dialectic, logic and epistemology – were seen to be tightly interwoven and even – for some

Soviet philosophers – identical. Because of its generality the Marxist dialectical method is qualified as philosophical[23] and, therefore, must be integrated into the over-all Marxist-Leninist philosophic context. This integration normally takes the form of an identification of the Marxist dialectical method with one or another of the three Marxist-Leninist philosophic disciplines or – in the case of their identification – with all three.[24] Since the Marxist dialectical method is the 'analog of reality' and the 'reflection of the laws of the real world' it pertains to the subjective dialectic, and must be distinguished from and correctly related to epistemology and logic. Previous to the extensive development of dialectical logic which began around 1960, the standard Soviet explanation was quite simple. The subjective dialectic as the reflection of dialectical reality was presented as the science on the most general laws of reality. Because it also included the operations of thought, it formed 'Marxist-Leninist epistemology', and as dealing with the laws of thought it became 'Marxist-Leninist logic'. All these taken together – according to the dialectical-materialist philosophers – presented a complete image of reality and, as such, were known as the Marxist dialectical method – on the argument that a totally correct view of reality (Marxism-Leninism's three components) guaranteed the correctness of further views of reality.

The recent developments in dialectical logic have simplified the question by coalescing logic and Marxist-Leninist epistemology but have not, it seems, brought Soviet philosophers any closer to a solution. Even the most recent Soviet accounts of the Marxist dialectical method are obviously talking not about a method but about an *a priori* conceptual schema.[25] The subjective dialectic reflects the objective dialectic. Through dialectical logic the dialectical laws which constitute the objective dialectic are codified in the 'dialectic' and in 'materialism'. These codified laws serve as methodological guide-lines for further acts of knowing the objective dialectic. Because the Marxist dialectical method is held to be universal – i.e. whatever is known is known in function of the laws of the dialectic – the ontological premiss on which it is based must also be universal: all of reality has to belong to the objective dialectic and to conform to the laws of the dialectic. An interesting question which has hardly been touched by Soviet philosophers would be to know if the dialectical character of thought as a universal method pertains only to the content of thought or also to the knowing process and, if the latter, whether this mechanism is acquired or infused.[26]

In practice, the Marxist dialectical method is made up of the elements and modes which we have described above. The use of any of them – singly or in combination – constitutes a use of the dialectical method provided the recommendations are observed. In addition to the general recommendations which we mentioned above (p. 85) there are specific recommendations for the various modes and elements. For example, the dialectical unity of induction and deduction must be strictly respected; concepts and judgements are dialectically interrelated and one must never 'metaphysically' separate them, and so on.

REFERENCES

1. Exceptions are J. M. Bocheński: *Diamat*, and his articles in *Studies in Soviet Thought*, and Wetter: *Diamat*.
2. T. J. Blakeley: *Soviet Scholasticism*. Dordrecht, Holland. 1961.
3. Cf. Engels: *Dialectics of Nature* (English), p. 282.
4. "As soon as each special science is required to make clear its position in the totality of things and of knowledge as a whole, a special science dealing with the totality is superfluous. What still independently remains of all earlier philosophy is the study of thought and its laws – formal logic and dialectics. Everything else is absorbed in the positive science of nature and history." (Engels: *Anti-Dühring* (English), p. 23).
5. Cf. B. M. Kedrov: 'O klassifikacii nauk' (On Classification of Sciences). *VF* 1955, 2, 49–68. and I. S. Kon: 'Nauka kak forma obščestvennogo soznanija' (Science as a Form of Social Consciousness). *VF* 1951, 1, 41–58.
6. Cf. V. V. Orlov: 'Materializm kak metod poznanija i praktičeskoj dejatel'nosti' (Materialism as a Method of Knowledge and of Practical Activity). In *Voprosy teorii poznanija*. Perm'. 1960. p. 3.
7. Cf. Blakeley: *op. cit.*
8. A. A. Zinov'ev (in *VF* 1957, 4, 189) rebukes Rozental' for tying growth of the concept univocally to growth of the object. According to Zinov'ev, there is a deepening of knowledge caused by the very process of investigation itself.
9. Cf. B. M. Kedrov: *Klassifikacija nauk*. Moskva. 1961. This book is basic and has been used freely in writing this section (cf. note 13, below).
10. Kedrov: *VF* 1955, 2, 49–68.
11. Cf. Andreev: *Dialektičeskaja logika*, p. 110. Rozental': *Principy dialektičeskoj logiki*, p. 198f. Kedrov describes, in the context of the negation of negation, the ontogenesis-phylogenesis which are responsible for this state of affairs (s. Blakeley: *Soviet Scholasticism*. p. 29 note).
12. Orlov: *op.cit.*
13. B. M. Kedrov: *Klassifikacija nauk. I: Engel's i ego predšestvenniki*. (Classification of Sciences. I: Engels and his Predecessors). Moskva. 1961. 471 str. This is to

be the first in a series of three volumes. Cf. bibliography for Kedrov's numerous works on classification of sciences.

14. *Ibid.*, p. 318ff.
15. *Ibid.*, pp. 279–280.
16. Cf. Blakeley: *Soviet Scholasticism.*
17. This anthropomorphic aspect of the Marxist dialectical method has persisted even in post-Stalin Soviet writings. There is some variation in the number and types of recommendations. The list quoted here is from G. A. Podkorytov: 'Sootnošenie dialektičeskogo metoda s častnonaučnymi metodami' (Relation of the Dialectical Method to the Methods of the Single Sciences). *VF* 1962, 6, 36–47.
18. In 'K voprosu o sootnošenii ob"ektivnoj, otnositel'noj i absoljutnoj istiny v matematike' (On the Question of the Relationship of Objective, Relative and Absolute Truth in Mathematics). *V MGU* 1962, 2, 54–68.
19. 'Matematičeskie abstrakcii kak otraženie zakonomernostej ob"ektivnogo mira'. *FN* 1960, 2, 94–104.
20. Cf. 'O roli modelej v kvantovoj mexanike' (On the Role of Models in Quantum Mechanics). *VF* 1958, 12, 67–79. 'K voprosu o roli model'nyx predstavlenij v naučnom poznanii' (On the Role of Modelling Representations in Scientific Knowledge). In *Dialektičeskij materializm.* Leningrad. 1958. pp. 117–135. 'Gnoseologičeskie funkcii modeli' (The Epistemological Functions of the Model). *VF* 1961, 12, 53–65.
21. Štoff: *VF* 1958, 12, 67–79.
22. Cf. especially the works on hypothesis and induction cited in the previous chapter.
23. Cf. *Bol'šaja sovetskaja enciklopedija* (Great Soviet Encyclopedia). Moskva. 1952f. vol. 14, p. 284. *Osnovy*, p. 230. *Dialektičeskij materializm* (edited by G. F. Aleksandrov). Moskva. 1953, p. 65.
24. Cf. Alekseev: *Dialektičeskaja logika.* p. 25. and G. M. Kalandarišvili in I. K. Tavadze, G. M. Kalandarišvili: *V. I. Lenin o "Nauke logiki" Gegelja* (Lenin on Hegel's *Science of Logic*). Tbilisi. 1959. pp. 237–238.
25. Cf., e.g., G. A. Podkorytov: 'Istoričeskij i logičeskij metody poznanija' (Historical and Logical Methods of Knowledge). In *Dialektičeskij materializm.* Leningrad. 1958. pp. 190–205. and 'O ponjatii naučnogo metoda' (On the Concept of Scientific Method). *V LGU* 1962, 11, 72–82. A. A. Vetrov, V. V. Orlov: 'Protiv diskreditacii metoda materialističeskoj dialektiki' (Against Discrediting the Method of the Materialist Dialectic). *VF* 1961, 12, 151–155. P. V. Kopnin: 'Marksistskaja filosofija kak metod naučnogo poznanija' (Marxist Philosophy as a Method of Scientific Knowledge). *VF* 1960, 5, 135–144. Kalandarišvili: *op.cit.*, p. 310.
26. Alekseev has written on the subject (cf. his *Dialektičeskaja logika.* p. 25ff.) but his views are not widely espoused.

CHAPTER VII

CRITIQUE OF 'BOURGEOIS' THEORIES
OF KNOWLEDGE

The massive attacks made by Soviet philosophers on the philosophers and philosophic systems of the non-Communist world contain a wealth of information on the exact conception which contemporary Soviet philosophers have of their own system. This seems due to two causes. First, these attacks are officially sanctioned and encouraged by the ideological pontiffs and political leaders. As a result, 'inaccuracies' in the presentation of Marxism-Leninism – which are often fruitful developments of dialectical materialism and, therefore, would hardly be allowed in a non-polemical context – are passed over for the sake of victory. In the second place, the need of meeting and defeating other philosophies puts the Soviet philosopher in the presence of philosophical problems with which he is unfamiliar or which he has not been able to openly discuss since they were not mentioned by the classical sources.[1]

This chapter is devoted to a description and interpretation of Soviet attacks on 'bourgeois' theories of knowledge. These attacks participate in the three general characteristics of Soviet treatment of the non-Soviet world: aggressivity of tone, low scientific level, and a cabalistic terminology.

The distant roots of the aggressive tone used by contemporary Soviet philosophers in their discussions of non-Communist philosophic doctrines are to be found in the invectives and vituperations which fill many of the works of the classics.[2] More immediately, however, the sources of this attitude are the so-called revolutionary character of Marxism-Leninism, the Messianic world-view of Communism, and the doctrine of *partijnost'*. Of the revolutionary character of Marxism-Leninism, little remains today except the methodological principle that any true construction must be preceded by a total destruction of the old. Whence the Soviet attitude toward 'bourgeois' philosophy is based on the dogma that, although there are some valuable elements in it, a total reconstruction of the world on Marxist-Leninist lines requires the total annihilation of it and the society for which it provides foundation and justification.

90

The Messianic outlook of Communism produces a bipolar division of the world into good and bad. Because this division is not a matter of cold, clear analysis but of Messianic involvement, all that is 'non-good' (i.e. non-Communist) is assimilated to the bad. The doctrine of *partijnost'* is based on the Marxian sociological dogma that every man in a class-society shares the ideology of the class to which he belongs. The ideology of the progressive class (the proletariat) is incompatible with that of the 'reactionary' class (the bourgeoisie, imperialists, monopolists, etc.) and will – with historical inevitability – triumph over it. The authors of this triumph are the Soviet philosophers whose task it is to ideologically annihilate 'bourgeois' philosophy.[3]

The low scientific level of Soviet philosophy – it's frequent resort to irrelevant political arguments and to personal abuse – is too proverbial to need extensive description here.[4] It is satisfying to note, however, that the situation in this regard has significantly improved in the past few years. In the Soviet philosophical texts of ten to fifteen years ago one read of the "cesspool" of bourgeois philosophy, the "strike-breaker-ism" of American philosophy[5], the "racist character" of pragmatism[6], etc. Today bourgeois philosophy has not ceased to be "war-mongering", a "tool of capitalism", etc.[7], but these accusations have the character of *pro forma* designations of the enemy and are no longer considered the decisive philosophic arguments. Another improvement has to do with the sources of information which the Soviet philosophers possess in regard to contemporary non-Communist philosophy. In the old days, the standard procedure was to describe a given philosopher as the classics had and condemn him by means of the same arguments as the classics had used. In the case of philosophers not mentioned by or subsequent to the classics, condemnation was effected by assimilating them to a philosophic school on which the classics' arguments could be brought to bear. Today's Soviet philosophers have greater access to non-Communist philosophic works both in translation and in the original.[8] As a result of being better informed – coupled, perhaps, with the general decline of the Soviet inferiority complex[9] – contemporary Soviet philosophers have begun to discard the expedient of quoting out of context. Now we find Russell, Carnap, Maritain, Jaspers and even Aquinas quoted *in extenso*.[10] Finally, although bibliography is still a sadly neglected aspect of contemporary

Soviet philosophy, there is definite progress in the matter of correctly documenting books and articles.[11]

Cabalistic terminology marks all domains of Soviet activity but in Marxist-Leninist theory of knowledge it is particularly noticeable for several reasons. First of all, the use of such terms as idealism, materialism, rationalism, empiricism, etc., is not at all uniform even in the non-Soviet philosophic world. 'Cartesian idealism' means one thing for the existentialist and another for the positivist. In the second place, the classics themselves were not consistent in their use of epistemological terms. The meaning of 'idealism' as used by Lenin in *Materialism and Empirio-Criticism* often depends on whom he happens to be attacking at the moment. And Engels gives an interpretation to materialism which is quite more positivist and less metaphysical (philosophical) than that of Lenin. Finally, all the epistemological terminology has undergone a tremendous evolution since the turn of the century, rendering the Marxist-Leninist vocabulary not only heterogeneous but also dated. These terminological confusions make an account of the Soviet attitude toward contemporary Western philosophy both complex and interesting: complex because of the constant necessity of translating; interesting because of the light it throws on the real character of Soviet philosophic views.

A specific trait of Soviet philosophy's treatment of other theories of knowledge is its utilitarian opportunism. This comes out in the fact that very little attention is paid to ancient and medieval philosophy. The philosophers of these periods are usually brought in only for the sake of refuting a modern or contemporary philosopher who pretends to represent one or another ancient or medieval philosophic school. Another sign of this opportunism is the ease with which Soviet philosophers join one 'bourgeois' school in condemning another: for example, they will side with the positivists (whom they here quote approvingly) against the scholastics (and modern counterparts) on questions of faith and reason; but they will join the spiritualists (including neo-Thomists) against the positivists on the question of the transcendent character of knowledge. The following chapter's description of the contemporary Soviet attitude on non-Marxist-Leninist epistemology exemplifies the spotty coverage caused by these considerations: hardly anything is said about the first period, less about the second;

the third receives a quasi-normal coverage, and the fourth is treated all out of proportion to its intrinsic philosophic worth.

In this chapter we will take up questions of terminology and method pertinent to the Soviet treatment of other epistemologies; in the next we will take a closer look at the actual historical applications of this terminology and these methods.

30. A TERMINOLOGICAL AND PHILOSOPHICAL POINT OF VIEW

Soviet phenomena in general and Soviet theory of knowledge in particular can be dealt with in one of three ways: the purely objective presentation which does little more than describe and which, in order to avoid surreptitious interpretation, is forced to couch the description in Marxist-Leninist terminology[12]; the immanent critique which presents and critizes Marxism-Leninism 'from within', i.e. on the basis of its own principles[13]; criticism from a definite, non-Marxist-Leninist point of view.[14] Heretofore, we have restricted ourselves to the first or objective presentation. In this section we establish a philosophical point of view and a uniform terminology on knowledge, theory of knowledge and cognate philosophical domains. This procedure is justified, on the one hand, by the heterogeneity of Soviet epistemological views and terminology and, on the other, by the lack of consensus of opinion among Western philosophers on a uniform epistemological doctrine which could serve as basis for comparing the Marxist-Leninist view with a non-Soviet opposite number.

Knowing is an act. The act of knowing is the coming-together of the knower (the agent) with the known (the term of the act). All the 'reifications' used in interpreting this cognitive coming-together (sensations, sense-data, images, concepts, etc.) are intermediaries – and nothing more – between the knower and the known. The coming-together involved in knowing is of such a kind that the knower internalizes the known within himself, in one form or another; the known, on the other hand, remains unaffected by having-been-known. In knowledge had by man, which is the sole form interesting us here, the knower knows not only the known but also the fact-of-knowing-the-known; in other words, human knowledge is reflexive, in knowing it knows its own act of knowing. Knowledge is the result of the knowing-act.

Now, theory of knowledge, in its widest sense, would be – as the words themselves indicate – a description and analysis of the knowing act and/or its product; this seems to be the explicit view of Cassirer[15] and, implicitly, that of Cornford.[16] In this sense, every philosophy and every philosopher would necessarily have a theory of knowledge. This view is open to the objection that, if all aspects of knowing – the knower as knowing, the knowing as a knower-known relation, and the known as known – are included in theory of knowledge, then this latter is, to all intents and purposes, identical with philosophy. The ready answer to this objection is that theory of knowledge restricts itself to what is properly cognitive in the knowing situation. But, the properly cognitive aspect of man's knowing – that which distinguishes it from all other acts, human or other – is precisely its reflexive character. It would seem, then, that a theory of knowledge which is not just another name for philosophy has as its specific object of investigation the reflexive character of human knowledge or – in more precise terms – the conditions, the prerequisites, which make it possible that man's act of knowing be what it is, i.e. the knowing of the known and of the fact of knowing the known.

This is precisely the 'critical question' of Immanual Kant; and, it is precisely from the appearance of his major work, *Critique of Pure Reason*, that one can date the formation of theory of knowledge as a distinct domain of philosophic activity. The fact that Kant's entire philosophy could be – and, has been – dismissed as 'nothing but theory of knowledge' is beside the point; the significant fact is that, once the question had been posed in the way Kant did it, no philosopher could afford to ignore it and was, therefore, forced – at least as a defensive measure – to develop some sort of a theory of knowledge; and this in the narrow sense of a speculation on the prerequisites conditioning the reflexive nature of knowing.

Does theory of knowledge, as an independent domain of philosophic activity, exist? There are, as a matter of fact, quite a number of reasons for doubting that any such thing is necessary or even legitimate. The principal among them can be stated as follows: each of the separate questions which are said to fall under the purvey of theory of knowledge can be shown to pertain – properly and strictly – to the competence of one or another of the already existing domains of philosophic

94

activity; therefore, a distinct domain of philosophic activity, called theory of knowledge, is superfluous. Thus, for example, the analysis of the knower as knowing belongs to psychology, the question of the intelligibility of the known to ontology, and the question of the validity of knowledge to logic. It seems, however, that this whole discussion deals rather with a question of convenience and terminology than with a matter of fundamental principles. There are questions where neither logic nor psychology, for example, can claim complete competence; and it seems that this no man's land can be conveniently called theory of knowledge.

Among the confusing terms used in philosophic discourse those which try to describe the over-all character of a system or point of view are often the most confusing. Such designations as idealist, realist, materialist, positivist, sensualist often have no clear meaning and their application to one or another philosopher depends more on the views of the person making the judgement than on the intrinsic character of the philosopher's own views. Thus, Plato has variously been called 'idealist', 'ultra-realist' and 'conceptualist' – all of which may be the case, but confusing. It is to be hoped that the following effort at classification will simplify matters – at least for the remainder of the present work.

Philosophic discourse makes use of three general classes of statements. In other words, that which philosophers discuss can be distributed into three general 'problem areas': the *ontological*, dealing with being in terms of 'ideal' and 'real'; the *psychological*, dealing with psycho-physical phenomena in terms of 'matter' and 'spirit' (or 'mind'); the *epistemological*, dealing with cognitive phenomena in terms of 'immanence' and 'transcendence'.

The basic ontological question may be stated as follows: is being exclusively real or exclusively ideal or, if there are both, is there a primacy of some kind of one over the other? 'Real' is that which is in space and time, is changeable, individual and contingent (e.g., a table). 'Ideal' is that which is non-spatio-temporal, unchanging, general and essential (e.g., a mathematical law).

The basic psychological question may be formulated: is every being material or spiritual; if there are both types, is there a primacy of one over the other? 'Material' is that real being which is – in addition to

95

the above characteristics – 'corporeal', i.e., has bodily existence. 'Spiritual' is that real being which is evidenced through material effects but which cannot be explained by purely material causes. For example, the purely physical make-up of the spoken or written word is not sufficient to explain the transfer of meaning which is effected through it.

The basic epistemological question has to do with an act – that of thinking – rather than with entities as is the case in the ontological and psychological domains; more precisely, it deals with the relational status of entities which owe their being such and such (e.g., knower and known, subject and object, mental and physical) necessarily to being included in the cognitive act. It can be formulated as follows: is thought immanent or transcendent; if the latter, is one of the elements (entities) primary in some respect? 'Immanent' means that the two cognitive correlates (e.g. knower and known) pertain to the same 'level of being' (in the 'ontological' sense as described above). 'Transcendent' means that they belong to different 'levels of being'.

Thus, on each of the three questions there are four fundamental positions: only the first term; only the second; both, with primacy of the first term; both, with primacy of the second term. In each of the three domains, therefore, there are two 'monist' positions and two 'dualist' positions. In theory at least, it seems that there could be 'triadist', 'quadratist' and, in general, 'n-ist' positions. In practice, however, such positions can be, and have been, reduced to a basically dualist point of view.

The twelve possibilities are as follows (m subscript stands for 'monist', d subscript for 'dualist'):

Ontological
real being	realism$_m$	realism$_d$
ideal being	idealism$_m$	idealism$_d$

Psychological
material being	materialism$_m$	materialism$_d$
spiritual being	spiritualism$_m$	spiritualism$_d$

Epistemological
cognitive immanence	immanentism$_m$	immanentism$_d$
cognitive transcendence	transcendentism$_m$	transcendentism$_d$

Only two of the twelve seem *a priori* to be untenable: immanentism$_d$ because if the two cognitive correlates pertain to the same level of being the adjunction of dualism implies an 'immanent transcendence', which is contradictory; on a similar basis transcendentism$_m$ is to be eliminated.

Any such system of classification will falsify by over-simplification. But the procedure is justified to the extent that this system of terms provides an unambiguous frame of reference in which contemporary Soviet philosophy in general and its theory of knowledge in particular can be compared to other philosophic systems, past and present.

31. 'IDEALISM' AND 'METAPHYSICS'

Returning to contemporary Soviet philosophy and its theory of knowledge, there are four basic classification-terms which are available for the characterization of all possible philosophic systems: 'idealism', 'materialism', 'dialectical', 'metaphysical'.

First Principle: all philosophers, philosophies, philosophic opinions, etc., are basically idealist or basically materialist.[17] Although there have been some philosophers who 'oscillated' between materialism and idealism, any efforts to reconcile the two views or to find a 'third path' ('above' the distinction between materialism and idealism) must necessarily end in idealism.

Definitions

Idealism is the philosophic view which affirms the primacy of soul, idea, consciousness, the subjective.

Among the other statements characterizing idealism as a whole we find: it is a refined form of religion; it is an impediment to science; it is irreconcilable with materialism in general and with dialectical materialism in particular. From this last trait, follows a series of more specific characteristics of idealism (e.g., exclusion of work as an epistemological category) but these will come under consideration in the discussion of the various historical forms taken by idealism.

There are three species in the genus idealism.

Subjective idealism is the philosophic view which to the doctrine on the primacy of the soul, etc., adds the affirmation that the object of knowledge (the known) is ideal and is located within the knower.

Objective idealism is the philosophic view which to the doctrine on the primacy of the soul, etc., adds the affirmation that the object of knowledge is ideal and is located outside the knower as a reified projection of the knower's consciousness.

In both definitions 'ideal' means 'created by the knowing subject'.

Masked idealism is the philosophic view which refuses the distinction between idealism and materialism as fundamental and, above all, refuses to let itself be classified as one or the other.

There are three major forms of 'masking': (1) the restriction of philosophic enquiry to epistemological questions so as to avoid having to make the ontological and psychological decisions which would necessarily imply – according to Marxism-Leninism – either idealism or materialism; (2) the relegation of idealism to the category of super-annuated philosophic doctrines which are inapplicable today; (3) the search for the 'third path' rising above the distinction between materialism and idealism. Basic to all forms of 'masking' – in the current Soviet interpretation – is the refusal to answer the 'basic question of all philosophy'; a refusal which automatically liberates the creative ability of thought and, therefore, leads to one or another form of idealism.

Each of these types of idealism can be individualist, pluralist or collectivist; sensualist, rationalist or irrationalist; absolute, monistic, panlogistic, voluntarist, etc.

Materialism is the philosophic view which affirms the primacy of matter, nature, objective reality.

Since it is in complete opposition to idealism, materialism is fully antagonistic to any form of religion and is the philosophic basis of genuine science.

For the definition of the various species of materialism, the time-factor is of some importance. There are three major forms of materialism.

Mechanicist materialism is the philosophic view which in affirming the primacy of matter, etc., over soul, etc., reduces all complex phenomena (including soul, etc.) to the mechanical combination of material particles.

This is pre-Marxist or 'metaphysical' materialism which has been superseded by 'Marxist' materialism, otherwise known as dialectical materialism.

Dialectical materialism is the philosophic view which in affirming the primacy of matter, etc., over soul, etc., refuses the mechanicist reduction and recognizes the fundamentally dialectically structured nature of a reality in constant evolution.

Vulgar materialism is the philosophic view which maintains the doctrines of mechanicist materialism despite the essential corrections made in this doctrine by Marxism-Leninism.

The time-factor in the distinction between the two versions of non-dialectical materialism also conditions contemporary Soviet attitudes towards these two views. The mechanicists are generally treated with paternal benevolence; they were in invincible ignorance since diamat had not yet been discovered. The vulgar materialists, on the other hand, are worthy only of contempt since they are in vincible ignorance of the true, dialectical-materialist, explanation of reality.

Second Principle: all philosophers, philosophies, philosophic opinions, etc., are basically metaphysical or basically dialectical. Exception to this rule is formed by a small number of metaphysical systems which have contained 'elements' or 'traces' of dialectic.

Definitions

Metaphysics is the philosophic point of view which eliminates motion, artificially abstracts from the real relations between real things, and separates the ideal from the real.

Seen in the light of the evolution of the use of the term 'metaphysics' in the history of philosophy, dialectical-materialism's almost exclusively methodological interpretation of it seems directly due to Kant. Thus, for Aristotle's editor it meant 'beyond physics'; for the scholastics, 'on being *qua* being'; for Locke, 'on extra-sensory reality'; for Humean neo-positivism, 'on extra-experiential (senseless) questions'; finally, for Kant, 'on futile manipulation of vacuous cognitive categories'. This would explain the fact that metaphysics appears in the writings of contemporary Soviet philosophers almost exclusively as a way of viewing reality rather than as a doctrine on the real (ontological) constitution thereof.

Dialectic is the philosophic view which affirms that reality is in constant motion (as described by the basic laws of the dialectic), that its components are all inter-related, and that all bipolar aspects of reality (like real and ideal) are complementary.

Like metaphysics this term has a long and venerable tradition from which the dialectical-materialist meaning seems to be directly derived. For the ancients – especially the Socratics – dialectic was 'discursive argumentation through counterposition'; for some historians of philosophy, Abelard's *sic et non* and Nicholas of Cusa's *coincidentia oppositorum* continue the tradition; finally, for Hegel it constitutes both a mode of being and a mode of thought and it was from him that the classics took it as a component of dialectical materialism. Again, the Hegelian idealist origin of the dialectic of dialectical materialism offers an explanation for the fact that its main significance has been – at least up to very recently[18] – as a way of viewing reality.

From these definitions contemporary Soviet philosophers draw up a classification with four basic elements: subjective idealism, objective idealism, mechanicist materialism, and dialectical materialism. In cross-classification through designation as either metaphysical or dialectical, since mechanicist materialism is necessarily metaphysical and dialectical materialism necessarily dialectical, the resultant philosophical systems are: metaphysical subjective idealism, dialectical subjective idealism, metaphysical objective idealism, dialectical objective idealism, mechanicist materialism, dialectical materialism.

For most of these systems it is easy to point out the correspondence to the terminology which we established above and, thereby, to systematize Soviet views of other systems.

Metaphysical subjective idealism = idealism$_m$ + spiritualism$_m$ + immanentism. Explanation: the subject – itself a 'bundle of sensations' or the like – creates its material counterpart and the object of knowledge.

Dialectical subjective idealism = idealism$_m$ + spiritualism$_m$ + immanentism. Explanation: dialectical subjective idealism differs from the metaphysical variety of subjective idealism only by the injection of the dialectic. But, as long as everything is created by the subject, dialectic can only mean a mode of thought which provides a pseudo-dualism but no essential difference.

Metaphysical objective idealism = idealism$_m$ + spiritualism$_m$ + transcendentism. Explanation: the idealism$_d$ and spiritualism$_d$ of the metaphysical objective idealist are only an apologetic 'front' since, in the end, he holds that the real is created by an ideal being (e.g., God) and that only the 'spiritual' form of matter is real (intelligible). This leaves only the transcendent theory of knowledge to distinguish him from the metaphysical subjective idealist.

Dialectical objective idealism = idealism$_m$ + spiritualism$_m$ + transcendentism. Explanation: as in the case of dialectical subjective idealism, the injection of the dialectic only adds a mode of thought and the resultant is a pseudo-dualism.

Mechanicist materialism = realism$_m$ + materialism$_m$ + immanentism.

Dialectical materialism = realism$_m$ + materialism$_m$ + transcendentism. Explanation: dialectical materialism differs from mechanicist materialism only in that the former does not permit a simple reduction of complex phenomena (especially the cognitive function) to a mechanical combination of homogeneous particles.

Several conclusions – which will later be exemplified in the Soviet treatment of non-Marxist-Leninist epistemologies – follow from this schematization:

(1) Diametrical opposition exists between dialectical materialism and metaphysical subjective idealism;

(2) Dialectical materialism does not admit the existence of any form of dualism. All forms of dualism contain a refusal or failure to accept and answer the 'basic question of all philosophy' and, therefore, are surreptitious efforts to find a 'third path'[19];

(3) All of these philosophical systems – with the exception of dialectical materialism – are ultimately reducible to metaphysical subjective idealism and, therefore, are all diametrically opposed to dialectical materialism. Dialectical subjective idealism differs only verbally from metaphysical subjective idealism. Both metaphysical objective idealism and dialectical objective idealism are distinguished only by their transcendent interpretation of knowledge. Since, however,

the object of knowledge is a reified projection of the knowing subject, both doctrines are ultimately forms of subjective idealism. In addition, dialectical objective idealism is really not dialectical; so that the reduction finishes in metaphysical subjective idealism. The situation of mechanicist materialism is somewhat more complicated but the central point is its explanation of knowledge. If knowledge is explained as the purely mechanical interactivity of material particles – thus in effect renouncing to a philosophical theory of knowledge – philosophy is eliminated and agnosticism sets in – a sure sign of metaphysical subjective idealism. If, on the contrary, the philosophical explanation of the rest of reality is anthropomorphically reinterpreted to admit a genuine theory of knowledge, the 'idealization' and 'spiritualization' typical of metaphysical subjective idealism are the result.

32. THE 'EPISTEMOLOGICAL ROOTS OF IDEALISM AND RELIGION'[20]

That these diverse erroneous philosophic interpretations of reality are not accidental occurrences is a necessary consequence of Marxist-Leninist historical determinism.[21] According to current Soviet doctrine idealism has both epistemological and social roots.[22] Since these 'roots' are also those of religion, a few words on the distinction between the two are in order. Idealism is the refined form of religion. This means that, whereas idealism is a philosophic doctrine – therefore, essentially a matter of thought, religion is a mixture of thought (idealist philosophy, precisely) and social behaviour based – according to dialectical materialism – on the use of emotive images and acts of worship. Because of the intimate connection between the two, Marxism-Leninism maintains that all forms of religion are based on and lead to idealism in its purest form, i.e. metaphysical subjective idealism. And, in philosophy, any concession to idealism is viewed as a first and fatal step on the road toward religion. The ferocious anti-idealism of contemporary Soviet philosophy is a bedfellow of their fanatic atheism.[23]

The basic identity of idealism and religion is evident – so say Marxist-Leninist historiographers of philosophy – throughout the history of thought. Early man was spontaneously materialist in a classless society. The rise of class-conflict in the form of slave-holding society saw the appearance of religion as an escape mechanism from the harsh realities of life. There immediately followed a materialist philosophical reaction against religion and throughout the three periods of class-society (slave-holding, feudal, capitalist) religion and the idealism which it engendered in order to crush early philosophic materialism worked hand in hand for the exploiting classes. Dialectical materialism represents the ultimate stage in the development of that materialist philosophy which has already begun to annihilate both idealism and religion.

The roots of idealism and religion are epistemological and social. They are the objective conditions which are always present and which – when the propitious moment presents itself – can always turn into idealism or religion. The epistemological roots are of two types. In the strict sense they are the characteristics in the structure of reality and in the operation of the cognitive apparatus which under normal conditions cause no difficulty; each in its own way, however, is open to abuse and this produces idealism. In the wide sense, the epistemological roots of idealism and religion are the innumerable arguments, based on these characteristics of reality and knowledge, brought by the idealists in favor of their philosophic position. The epistemological roots in this wide sense can be catalogued only by completely surveying the history of idealism in the history of philosophy – which we will undertake in the next chapter. Here we will examine the three main classes of epistemological roots of idealism, in the narrow sense of the term.

Idealism based on insufficient knowledge: insufficient knowledge in dialectical materialism can be either objective or subjective. Objective insufficiency means that the real objects have not attained a stage in their development where the problem posed by man can be solved on the basis of objective evidence. These are classed in the third category of epistemological roots of idealism (see below). The subjective insufficiency of knowledge refers to the effort to solve problems dealing with things which have not yet been studied to the point where they can be completely explained. There are three such problems which have been particularly significant in facilitating the formation of idealism:

(a) The absolutization of the differences between living matter and non-living matter. The metaphysical isolation of the living leads to vitalistic idealism; metaphysical stress on non-living matter is characteristic of the idealism of mechanicistic materialism.

(b) The absolutization of the differences between matter and consciousness. This leads, on the one hand, to mechanicistic materialism and, through it, to subjective idealism and, on the other, directly to idealism itself.

(c) The absolutization of seemingly uncaused natural events. Idealism arises when the scientist, faced by an event which has no apparent cause, begins to speak of indeterminism. This leads, through scepticism and agnosticism, to one form or another of idealism.

Idealism based on the contradictions of sense-knowledge: sensation, like all other things and processes of the objective dialectic, is essentially contradictory. These contradictions of sense-knowledge offer the possibility of idealism to the metaphysical thinker who stresses one pole of a given contradiction while excluding the other pole from view. There are three types of idealism which develop from the contradictions of sense-knowledge:

(a) The absolutization of sense-knowledge as the primary and sole cognitive given. It is true – says dialectical materialism – that the immediate source of all knowledge is sense-contact with reality *(nihil in intellectu nisi prius fuerit in sensibus)*. In this sense, the primary cognitive datum is sensation. Artificially separating sense-knowledge from intellectual knowledge, the metaphysically minded philosopher reasons as follows: sensed things are ideas; ideas are only in the mind; therefore, sensed things are only in the mind. Whence to idealism is – according to dialectical materialism – not even a half-step. This is sensualist idealism.

(b) The absolutization of the subjective aspect of sensation. When the subjective aspect of sensation is artificially (metaphysically) separated from its objective aspect as contact with reality, agnostic idealism results. The reasoning is: sensations are not things; we know only sensations; therefore, we do not know things.

(c) The absolutization of the synthetic operation of the subject in the process of the formation of perceptions. As we have seen, perceptions are combinations of sense-data from several distinct sense-organs. Overemphasis on this ability of man's sensory faculties leads to the 'logification' of sense-knowledge, i.e. attributing to sense-knowledge characteristics which are reserved to logical thought. This leads to idealisms of the panlogistic variety.

104

Idealism based on the contradictions of logical knowledge: the possibilities of idealism in this area are – according to Soviet philosophers – as numerous as the forms of perversion to which the constitutents of knowledge (Chapters IV and V) are subject. Nevertheless, there are four roots of idealism which are singled out as fundamental in this category:

(a) The absolutization of the singular or general in the concept. The absolutization of the singular is the rejection of the universal and is the basis of nominalist idealism. Inversely the absolutization of the general is Platonic idealism. It is to be noted that this absolutization is not restricted to the level of concept; but its perpetration at the concept level is fundamental to its appearance at the other levels.

(b) The absolutization of abstract thought's 'distance from matter' in judgement, syllogism, scientific theory, etc. All the higher forms of thought are abstract to a greater or lesser degree. Undue emphasis on the removal of abstract thought from direct contact with material reality can lead to various forms of idealism – above all to panlogism and monistic idealism.

(c) The absolutization of the creative ability of logical thought. Although thought is a reflection of reality, it benefits – in dialectical materialist philosophy – from a relative independence from its material base; in practice man applies his thought to the transformation of reality. If this ability of thought to detach itself from the 'real' control of its material progenitor is rendered absolute the resultant is an absolute idealism centered around subjective creativity.

(d) The absolutization of the relative character of truth. For dialectical materialism, as we have seen above, human knowledge is a mixture of relative and absolute truths. The absolutization of the relative side of knowledge leads to relativism which is a scepticist variety of subjective idealism. The absolutization of the absolute side leads to objective idealism and to religion, both of which are reducible to subjective idealism.

This by no means exhausts the possible litany of epistemological cores of idealism but the others (ignorance of the plasticity of concepts, of the dialectical nature of thought and of practice, etc.) are – at least according to current Soviet views – all reducible to one of these.

The social cores of idealism and religion are the catalysts which trigger the formation of idealist philosophy. They are the historical conditions which put man in a position which favors the espousal of idealist views. Social conditions affecting the rise and fall of philosophic views are multiple; they are all resultants of the formation of class-society with all of its inter-class tensions. Those which are fundamental enough to be termed 'roots of idealism and religion' are the immediate existential situations which are propitious for the development of one or another idealism on the basis of one or more of the epistemological roots.

(a) The separation of mental and physical work in class-society. Class-society is divided into two main classes: the exploiters and the exploited. Among the multiple differences which separate the two groups is the fact that the exploiters as the dominant power in society reserve to themselves the intellectual work and leave the manual labor to the exploited class. This means that theory is separated from practice, thought from reality, and the basic prerequisite for idealism is present. This idealism may be (1) that of the exploiting class which, in order to prevent revolutionary change and maintain the *status quo*, is interested rather in structuring reality according to its desires than in seeing it in its naked, revolutionary actuality; (2) that of the exploited classes who, deprived (at least, previous to the appearance of Marxism-Leninism) of any possibility of escaping their enslavement, seek refuge in the palliatives of idealism and religion. The exploiters will tend to espouse subjective idealism which gives them free rein to compose reality according to their desires. The enslaved class tends more toward objective idealism and religion.

(b) The dependence on the blind forces of nature. Before science had learned to satisfactorily explain many of the more terrifying natural phenomena man was totally incapable of influencing his natural environment. This occasioned an escapism which expressed itself in the formation of various idealist doctrines.

(c) The dependence on the blind forces of society and history. Before scientific sociology (the historical materialism of Marxism-Leninism) had opened to man the secrets of the operation of the basic laws of society, man's only recourse in the face of war, famine, etc., was to escape to an idealist world where these phenomena were excluded by definition.

(d) Social-weight. The mere fact of living in class-society puts the members of all classes under unnatural pressure which can express itself in the formation of idealistic philosophic systems.

106

(e) Class-motives. In a class-society each member of a class is an adherent and potential defender of the ideology of his own class. According to the principle of *partijnost'* the ideologist of the exploiting class will develop an idealist philosophy of some kind as the theoretical justification of his class-position; the ideologist of the exploited class will, of course, turn to materialism.[24]

Recapitulation: both the epistemological and social roots of idealism are objective, i.e. they are real factors or situations opening the door to idealism. The social roots are existential situations in which the development of the epistemological roots is favored. The social roots are necessary concomitants of class-society and every class-society has them in one form or another. Finally, there is no necessary correspondence between one epistemological root and one social root; likewise, there is no necessary correspondence between any one root – be it epistemological or social – and any one form of idealism. Soviet theory in this regard has not developed to the point where a one-to-one correspondence can be made; a given idealism may be explained as the result of one or of a combination of roots.

REFERENCES

1. A striking example is the development of a Marxist-Leninist semantics (not to be confused with the linguistic questions discussed during Stalin's time) in answer to developments in the West. Cf. P. S. Popov: *Istorija logiki novogo vremeni.* Moskva. 1960.
2. Examples are to be found throughout the works of Lenin but especially on almost every page of *Materialism and Empirio-Criticism.*
3. This attitude gives a peculiar flavor to the titles of Soviet philosophic works which include appeals for a "fighting philosophic journal" (*VF* 1949, 1, 7–10), for a "militant materialism" (*VF* 1952, 2, 4–13), etc. The predecessor of *Voprosy filosofii* was *Pod znamenem marksizma* (Under the Banner of Marxism); the words "banner", "battle", "against", "fight", "defeat" recur throughout this writing – especially up to 1956.
4. Cf. Bocheński: *Diamat,* pp. 52–53.
5. Cf. I. Lingart: *Amerikanskij pragmatizm* (American Pragmatism). Moskva. 1954. p. 107.
6. Cf. M. B. Mitin: ' "Materializm i empiriokriticizm" V. I. Lenina i bor'ba protiv sovremennoj idealističeskoj reakcii' (Lenin's *Materialism and Empirio-Criticism* and the Fight Against Contemporary Idealist Reaction). *VF* 1949, 1, 72.
7. Cf. A. P. Gagarin: *Pragmatizm SŠA* (US Pragmatism). Moskva. 1963. p. 57f. See also the articles by T. I. Ojzerman, B. E. Byxovskij, T. A. Saxarova, Ju. P.

Mixalenko, E. D. Modržinskaja, and L. N. Velikovič in *Sovremennye religiozno-filosofskie tečenija v kapitalističeskix stranax* (Contemporary Religious-Philosophic Currents in Capitalist Countries). Moskva. 1962.

8. Recent translations include works by R. Ingarden, P. Teilhard de Chardin and M. Bunge. Earlier, Hilbert-Ackerman, Tarski and Kleene had been translated by the logicians.

9. This has been a positive side-effect of the Soviet accomplishments in the space-race.

10. Cf., e.g., I. D. Pancxava on Aquinas' five proofs for the existence of God in *Osnovnye voprosy naučnogo ateizma* (Basic Questions of Scientific Atheism). Moskva. 1962. pp. 220–226.

11. In the *Voprosy filosofii* K. X. Xanazarov complains that the Soviet Union possesses no bibliography of Soviet philosophy comparable to that published by the Institute of East-European Studies of the University of Fribourg. Cf. 'O sostojanii bibliografie filosofskoj literatury v SSSR' (On the Situation of Philosophic Bibliography in the USSR). *VF* 1962, 12, 173.

12. E.g., Wolfgang Leonhard's *Sowjetideologie heute II*. Frankfurt. 1962.

13. E.g., Herbert Marcuse: *Soviet Marxism*. New York. 1958.

14. E.g., G. A. Wetter: *Sowjetideologie heute I*. Frankfurt. 1962.

15. Cf. E. Cassirer: *Das Erkenntnisproblem in der Philosophie und Wissenschaft der neueren Zeit*. Berlin. 1922.

16. Cf. F. M. Cornford: *Plato's Theory of Knowledge*. London. 1960.

17. These definitions are, for the most part, taken directly from the works quoted in the bibliography. But, their arrangement as a system is not to be found as such in any Soviet work.

18. The development of dialectical logic has evoked speculation on the ontological status of the dialectic. There is a mild controversy on the subject going on now. Cf. H. Fleischer: 'Auf dem Bauplatz der materialistischen Dialektik', *Studies in Soviet Thought II* (1962) 269–288, and the same author's reviews and notes in the same journal for 1962–1963.

19. Cf. V. F. Asmus: 'Dualizm'. In *Filosofskaja enciklopedija*, vol. 2, pp. 79–81.

20. This section is based principally on P. Čerkašin: *Gnoseologičeskie korni idealizma* (Epistemological Roots of Idealism). Moskva. 1961. Cf. also G. P. Alekseev: 'V. I. Lenin ob utončennyx formax religii' (Lenin on the Refined Forms of Religion). In *Kniga V. I. Lenina "Materializm i empiriokriticizm" – važnejšij etap v razvitii marksistskoj filosofii*. Moskva. 1959. pp. 425–440. and A. D. Suxov: 'Gnoseologičeskie korni religii' (The Epistemological Roots of Religion). *FN* 1958, 4, 102–112. See Čerkasin's article in *VF* 1954, 1, 59–77.

21. On this subject, see H. Fleischer: 'Die Idee der historischen Notwendigkeit im historischen Materialismus'. *Studies in Soviet Thought II* (1962), 181–203.

22. *Koren'* could also be translated as 'cause' but we have retained 'root' because it corresponds more closely to the Soviet idea as will appear in the sequel.

23. There may be some correlation between the epistemological revival in contemporary Soviet philosophy and the recent serious attention being paid to 'scientific atheism'. Cf. *Osnovy naučnogo ateizma* (Principles of Scientific Atheism). Moskva. 1961. *Istorija i teorija ateizma*. (History and Theory of Atheism). Moskva. 1962. *Osnovnye voprosy naučnogo ateizma* (Basic Questions of Scientific Atheism). Moskva. 1962. *O religii. Xrestomatija* (On Religion. A Reader). Moskva. 1963.

24. Cf. V. Kelle, M. Koval'zon: 'Ideologija' (Ideology). In *Filosofskaja enciklopedija*, vol. 2, pp. 229–233; and H. Fleischer: 'The Limits of "Party-mindedness" ' *Studies in Soviet Thought* II (1962), 119–131.

CHAPTER VIII

SOVIET HISTORIOGRAPHY OF KNOWLEDGE

Because of the basic question of all philosophy, the history of knowledge plays an inordinately large part in contemporary Soviet historiography of philosophy. This means that past and present philosophers and philosophies are judged primarily or even exclusively on the basis of their philosophical explanation of knowledge. In this chapter we take up the question of knowledge in the history of philosophy in its broad outlines and compare it to the contemporary Soviet version on the same men and philosophical events.

The periodization of contemporary Soviet history of knowledge follows the general pattern of Marxist-Leninist historiography of philosophy[1] which *mutatis mutandis* can be made to conform to the periodization of the history of philosophy commonly used in the West. Marxism-Leninism distinguishes five historical periods: primitive, slave-holding, feudal, capitalist, socialist. Since primitive society is considered pre-philosophical, there are four major periods in the history of philosophy: slave-holding which corresponds to what the rest of philosophers call ancient philosophy; feudal or medieval; capitalist or modern; and, 'philosophy of the period of the general decline of imperialism' or contemporary. The limits of these periods are as ill-defined in contemporary Soviet philosophy as they are in Western treatises on the subject and this is aggravated by the fact that very little of Soviet history of philosophy deals with the centuries between Aristotle and Descartes.[2] However, the general tendency is to consider the first period (ancient philosophy) closed with Augustine, the second with Descartes, and the third with the turn of the last century.

33. KNOWLEDGE IN ANCIENT PHILOSOPHY

In as far as their treatment of knowledge is concerned, all philosophic systems previous to Descartes can be collectively designated by the terms 'ontological realism' and 'naive dogmatism'. Ontologically realist

110

means that for the pre-Cartesians, (a) knowing, as an act of the knower, is an integral part of the total philosophic explanation of reality; (b) there is a 'real' which is – in some sense – external to and independent of the knower and which, when implicated in the act of knowing, becomes the known. Naive dogmatism means that they (a) held knowledge to be generally trustworthy – at least to the extent of rejecting the possibility of all knowledge being invalid for this would destroy any distinction between validity and invalidity; (b) did not analyse knowledge 'critically', i.e. in regard to the prerequisites of its proper coming-to-be.

Ancient Greek discussions on knowledge revolved around the distinction between ἀλήθεια and δόξα, between certitude and opinion. Although this same problem can be posed ontologically as the 'one and the many', logically as 'the universal vs. the singular', methodologically as 'the empirical vs. the rational', the ancients seem to have taken it psychologically as the opposition of dogmatism and scepticism. But, this certainly was not a central concern of any of these philosophers; in the process of developing their philosophies of nature, the pre-Socratics were generally content with a description of intellectual knowledge in terms of some sort of participation in a universal mind (νοῦς), and of sense-knowledge as a transfer of material particles from the known to the knower. Protagoras was the first Western philosopher to offer a rather well-rounded philosophical description of knowledge. On the basis of the atomist ontological doctrine of the continual change of all being and of Empedocles' theory of sense-knowledge as the reception by the knower of 'similars', i.e. elements emitted by the known which meet cognate elements in the sense-receptors, he came to the conclusion that (the individual) man is the epistemological measure of all things, for: (a) if all is in a state of change, the 'causes' which are the object of knowledge are in flux also and this means that they are seized differently by different people; (b) if knowledge is through emitted similars which meet their counterparts in the knower, then everything perceived is dependent on the perceiver and his states, i.e. there is a strict epistemological identity and man is the measure of the known.

In the hands of Plato the distinction between ἀλήθεια (ἐπιστήμη) and δόξα becomes that between true intellectual knowledge and deceptive sense-knowledge. The 'Ideas' or forms are objective essences;

the 'lower world' contains beings which are participations in these; knowledge is reminiscence of things known in previous lives, occasioned by meeting their 'shadows' in this life; a statement is true if its predicate and the property of the real object participate in the same 'Idea'.

Outside of his contributions to logic – which were considerable – Aristotle's prime epistemological merit was his ontological doctrine of act and potency (and of their analogical correlates, matter and form) which, by giving a viable philosophic explanation of the problem of permanence and change, permitted a satisfactory solution to the Platonic antithesis between true intellectual knowledge and deceptive sense-knowledge as providing, respectively, the form and the matter of knowing.

Post-Aristotelian scepticism based its version of knowledge on a sophism which even today has many adherents: all knowledge comes from the senses; the senses are fallible; there is no criterion which does not come from the fallible senses; therefore, there is no decision-system for separating knowledge from belief, truth from error, or being from appearance.

Contemporary Soviet philosophers generally begin their treatment of ancient philosophy with a few slogans on ancient Indian and Chinese philosophic systems. The Brahmanism of the Vedas and the Upanishads as well as the vedanta, mimansa and yoga are classified along with Confucius as idealist[3] but no distinction into subjective or objective is made and little evidence is offered to substantiate the classification.

Ancient Greek philosophy came to be – according to dialectical materialism – as a result of the appearance of classes in society. The separation of mental and physical labor between masters and slaves, the embryonic state of natural science, the complete lack of social sciences, and the predominance of religion gave this period a dominantly idealist character, with only some elements of dialectic. With some materialist (notably the Atomists) and subjective idealist (e.g. Protagoras and Socrates) exceptions, the majority of ancient philosophers are classified by the Soviets as objective idealists. Thus, the $\nu o\tilde{\upsilon}\varsigma$ of the pre-Socratics, Eleatics and Pythagoreans, the 'Idea' of Plato, the 'form' of Aristotle, the 'One' of Plotinus and the neo-Platonics, and the 'God' of the Church Fathers, are all alienated reifications and the accounts of knowledge based on them are all objective idealist in that ultimately it is the subject who extrapolates the object of his knowledge. Therefore, whereas we would classify Plato as realist$_m$ + spiritualist$_d$ + transcendentist and Aristotle as idealist$_d$ + spiritualist$_d$ + transcendentist, the Soviet classification reads idealist$_m$ + spiritualist$_m$ + immanentist for Plato and realist$_m$ + materialist$_m$ + transcendentist for Aristotle.

The link between ancient philosophy and medieval scholasticism was formed – at least as regards knowledge – by the Christianized neo-Platonism of Augustine. The problem to be resolved was: how, with fallible senses and a contingent (limited) intellect, does man know eternal, necessary 'forms' (Plato's 'Ideas')? The answer reads: divine illumination renders 'luminous' the form of the known, making it accesible to the human knower.

But, the central problem of medieval scholasticism was the problem of the 'Universals'. Although we are today accustomed to considering this as an epistemological problem, it was formulated in the Middle Ages as a primarily ontological one: are the genus and species used in thought also something real? In other words, can the mind's capacity to understand universally what is actually particular be explained in terms of something universal in the known? The Platonic, ultra-realist answer is obvious: the real 'reals', the 'Ideas', are universal and any traces of universality found in the empirical world are due to the fact that the 'shadows' retain some resemblance to the 'Ideas'. Medieval nominalism reduced the universal to a *flatus vocis* (mere word). The intermediate solution – the universal is properly mental but has a *fundamentum in re* ('a basis in the thing') – is often called 'moderate realism' to distinguish it from Platonic 'ultra-realism'. The eighty-fourth question of the *Prima Pars* of Thomas Aquinas' *Summa Theologica* is the best, succinct presentation of this position on knowledge. Corporeal objects affect the organs of sense; sensation is an act of the human *compositum*, determined by nature to the apprehension of particulars. Human (intellectual) knowing is, however, of the universal (the natural objects of intellectual knowledge are the essences of material objects); the 'active intellect' abstracts 'intelligible species' from the particular sense-image *(phantasma)*, producing in the 'passive intellect' the *species impressa* which, in the form of *species expressa*, becomes the *verbum mentis*. There are no innate ideas; the concept is that which, by being known, renders the thing known *(quod in quo cognito cognoscitur res)*.

113

For contemporary Soviet philosophers, medieval philosophy is a product of the separation of mental and physical labor between master and serfs and of religion's complete domination over all other aspects of human life. The predominant characteristic of the philosophy of this period is its subservience to religion and, consequently, its objective idealist character. This explains Soviet philosophy's almost total lack of interest for this period; what little writing is done on the philosophy of the Middle Ages is intended as basis for refutation of neo-scholasticism, neo-Thomism, etc. Early scholasticism, medieval Arabic thought, Anselm, Aquinas, Averroes and Avicenna are all lumped together as objective idealists because they all, in one way or another, base their philosophies and accounts of knowledge on reified extrapolations of subjective thought-categories. The whole scholastic movement is dismissed as 'pseudo-rational irrationalism' because the ultimate guarantee of knowledge is a 'non-existent supreme being'. Avicenna and Averroes are said by the Soviets to combine materialism and neo-Platonism but both are fundamentally objective idealists – the first, it seems, because of his separate intelligences and the second because of the doctrine of a common active intellect. Whereas we would classify the mainstream of medieval philosophy as realism$_d$ + spiritualism$_d$ + transcendentism, the contemporary Soviet designation is idealism$_m$ + spiritualism$_m$ + transcendentism.

34. MODERN PHILOSOPHY AND THE RISE OF EPISTEMOLOGY

The breakthrough from scholasticism to modern philosophy – as concerns knowledge – is due to Scotus and Ockham. The former posited, in the place of Aquinas' abstraction of essence from individual things, a type of direct intuition of the individual coupled with a strict interpretation of *nihil in intellectu nisi prius fuerit in sensibus*, according to which sensation is the unique and immediate source of intellectual (rational) knowledge. The latter considered as fundamental an intuitive knowledge of the thing as existing, which allows the mind to form a contingent (not necessary) proposition concerning the existence of that thing; statements are analytic or empirical; propositions asserting a causal relation or based on an inference from one existent to another are hypothetical.

114

The principal preoccupation of the founders of modern philosophy was methodological: to find a philosophic method which would permit philosophy to achieve results as brilliant as those attained by the then nascent physical sciences. Philosophic empiricism drew ammunition from the conviction that science was successful because it was based on actual observation, justifying the empiricist thesis that factual knowledge is ultimately based on sense-perception. The success of the application of mathematics in science lead to the formation of a rationalism in philosophy, using *a priori* deduction from axioms analogous to those used in mathematics. Because questions of knowledge and method came to be considered as necessary preambles to any philosophizing, modern philosophy was neither ontologically realist nor naively dogmatic: neither the ontological status of knower and known nor the general trustworthiness of knowledge could any longer be taken for granted.

According to Francis Bacon, the value and justification of knowledge consists, above all, in its utility for the extension of man's dominion over nature. Physics treats of efficient and material causes, metaphysics of formal and final causes; but, speculation on final causes is futile; therefore, metaphysics deals with the laws of nature, with the axioms and concepts common to the various sciences. Induction from the perception of particulars to the most general axioms and, from these, to the deduction of less general propositions has only produced *anticipationes naturae;* properly, induction should proceed from the perception of particulars to immediately attainable axioms and, thence, gradually and patiently, to the more general axioms. This procedure will render an *interpretatio naturae.*

Descartes' search for 'certain and easy rules' for philosophic enquiry may be considered the beginning of the 'epistemological period' in the history of philosophy. From innate ideas and immediate apprehensions are formed simple propositions from which, by induction, the mind proceeds to other propositions; complex propositions are to be reduced to immediately evident simple propositions. Clear and distinct perception is the criterion of truth; error has its roots in the will's tendency to force the intellect beyond the domains where it is competent, i.e. beyond the clear and distinct.

Locke, defining idea as "whatever is meant by phantasm, notion, species, or whatever it is which the mind can be employed in thinking", rejected innate ideas; all knowledge comes from experience which is twofold: sensation, and reflection on the operations of the mind. Ideas are simple (stemming from one sense only) or complex (space, figure, motion) and all are received passively through emanations from the known. Knowledge consists in perceiving the agreement or disagreement between ideas or between ideas and things; truth is the self-evidence of immediate experience, the immediate constatation of the agreement or disagreement of ideas. General ideas are fabricated by removing (abstracting) determinations of time and place from ideas of particular things.

Berkeley used the word 'idea' to indicate what is normally called 'thing', his basic thought being that the only existence we can legitimately attribute to that which we know is the fact of being known – *esse is percipi*. Berkeley further rejects Locke's general ideas; there are general terms which serve as convenient abbreviations for the designation of sets of particulars.

Hume uses the word 'perception' to cover the mind's contents in general; perceptions are impressions (the immediate data of experience) or ideas (faint copies of impressions); impressions are 'of sensation' or 'of reflection', the former being the ultimate constituents of knowledge. Certain knowledge is that concerning 'relations of ideas' (contained in propositions whose truth or falsity is evident from the definition of the terms); knowledge of 'matters of fact' remains only more or less probable. Abstract, general, ideas are founded on 'custom' or habit.

Spinoza's infinite system is unique, but has two aspects; to every mode under the attribute of extension corresponds a mode under the attribute of thought, called 'idea'. Knowledge is, therefore, basically infused and needs no criterion.

Every monad in the system of Leibniz reflects in itself the whole universe from its own finite point of view; in addition to this 'perception', enjoyed by all monads, the rational monads have 'apperception', i.e. the ability to reflect on their own acts of 'perception'. 'Truths of reason' – themselves self-evident or reducible to self-evident propositions – are necessarily true and are based on the principle of contradiction; 'truths of fact' are not necessary and are based on the principle of 'sufficient reason'.

116

Kant sought to explain the 'inconclusiveness' of all previous meta-physics by seeking out the pure conditions of the human subject – as such – for knowing the known, among which the principal are the *a priori* universality and necessity of some propositions (e.g., of those of mathematics). Kant's 'Copernican revolution' was the posing of the 'critical question': since the supposition that knowledge must conform to the known has lead nowhere in explaining how *a priori* ideas are there, one can try the opposite to see if the known does not in some way conform to knowing. In order to make room for synthetic (bringing new knowledge) *a priori* (being necessary) judgements, Kant constructed the following theory of knowledge. Primitive sense-intuition – behind which stands the inscrutable 'thing-in-it-self' *(Ding-an-sich)* – is already conditioned *a priori* by space and time. The understanding *(Verstand)* turns this appearance *(Erscheinung)* into a phenomenon through ap-plication of the categories. Sensibility and understanding cooperate in constituting experience and in determining objects *as* objects; the connection between the intuitions of sense and the categories of under-standing is provided by the imagination *(Einbildungskraft)* which makes use of *schemata*, methodological rules for the application of the categories. Finally, reason *(Vernunft)*, because it deals with transcen-dental ideas (God, soul, world) which are beyond the categories, plays not a cognitive but a regulative role. Involved in every act of knowledge is 'pure apperception' which is the unity of the subject with the manifold of intuition; thus, the complex of possible objects of experience forms *one nature* in relation to the unity of consciousness in general.

Among the post-Kantians who rejected the 'thing-in-itself' but retained most of the rest of Kant's view of knowledge, Fichte affirmed a basic dialectic (identity, diversity, limitation) of the self-positing '*Ich*'; Schelling's 'absolute' is above the opposition of subject and object – in it they are identical; Hegel's absolute is 'spirit' *(Geist)* which pursues a 'dialectical' development; since the logical, the 'idea', is immanent to spirit, the dialectic as the form of the self-development of spirit is, at the same time and therefore, the logical form of thought. Theory of knowledge is, on these latter premises, fully identical with ontology.

Parallel to this distinctly epistemological philosophy there was a continuation of the empiricist tradition which, in the form given it by Auguste Comte and J. S. Mill, took on the name 'positivism'. Its basic

117

tenet on knowledge was that all knowing can be reduced to sense-knowledge and all 'universal' concepts or terms are some variety of fiction, illusion or convention. The empirio-criticism of Richard Avenarius and Ernst Mach reduced all of reality to 'sense-contents' (elements); the laws of nature (like all universal statements) are mere abbreviations of the manifold nature of sense-contents; true knowledge is that which is most economical.

For Soviet historiography of philosophy modern philosophy was marked by the decline of the concrete and intimate connection between idealism and religion. As a result, a strong school of subjective idealism developed wherein fideism, agnosticism and scepticism were used to fill the gap where objective idealism had put its reified alienation. Thus, whereas in pre-Cartesian philosophy objective idealism had held almost complete sway, in the modern period there is a more or less equal distribution of objective and subjective idealists. The objective idealists include, on the one hand, philosophers like Nicholas of Cusa, the Cambridge Platonists and the Occasionalists, whose doctrines are still intimately bound up with religion and, on the other, Descartes (at least as regards his ontology), Leibniz, Schelling and Hegel. The subjective idealism of this period is represented by Descartes (in epistemology), Berkeley (who "later sought refuge in objective idealism"), Hume, Kant and Fichte. Although all of the philosophers of this period were 'metaphysicians', a great number of them had some notions of the dialectic and tried to use it in their philosophizing, e.g. Nicholas of Cusa, Descartes, Leibniz, Kant, Fichte, Schelling, Hegel.

However, the salient characteristic of the modern period in philosophy was the appearance of Marxism-Leninism in the form of Marx' 'revolutionary upheaval in philosophy'. Pre-Marxian modern philosophy is seen, therefore, exclusively in its capacity as immediate preparation for this upheaval. Philosophies between Marx and Lenin are assimilated to 'contemporary bourgeois philosophy'. Thus, Hume and the neo-Kantians are of purely historical interest as forerunners, respectively, of contemporary positivism and irrationalism. Hegel and Kant (to a lesser degree), on the other hand, are important for their contributions to the formation of dialectical materialism. Hegel's contribution was the dialectic as a mode of being and method of thought and his mistake was to limit the dialectic to spiritual being.[4] Kant's contribution was a

118

fundamentally transcendentist ('materialist' in Lenin's words) view of knowledge and his subjectivist error was the affirmation of the unknowability of the *Ding-an-sich*. The following list of eminent modern philosophers contains our characterization of them (a) and a résumé of the Soviet judgement on them (b).

Descartes: (a) $realism_d$ + $spiritualism_d$ + transcendentism
   (b) $idealism_d$ + $spiritualism_d$ + transcendentism = an incoherent combination of subjective and objective idealism.
Spinoza[5]: (a) $realism_m$ + $spiritualism_m$ + immanentism
   (b) $realism_m$ + $materialism_m$ + immanentism = metaphysical materialism.
Leibniz: (a) $realism_m$ + $materialism_d$ + immanentism
   (b) $idealism_d$ + $spiritualism_d$ + immanentism = dialectical objective idealism.
Locke[6]: (a) $realism_d$ + $materialism_d$ + transcendentism
   (b) $realism_d$ + $materialism_d$ + transcendentism = metaphysical materialism.
Berkeley: (a) $idealism_m$ + $spiritualism_m$ + immanentism
   (b) $idealism_m$ + $spiritualism_m$ + immanentism = metaphysical subjective idealism.
Hume[7]: (a) $realism_m$ + $materialism_m$ + immanentism
   (b) $idealism_m$ + $spiritualism_m$ + immanentism = metaphysical subjective idealism.
Kant[8]: (a) $realism_d$ + $spiritualism_d$ + transcendentism
   (b) $idealism_d$ + $spiritualism_d$ + immanentism = dialectical subjective idealism.
Fichte: (a) $idealism_m$ + $spiritualism_m$ + immanentism
   (b) $idealism_m$ + $spiritualism_m$ + immanentism = dialectical subjective idealism.
Schelling: (a) $idealism_m$ + $spiritualism_m$ + transcendentism
   (b) $idealism_m$ + $spiritualism_m$ + transcendentism = dialectical objective idealism.
Hegel: (a) $idealism_m$ + $spiritualism_m$ + transcendentism
   (b) $idealism_m$ + $spiritualism_m$ + transcendentism = dialectical objective idealism.
Marx: (a) $realism_d$ + $materialism_d$ + transcendentism

(b) realism$_m$ + materialism$_m$ + transcendentism = dialectical materialism.

In interpreting the differences between our classification and that of contemporary Soviet philosophers it is important to keep in mind, first, that any dualism automatically entails for them some brand of idealism and, second, the main criterion used in classification is the given philosopher's view on the object of knowledge. Locke was not at all a materialist in the all-is-matter sense of the term but he did hold that knowledge is the sense apprehension of the material particular; hence, he is a materialist. Hume was a professed materialist in the only-matter-can-be-known sense but he held that the object of knowledge is made up of sense-impressions which, for diamaticians, are creations of the knowing subject; hence, he is a subjective idealist of the metaphysical variety.

In addition to the general classificatory terms – the various forms of idealism and materialism – contemporary Soviet philosophers make use of a number of specifically epistemological classifications which, although drawn from the general philosophic tradition, have their own specific dialectical materialist flavor and use.

Monism: is accepted by the Soviets in its ordinary meaning as indicating a doctrine which postulates one level of being; according to dialectical materialism, monism is rigorously necessary in ontology and psychology but strictly nonsensical in epistemology. Eminent monists, in addition to the classics of Marxism-Leninism, include Plato, Scotus Eriugena, the neo-Platonics, scholasticism, Spinoza, Fichte, Schelling and Hegel.

Dualism: is rejected in any form as being or leading necessarily to some form of idealism. Among the philosophers who have erred in this direction, contemporary Soviet philosophy includes Aristotle, Avicenna, Averroes, Aquinas, Descartes and Kant.

Rationalism: is literally interpreted in contemporary Soviet philosophy as the affirmation of the absolute ability of human reason to cognitively conquer anything and everything, and as the negation of any form of unknowability. The Eleatics, Plato, Aristotle, Descartes, Kant, Leibniz and Hegel are cited in contemporary Soviet philosophy as the forebears of the absolute rationalism of the classics.

120

Irrationalism: is very broadly interpreted by Soviet philosophy to include any doctrine which puts any limit whatsoever on the 'sovereignty' of human reason. The most discussed irrationalists are the neo-Platonics, Augustine, Rousseau, Hamann, Jacobi and Schelling. The scholastics are classed as 'pseudo-rationalist irrationalists'.

Sensualism: in the broad sense, dialectical materialism classes as sensualist any philosopher who puts sense-knowledge at the base of his epistemological speculations. Protagoras, Aristotle and Ockham are often-cited examples. In the more pejorative and strict sense, a sensualist is a philosopher who artificially ('metaphysically') separates sense-knowledge from rational knowledge and pretends that sensation is the only form of (valid) knowledge. Locke, Berkeley and Hume fall into this category.

Agnosticism: is a form of 'masked' idealism, a result of the effort to avoid answering the 'basic question' and to find a 'third path'. Irrationalism happens by default; agnosticism is the result of a conscious refusal.

Scepticism[9]*:* is also a form of 'masked' idealism, resulting from the same two causes as given for agnosticism. According to dialectical materialism, the specific trait of the sceptic is that he artificially ('metaphysically') separates relative and absolute truth in human knowledge and interprets all knowledge as a mere approximation to an essentially unknowable known.

35. CONTEMPORARY BOURGEOIS EPISTEMOLOGY

Contemporary Soviet philosophy's criticism of contemporary bourgeois philosophy consists in both massive rejection and detailed refutation.[10] For this reason we will not attempt a description of contemporary Western philosophy; the reader will find an adequate description of the innumerable contemporary Western philosophical trends in J. M. Bocheński's *Contemporary European Philosophy*[11], on which the vast majority of contemporary Soviet philosophers depend for their information on the subject.[12] This section is devoted to an examination of the contemporary Soviet characterization of those contemporary Western philosophical trends which are considered by them to be worthy of attention. This attention is predominantly epistemological.

Contemporary bourgeois philosophy is the ideology of the imperialist bourgeoisie. In the imperialist stage of capitalism, class-conflict has reached a 'meta-historicist' level: it is no longer simply a conflict between the proletarian class and the capitalist class but also a fight to the death between the imperialist nations and the proletarian ('socialist') nations and their colonial and semi-colonial allies. From this general description of the present-day situation, Marxist-Leninist philosophers draw upon five social factors which are the 'cores' of contemporary 'bourgeois' idealism:

(1) Contemporary bourgeois philosophy is the ideology of the 'capitalist system in its final crisis'. Whence, according to Soviet philosophers, the 'fear and trembling' of the existentialists, the 'flight unto God' of the Thomists, and the 'linguistic scientism' of the positivists.

(2) Contemporary bourgeois philosophy is the theoretical content of the decadent and dying bourgeois culture. Whence its flight into poetry, prayer and etymology.

(3) The rise of the working class as an intellectual force, armed with Marxist-Leninist philosophy, has deprived bourgeois philosophers of their monopoly on knowledge and has set, over against the distortions of bourgeois idealism, a true and scientific picture of the world.

(4) The increase in intensity of the class-war – because of the general crisis of capitalism and the rise of the world-wide 'socialist' bloc – and its extension to the international scene have completely derailed the thinking of bourgeois ideologists and created a state of *sauve qui peut* in the bourgeois philosophical world.

(5) The defeat of fascism – the political expression of aggressive bourgeois ideology – has completely broken the self-confidence of contemporary bourgeois philosophy. Thus has been practically demonstrated the steeling influence of true and scientific Marxist-Leninist philosophy.

These social factors explain the philosophic and methodological characteristics common to all trends of contemporary bourgeois philosophy:

(1) Contemporary bourgeois philosophy is completely idealist. There are many varieties of idealism in contemporary bourgeois philosophy but the 'masked' version seems to be the most popular. The only non-idealist philosophers outside of the Iron Curtain are the 'progressive

philosophers', like Roger Garaudy and Maurice Cornforth, and some inexplicable throwbacks, like Roy Wood Sellars.

(2) There is absolute confusion in the ranks of contemporary bourgeois philosophy on the precise nature of philosophy: some call it 'existential fear and trembling'; others, 'linguistic analysis'; still others 'the metaphysics of God'. This is due to the failure or inability to recognize and answer the 'basic question of all philosophy'.

(3) The complete disorientation among bourgeois philosophers – coupled with the fact that the proletariat has now assumed the initiative in philosophy – has resulted in a general return to philosophical systems of the past, especially to scholasticism and Platonism.[13]

(4) All contemporary bourgeois philosophers are – by definition – hostile to dialectical materialism. In this hostility, they forget their philosophical differences in an effort 'to crush diamat'.

For convenience the contemporary Western philosophies attacked by the ideologists of Marxism-Leninism can be grouped under three headings: positivism along with any doctrine in any way derived from it, Thomism, and existentialism.

Positivism[14]

The proverbial inability of the contemporary Soviet philosopher to distinguish an Ayer from a Russell or an Aquinas from a Tarski belongs to the past – although remnants of it are still to be found in the works of the Mitins and Rozental's. The professional philosopher in the Soviet Union today recognizes that properly speaking 'positivism' applies to the doctrines of such philosophers as Comte and J. S. Mill. When he uses it in reference to such diverse tendencies as logical empiricism and linguistic analysis this is no more than a recognition of their common origin and common tenets. According to Soviet historians of philosophy, the stages in the historical development of positivism are: logical empiricism, logical atomism, logical positivism, semantic idealism (of formalized language and of common language). Pragmatism, instrumentalism, neo-realism and analytic philosophy are classed as cognate, derivative or 'masked' forms of positivism.

The large place in Soviet polemics against contemporary Western philosophy given over to attacks on positivism[15] has its roots both in the Marxist-Leninist tradition and in the position of dialectical materialism in contemporary world philosophy. First and foremost, positivism is – according to the dogmatic affirmations of the diamaticians – a latter-day continuation of the 'Machism' to the refutation of which Lenin devoted the entirety of his *Materialism and Empirio-Criticism*. In other words, it is the main opponent of Marxist-Leninist fundamentalism. Secondly, positivism is to the capitalist monopolists of the war-mongering U.S.A. what diamat is to the proletariat of the peace-loving U.S.S.R. Against it, therefore, the full weight of ideological (philosophical) class-war must be brought to bear. Finally, there are a series of points – the outside observer would call them 'pretensions' – on which positivism and dialectical materialism meet head-on.

(1) Both positivism and dialectical materialism are embued with a 'scientism' which – although its roots are different in each case – inevitably leads to misunderstanding if not to outright contradiction. Contemporary positivism, even having attenuated its claims in this regard, still pretends to a sort of monopoly on the linguistic and methodological interpretation of the activities and findings of the natural sciences. Dialectical materialism, on the other hand, firmly maintains that its view of the world is the only one which permits the natural scientist to correctly pursue his work.[16]

(2) Both dialectical materialism and positivism have a strong methodological or 'logical' bias. Primitive neo-positivism claimed to be nothing more nor less than just the methodology of the natural sciences. Dialectical materialism touts its dialectical logic – and, consequently, its philosophy as a whole – as the only scientific method available to both philosopher and scientist. The opposition comes from the fact, of course, that each understands method in its own special way: for positivism method is once reduced to direct sense-observations of the immediately given and again to the purely logical analysis of artificial languages. Dialectical materialism understands by method – as we saw above – philosophy *tout court* and its philosophy is of the type stigmatized by the totality of positivists as 'metaphysics'.

(3) A common distaste for 'metaphysics' is another trait which puts dialectical materialism in fundamental opposition to positivism. Again, there is complete disagreement as to what the term means. For the dialectical materialist, metaphysics is the philosophic point of view

124

which eliminates motion, artificially abstracts from the real relations between real things, and separates the ideal from the real. In other words, for dialectical materialism metaphysics means, to all intents and purposes, 'positivism'. For positivism, on the other hand, the term 'metaphysics' is used to indicate the pre-positivist mode of philosophizing the main characteristic of which was juggling around abstract terms for which no real (sense) correlate could be indicated. The most prominent contemporary representative of this form of philosophizing is precisely dialectical materialism.

(4) Both of these philosophies claim to be, in one way or another, the 'modern' and 'progressive' trend in human thought. The claim is implicit in positivism's rejection of all other philosophy – past and present – and explicit in innumerable texts where Soviet philosophers explain that, as ideology of the 'forward-looking' proletariat, Marxism-Leninism cannot but be *the* philosophy of the present and future.

For dialectical materialism the basic diagrammatic of positivism is idealism$_m$ + spiritualism$_m$ + immanentism (i.e. that of Leibniz, Hume and Fichte). According to the contemporary Soviet historiography of positivism this philosophic doctrine is an amalgam of the primitive positivist insistence on attention to facts, combined with the empiricist restriction to 'sense-facts'; the 'Machist' variety added the postulate that the 'sense-facts' were epistemologically neutral; finally, came the adjunction of the preoccupation with semantic analysis. With the exception of the 'Machian neutrality', the dialectical materialist would give an 'incomplete but basically correct' rating to positivism if it were not for the fact that contemporary positivists have a general tendency to put logical correctness over empirical truth.

The basically epistemological nature of contemporary Soviet philosophy's objections to positivism is even more evident in the more detailed criticisms made of this doctrine. These can be grouped under eight headings.

(1) *The 'Basic Question':* The positivists make a profession of faith out of their refusal to consider the basic question in any form at all. Soviet philosophers are accustomed to explaining away with fatherly benevolence the absence of consideration of the basic question when it is a matter of pre-Marxist-Leninist philosophy. But, the positivists are contemporaneous to dialectical materialism and can and should learn

from it. Refusal to solve the 'basic question' vitiates all philosophic endeavor: only by answering the basic question can a philosopher gain clarity for the solution of more specific problems; inversely, the apparent solution of all the particular problems is useless unless the basic question has been previously solved.[17] The positivists are, therefore, guilty of voluntarily remaining on the level of what they themselves call 'metaphysics', i.e. idle speculation with vacuous terms.

(2) *Philosophy:* According to contemporary Soviet philosophers, by reducing philosophy to methodological or linguistic analysis the positivists have destroyed philosophy as a science. Philosophy is reduced to analysis and analysis restricted to the conceptual apparatus of natural science. This reduces philosophy to epistemology and then to mere philosophy (epistemology) of science.

(3) *The World:* Positivism refuses to categorically affirm the existence of an external (objective) world, denies the objective laws which are the proper object of philosophy, and reduces existence to the existential quantifier. According to dialectical materialism, the first is the worst form of idealism, the second is the death not only of philosophy but of any theoretical science at all, and the third is simple logicistic nonsense.

(4) *The Dialectic:* In an era when dialectical materialism has conclusively demonstrated the dialectical nature of reality and thought, the positivists with their 'metaphysical' logic of fixed concepts are an anachronism. This anti-dialectical point of view results from the refusal to recognize the validity of the 'Leninist theory of reflection' and a recourse to the *esse est percipi* of Berkeley.

(5) *The 'Third Path':* A trick popular among the positivists who are aware of their idealism and try to mask it is to make up for their inability to master dialectical reality by 'transcending' the various 'contradictions' of the objective world and of thought. This produces an artificial ('metaphysical') separation of the sensible and rational, of appearance and essence, of the abstract and concrete, of theory and practice, of the form and content of thought, etc.

(6) *Meaning:* By making the relative (dialectical) distinction between analytic and synthetic propositions a dogma of their system, the positivists have 'metaphysically' separated the subjective and objective, and have elevated solipsism (subjectivisation of meaning) to the rank of a philosophical virtue.

126

(7) *Truth:* The positivist doctrine on truth is similarly – according to the contemporary Soviet philosopher – a matter of rank subjectivism. Systems are built by convention, arbitrary selection of axioms, etc. True is what is verifi*able* or what is taken into the system. All of this puts the onus on the knowing subject and artificially ('metaphysically') excludes any reference to the real world.

(8) *Verification:* Even when the positivist does not hold a strictly logical theory of truth (e.g. systematic coherence) and speaks of 'verification', this is understood as the subjective act of the individual knower; epistemology and philosophy are reduced to logic and psychology. Social and historical conditions are completely excluded and there is an identification of existence, knowability and affirmability.

Pragmatism[18]

Contemporary Soviet philosophers stress the American origins of pragmatism. Among the most frequently quoted social causes responsible for the peculiar character of pragmatism, three stand out:

(1) Pragmatism is a result of the American philosopher's preoccupation with and absorption in 'the American way of life', with its rank individualism, worship of material wealth and cult of 'success'.

(2) Pragmatism is an expression of the basically imperialist outlook of modern America. It provides the justification for the expansionist and aggressive policies of the U.S. government.

(3) American big business and the rapacious American monopolies speak with the voice of pragmatism which ignores the social needs of man and justifies the exploitation of the American worker.

Many of the characteristics of contemporary pragmatism can also be explained – say the diamaticians – by the fact that philosophy in the U.S.A. has always tended to be religiously inclined, irrationalist, voluntarist and anti-intellectual.[19]

For dialectical materialism, pragmatism is an agglomeration of elements of positivism, empiricism and a few other stray philosophical trends (e.g. neo-Darwinism, Malthusianism, etc.).[20] It, therefore, participates in all the above-mentioned defects of positivism but exhibits certain peculiarities which are of particular interest to diamat philosophers. These have to do with the nature of knowledge and with the criterion of truth.

Since both pragmatism and dialectical materialism have a lot to say about the role of practice in knowledge, and dialectical materialism claims that the introduction of practice as an epistemological category was Marx' revolutionary upheaval in philosophy, contemporary Soviet philosophers insist that the practice of dialectical materialism has nothing at all in common with the practice which the pragmatists have in mind. Fortunately, the days are gone when one could find that pragmatist practice was bad because it served the interests of decadent capitalism and that of diamat good because it serves the progressive interests of the proletariat – and this was considered as a philosophical characterization. Today the practice of pragmatism is accused of a series of failings of a distinctly philosophic nature[21]:

(1) Practice for pragmatism is equivalent to human subjective experience; for dialectical materialism it is human material-productive activity. Diamat's practice, therefore, is objective and permits a concrete reconnaissance of the objective, external world. The practice of pragmatism remains the affair of the single individual who cannot transcend the subjectivist limits of his own experience.

(2) Pragmatist practice reduces to the subjective desires and biological needs of the knowing subject; it is blind, instinctive and abstractly removed from the external world. Marxist-Leninist practice is social-historical practice, not of the individual but of the totality of mankind. Again, practice in dialectical materialism serves to connect man with external reality and serves as the experiential base which unites all men and permits knowledge, communication, cooperation, etc. The practice of pragmatism is egocentric and conceives of knowledge as a purely selfish pursuit by man of his immediate biological needs.

(3) The practice of pragmatism leads to idealism and agnosticism. To idealism, because the subject's wants are his own private domain and the knowing activity, evoked as a response to them, remains in the closed circuit of his own subjective world. To agnosticism, because man has, for the same reasons, no access to the real world; knowing is imagining. Marxism-Leninism's practice leads naturally to materialism because it correctly conceives man as involved in 'practice' and as using knowing and practical activity as means of understanding and controlling the external, objective world.

(4) The irrationalist subjectivism of pragmatism opens the door to

128

religion since religious experience can be as 'satisfying' to man as are any of his other subjective experiences. Dialectical materialism gives religion no quarter, refuting it both in theory and practice.

On the subject of knowledge and truth, dialectical materialism finds itself in much the same type of opposition to pragmatism.

(1) For dialectical materialism – as we saw above – knowledge is a reflection of the external world, which is founded on practice and which leads to effective practice in function of the nature of the subject and of the object. For pragmatism, knowledge is subjectively created for the needs of practical activity. Diamat says that the object plays the dominant role in determining the act of knowing; it reproaches pragmatism for putting the entire cognitive onus on the subjectivity of the knower.

(2) Pragmatism (in conjunction with behaviorism) degrades man by making his intelligence a mere 'instrument' which serves to biologically adapt him to changing circumstances. Dialectical materialism recognizes man's privileged status by pointing out his ability to abstractly dominate reality in thought and then to concretely apply his knowledge to changing reality in practice.

(3) Pragmatism is guilty of rank relativism (whence its agnosticism and contribution to American scepticism) in that knowledge is always the knowing of the individual and, what is worse, truth is always individual – therefore, relative – truth. Knowledge in dialectical materialism is always social-historically conditioned and truth is always a combination of relative and absolute truths.

Dewey's *instrumentalism*[22] is classified by contemporary Soviet historians of philosophy as the ultimate in subjective idealist derivations of the basic tenets of pragmatism. For Dewey experience is reduced to the emotions of the individual; the intelligence serves as a simple instrument of adaptation relative to individual needs; logic is a purely subjective formalization of 'adaptability'; the 'principle of continuity' is an open establishment of philosophy on a purely subjective idealist basis.

Neo-realism[23]: This philosophic trend is considered by contemporary Soviet philosophy to be at the same time a derivative of and a reaction to positivism. As a derivative of positivism, neo-realism and its ultra-eclectic cohort, critical realism, shares in many of the characteristics

129

enumerated above: (1) it is oriented toward the natural sciences; (2) it seeks a 'third path' above the opposition of materialism and idealism and is, consequently, anti-dialectical; (3) it joins in the united front of bourgeois philosophy against dialectical materialism; (4) it marks a definite return to Platonism and neo-scholasticism.

In as far as it is a reaction to positivism, neo-realism contains – in the opinion of the dialectical materialists – one positive element: its insistence on the existence of 'external reals'. But, this praiseworthy reaction against subjective idealism is counterbalanced by the adjunction of three idealist postulates. First, when the neo-realists insist on the immanence of the object of knowledge they fall back into the subjective idealism from which the affirmation of 'external reals' had saved them. Second, their insistence on the total exclusion of the subject from the cognitive scene constitutes a 'metaphysical' separation of the subjective and objective and leads to agnosticism because it leaves man a helpless spectator instead of giving him his rightful place as knower and transformer of reality. Finally, the neo-realist postulate on the objective existence of universals and 'essences' (in the Platonic sense of the term) makes them guilty of a brand of objective idealism which furthers the cause of religion.

Ultimately the objections of contemporary Soviet philosophers against neo-realism, critical realism and related movements in contemporary Western thought are based on the lack of attention paid to the 'basic question' and the 'eclectic' composition of these doctrines.

Analysis: Despite the improvement which Soviet philosophy has recently undergone in respect to its knowledge of contemporary Western doctrines, the analytic movement remains for the most part completely misunderstood. Analysis for contemporary Soviet philosophers is a 'masked' form of neo-positivism and most of their criticism is aimed at the early Russell and Wittgenstein.[25]

In addition to the characteristics of positivism in which analysis shares, the analytic movement means for the diamaticians: (1) a stop-gap measure to prevent the complete disintegration of bourgeois philosophy in the era of 'general crisis of capitalism'; (2) a neo-Cartesian effort at clarity through 'reduction to simples'; (3) a determined and aggressive anti-materialist attitude (meaning anti-dialectical materialist).

130

Analysis is idealist – according to the dialectical materialist point of view – on three counts:

(1) Analysis begins its philosophical work with knowledge instead of with the thing: it proceeds 'word – fact – thing – fact – word' instead of 'thing – fact – word – fact – thing'.[26] This leads to divorce of thought from the object of knowledge and leads, through agnosticism, to subjective idealism.

(2) The followers of analysis remain in the Machist tradition of insisting on an ultimate reduction to sense-data: but, sense-data are, as Lenin showed, the product of the subject and cannot be the ultimate poles in the cognitive process – they must have an external, objective reference. Retaining this salient epistemological earmark of positivism, the analysts trap themselves in the same subjective idealist vicious circle.

(3) The use of 'sense-constructs' by many adherents of analysis does not essentially change matters. As Lenin pointed out, when Mach changed from 'sense-data' to 'elements', his subjective idealism remained unchanged.

But, the most serious objection which contemporary Soviet philosophy makes to analysis is that the method may be good and useful but it means nothing if it is not based on sound philosophic views. Thus far, they maintain, linguistic analysis has proved unfruitful for philosophy precisely because the context in which it was executed had a constantly subjective idealist character.[27]

Semantics[28]: As mentioned above 'semantic idealism' is one of the components which diamaticians attribute to positivism. The principle objection made specifically against any form of semantics is that operation with artificially created languages is a-philosophical and can only lead to a 'metaphysical' separation of thought and reality, of the subjective and objective, and thence to metaphysical subjective idealism. The semanticist reduces reality to a series of propositions, defines truth as the correspondence of propositions to propositions, and concludes by affirming that thing and thought differ only in their function. The first tenet subjectivizes reality by reducing it to what one says of it; the second renders truth a matter of definition; the third gives an absolute priority to the creativity of the knowing subject.

131

Thomism[29]

Positivism, pragmatism, instrumentalism, etc., represent the dominant metaphysical subjective idealist enemy of dialectical materialism in contemporary philosophy. Thomism represents – for contemporary Soviet historiography of philosophy – the dominant contemporary form of metaphysical objective idealism. The increasing place which Thomism is currently taking in Soviet anti-bourgeois literature seems due, on one hand, to recent stress on making 'scientific atheism' more scientific[30] and, on the other, to the gradual decline of positivism as a living philosophic trend.

Under 'Thomism' dialectical materialism gathers (a) the philosophy of Aquinas and of the early and late scholastics, (b) the neo-scholastic revival of the turn of the century, (c) the neo-Thomist movement of the last three decades, and (d) just about anyone who quotes any of these approvingly. As a first approximation, Thomism is identified as 'the philosophy of the Catholic Church'. In this capacity it represents the result of certain sociological influences.

(1) Thomism as a philosophy serving a religion is a direct result of the separation of mental and physical labor in a class society. As the expression of the views of the hierarchy – i.e. a portion of the exploiting class – Thomism officially prones an ecclesiastical form of objective idealism. Since, however, it is also the systematization of the views of the faithful – part of the downtrodden proletariat – there are definite signs of fideistic subjective idealism.

(2) Since the Church, as a social organization, is devoted to the repression of any science which does not support its dogmas (e.g. the Inquisition and Galileo), Thomism as its philosophic servant devotes itself to the repression of all that is progressive in the development of science and philosophy.

(3) The philosophy of the Church is devoted to maintaining the status quo and to frustrating any efforts at social change by relegating to a distant 'city of God' the full enjoyment by all men of their human rights and dignity. Thomism, therefore, is firmly against all progressive social ideas, especially those of historical materialism.

(4) Thomism is the philosophic marihuana corresponding to the religious opium with which the Church vainly hopes to stem the rise of class-war and the final liberation of the proletariat.

(5) Finally, Thomism is the most deadly opponent of dialectical materialism. Just as the Church has always been against progressive thinkers (de la Valla, Savonarola, etc.), so now a desperate 'return to Aquinas' is supposed to draw the masses and the intelligentsia away from the only true, scientific philosophy, dialectical materialism.

Notwithstanding its differences of opinion with positivism, dialectical materialism is not unwilling to join forces with positivism in order to refute Thomism. The bases of this 'unholy alliance' are to be found in the four resemblances between positivism and dialectical materialism which serve, as mentioned above, as points of friction between the two but which, *mutatis mutandis*, also serve as a common platform from which both movements criticize Thomism.

(1) Both positivism and dialectical materialism present themselves as 'scientific'; both reproach Thomism for being the apologist of a fundamentally anti-science point of view.

(2) The emphasis both in positivism and in dialectical materialism is on the methodological or logical aspect of philosophizing and both strive for a perfect rationalism. On both counts, the two schools condemn Thomism as being a relic of the past. Catholicism in general and Thomism in particular are based on faith, a faith which limits or denies the power of human reason and which, consequently, renders logic a simple mechanism for cataloguing already revealed truths.

(3) Thomism is an explicitly metaphysical doctrine. And it is condemned as such – although for entirely different reasons – by both dialectical materialism and positivism. Positivism condemns Thomism for 'metaphysics', meaning operation with vacuous concepts; diamat condemns Thomism for 'metaphysics', meaning operation with fixed concepts, i.e. an anti-dialectical view.

(4) Finally and most obviously, Thomism is distasteful to both positivism and dialectical materialism because it constitutes a return to a moribund medieval tradition. Thomism is neither 'progressive' nor 'modern'.

However, the situation is often reversed and we find dialectical materialists agreeing with Thomist criticism of positivism. This agreement – which is, of course, purely tactical – is based on the fact that both Thomism and dialectical materialism are complete philosophic explanations of reality while positivism is not (nor does it pretend to be!). There are three major areas of agreement.

133

(1) Both Thomism and dialectical materialism refuse to recognize positivism as a philosophy; at most it is an epistemology of scientific thought which, more often than not, is no more than a methodology of science. Both dialectical materialism and Thomism deal with science from a philosophic point of view, i.e. they both develop a philosophy of nature which deals philosophically with the same reality which science treats from its own point of view.

(2) Dialectical materialism and Thomism both represent metaphysical systems – metaphysics here meaning that they recognize the legitimacy of discourse on general characteristics and properties of the real, discourse which is not necessarily reducible to direct sense-perception. Positivism is, in the eyes of both, hopelessly a-philosophical with its logical atomism and epistemological nominalism.

(3) Both dialectical materialism and Thomism have a social doctrine. Positivism has recently developed one also but it is not an intrinsic component of the positivist world-view as is the case both for Thomism with its Catholic social doctrine and for dialectical materialism with its historical materialism.

For dialectical materialism the basic diagrammatic of Thomism is idealism$_m$ + spiritualism$_m$ + transcendentism (i.e. that of Aquinas, Schelling and Hegel). Behind every judgement which the contemporary Soviet philosopher makes in reference to Thomism is the conviction that the inclusion of God in the Thomist system deprives it of any rational (explanatory) content. More precisely, the anti-Thomist objections of the diamaticians fall under eight points, four ontological and four epistemological.

(1) Thomism takes an anti-subjective idealist stand over against positivism but even material things (those available to the senses) – not to speak of souls, angels, etc. – are such as they are because of their 'forms' which are creations of the 'divine mind', hence ideal. This is objective idealism.

(2) The anti-dialectical and 'metaphysical' character of Thomism is evident in its conception of beings as rigidly fixed and of categories as immutable elements of reality.

(3) Thomistic ontology is based on 'pure act', i.e. 'God'. God, however, is an alienated reification. Therefore, Thomism's whole structure of reality is based on an idealist fiction.

134

(4) In the course of 'Christianizing' Aristotle, Aquinas and his latter-day followers have succeeded in completely distorting the Philosopher's basically materialist doctrine. The search for a 'reality' which would represent the 'third path' between the idealism of Plato and the materialism of Aristotle has led to an inconsequent objective idealism.

(5) Both the knower and the known in the Thomist dispensation are ideal beings. Both are creations of a fictional 'divine being' and, therefore, are essentially mental.

(6) In the Thomist theory of knowledge the mind is said to abstract 'eternal essences' from their 'material envelope'. This is not only dualism (which leads to idealism) but also a solipsistic reduction of knowledge to the knowing of the known (i.e. the form which is essentially ideal, hence mental). The 'first principles' are found *a priori* in the 'mind of God'.

(7) Under the cover of 'rationalism' Thomism carries on an 'irrationalist pseudo-rationalism', the central element of which is the so-called proof of the existence of a non-existent 'God'.[31]

(8) For Thomism, reason is subject to faith, philosophy to theology. To this doctrine of double truth is added the affirmation that the criteria of truth are, on the one hand, Church dogmas and, on the other, the subjective conviction of the individual believer.

Existentialism[32]:

The heterogeneity of existentialism as a philosophic trend accounts for the little attention given to it – by contemporary Soviet philosophers – in comparison with that devoted to Thomism and to the varieties of positivism. In other words, existentialism is not a strong philosophic trend likely to endanger the dialectical materialist monopoly on truth.

For dialectical materialism, the basic diagrammatic of existentialism is $idealism_m$ + $spiritualism_m$ + immanentism (i.e. that of Hume, Berkeley and Fichte). Existentialism is the metaphysical subjective idealist expression of the irrationalism which marks contemporary bourgeois decadence, the fear and trembling of the bourgeois from the last war and from those to come, and the capitalist, imperialist, bourgeois inability to face a reality which is now predominantly socialist and favorable to the proletariat. All the diamatician's objections against

135

existentialism are also applied to *phenomenology*, and are of a completely epistemological character.

(1) Existentialism preaches a purely subjectivist view of absolute freedom of the individual with knowledge being conceived as strictly of the individual and, therefore, completely relative.

(2) Existentialism (and phenomenology) isolates science on facts from science 'on essences', knowledge from the thing, and knowing (and knowledge) from *any* knower.

(3) The process of knowing consists for the existentialist in deducing reality – in fear and trembling – from the idea, in view of biological preservation of the individual.

(4) Existentialism rejects the reflection theory of knowledge, denies practice any epistemological function, separates the logical from the historical, is resolutely opposed to any form of objective truth, and eliminates the distinction between the object and subject of the knowing process.

(5) Truth is – for existentialism – equivalent to existence. The concept is eliminated. Subjective existence is introduced as the criterion of truth, whereupon truth takes on the sense of biological preservation of the individual.

Finally, the existentialists do not answer the 'basic question' and their doctrine as a whole is an open invitation to religion.

Others

There are a number of modern and contemporary Western philosophers who do not fit easily into the three above-mentioned trends but whose doctrines are nevertheless discussed by contemporary Soviet historiographers of thought.

(1) *Croce's*[33] dialectic is dismissed as 'metaphysical' because it does not allow for the development (plasticity) of concepts. Other neo-Hegelians are classed as combining dialectical subjective idealism and spiritualism.

(2) *Frege's*[34] use of *Bedeutung* (*značenie* = meaning) for 'thing' (*predmet*) is wrong because things pre-exist (temporally) and are epistemologically prior to thought and meaning.

(3) *Gonseth*[35] has a basically correct view of the dialectic of relative and absolute truth but is hindered from arriving at full dialectical

materialism because of academic prejudices against materialism. He, therefore, remains a 'third path' eclectic, objectively near to diamat but subjectively not realizing it.

(4) *Bridgeman's*[36] operationalism is a corrected but unrepentant neo-positivist subjective idealism. Basically, all Bridgeman has done is to replace the sense-knowing subject by a 'series of operations'. As soon as the question: who does the operations? is answered, one is back in neo-positivist subjectivism.

(5) *Personalism*[37] as a continuation of the spiritualist-religious tradition in the U.S.A. is just another instance of metaphysical subjective idealism.

(6) *Piaget*[38] is a 'spontaneous materialist' *(stixinyj materialist)* but he metaphysically separates the 'inner equilibrium of the subject' from the 'equilibrium of subject and object'.

(7) *Sellars*[39] has a basically materialist view in that he conceives of knowing as a reflection and insists on the fact that it is physiologically based. He errs, however, in not recognizing that the cognitive act forms an inseparable whole and he lacks the social-historical view, without which one cannot correctly conceive the nature of knowing.

(8) *Whitehead's*[40] 'presentational immediacy' leaves the door open to arbitrariness and indeterminacy, thereby favoring the formation of subjective idealism.

REFERENCES

1. Cf. K. G. Ballestrem: 'Soviet Historiography of Philosophy'. *Studies in Soviet Thought* III (1963), 107–120.
2. In the five-volume *Istorija filosofii* (Moskva. 1957–1961) the first volume (717 pp.) covers the history of philosophy from the beginning to the French revolution, while the other four (a total of 2911 pp.) cover up to the First World War.
3. For specific details on thinkers and points of view surveyed in this chapter, see the corresponding sections in *Istorija filosofii* and *Filosofskaja enciklopedija*.
4. Cf. K. S. Bakradze: *Sistema i metod filosofii Gegelja* (System and Method of Hegel's Philosophy). Tbilisi. 1958. T. Ojzerman: *Filosofija Gegelja*. Moskva. 1956. I. K. Tavadze, G. M. Kalandarišvili: *V. I. Lenin o "Nauke logiki" Gegelja*. Tbilisi. 1959. See the newer works listed in Ballestrem: *op.cit.* note 32.
5. Cf. V. V. Sokolov: 'Racionalizm XVII veka i teorija poznanija Spinozy' (Rationalism of the Seventeenth Century and Spinoza's Theory of Knowledge). *V MGU* 1962, 5, 64–74. A. Karapetjan: *Kritičeskij analiz filosofii Kanta* (Critical Analysis of the Philosophy of Kant). Erevan. 1958.
6. Cf. G. A. Zaičenko: 'K voprosu o skepticizme v teorii poznanija D. Lokka' (On Scepticism in Locke's Theory of Knowledge). *FN* 1959, 4, 123–131.
7. Cf. Ju. P. Mixalenko: *Filosofija D. Juma – teoretičeskaja osnovy anglijskogo*

pozitivizma XX veka (Hume's Philosophy as Theoretical Base of Twentieth Century English Positivism). Moskva. 1962.

8. Cf. V. F. Asmus: 'Immanuil Kant'. *VF* 1954, 5, 92–108. and Karapetjan: *op.cit.*

9. Both 'agnosticism' and 'scepticism' are frequently used as ill-defined condemnatory terms for any sort of idealism.

10. Massive rejection used to be the standard Soviet procedure. It is still used by some members of the old guard, like Mitin. A more detailed and analytic refutation is characteristic of the younger generation.

11. *Europäische Philosophie der Gegenwart.* Bern. 1947 (second edition 1951). English: *Contemporary European Philosophy.* Berkeley. 1956.

12. Rumor has it that, although there is no official Russian translation of Bocheński's book, Soviet philosophers do dispose of a translation, mimeographed for private circulation. In any case, it is striking how the article on 'Idealism' in the *Filosofskaja enciklopedija* follows Bocheński's exposition.

13. The Soviets are referring here not only to Thomism but also to modern nominalism, neo-realism, etc.

14. Cf. W. F. Boeselager: 'Recent Soviet Works on Neopositivism'. *Studies in Soviet Thought* III (1963), 230–242 and IV (1964) 81–84.

15. *Ibid.*

16. This constant affirmation stems from Lenin's *Materialism and Empirio-Criticism* where he states that all scientists are turning to dialectical materialism.

17. Cf. *Osnovy*, pp. 10–11.

18. Cf. I. Lingart: *Amerikanskij pragmatizm* (American Pragmatism). Moskva. 1954. G. A. Kursanov: *Gnoseologija sovremennogo pragmatizma* (Epistemology of Contemporary Pragmatism). Moskva. 1958. Articles by: Ju. K. Mel'vil' (*VF* 1950, 2, 306–330), M. B. Mitin (*VF* 1949, 1, 60–84), Ju. G. Gajdukov (*VF* 1959, 6, 101–110), D. I. Dubrovskij (*VF* 1962, 4, 24–31), G. A. Kursanov (*VF* 1957, 2, 188–193), I. T. Jakuševskij (*FN* 1958, 4, 113–121), E. P. Nikitin (*FN* 1962, 3, 120–122). Also, Ju. A. Aseev, I. S. Kon: *Osnovnye napravlenija buržuaznoj filosofii i sociologii XX veka* (Basic Tendencies of Twentieth Century Bourgeois Philosophy and Sociology). Leningrad. 1961. p. 36ff.

19. Cf. Jan Bodnar: *O sovremennoj filosofii SŠA* (On Contemporary U.S. Philosophy). Moskva. 1959. p. 64f.

20. Lingart: *op.cit.*, pp. 38–74 *et passim.*

21. *Ibid.*, p. 98f. Gajdukov: *op.cit.* Jakuševskij: *op.cit.*

22. Kursanov: *Gnoseologija sovremennogo pragmatizma*, p. 75ff. Lingart: *op.cit.*, p. 24f., p. 83f.

23. Cf. Bodnar: *op.cit.*, p. 115ff.

24. A. F. Begiašvili: *Metod analiza v sovremennoj buržuaznoj filosofii* (The Analytic Method in Contemporary Bourgeois Philosophy). Tbilisi. 1960. A. I. Korneeva: *Kritika neopozitivistskix vzgljadov na prirodu poznanija* (Critique of Neopositivist Views on the Nature of Knowledge). Moskva. 1962. p. 137f.

25. For example, Begiašvili devotes some 160 pages to discussing just Russell and Wittgenstein.

26. Cf. *Filosofskaja enciklopedija*, vol. 1, p. 222.

27. Begiašvili: *op.cit.*, pp. 170–174.

28. Bodnar: *op.cit.*, p. 188ff. G. A. Brutjan: *Teorija poznanija obščej semantiki* (The Theory of Knowledge of General Semantics). Erevan. 1959. A. A. Vetrov: 'O semantičeskom ponjatii istiny' (On the Semantic Conception of Truth). *VF* 1962,

9, 63–74. D. P. Gorskij: 'O roli jazyka v poznanii' (On the Role of Language in Knowledge). *VF* 1953, 2, 75–92. I. S. Narskij: 'Kritika koncepcii jazyka v teorii poznanija "obščej semantiki"' (Critique of the Conception of Language in the Theory of Knowledge of "General Semantics"). In *Kritika sovremennoj buržuaznoj filosofii i sociologii*. Moskva. 1961. pp. 59–109.

29. Aseev and Kon: *op.cit.*, p. 54ff. I. M. Kičanova: 'Filosofija Fomy Akvinskogo' (The Philosophy of Thomas Aquinas). *VF* 1958, 3, 104–117. T. M. Jaroševskij: 'O tomistskom "gnoseologičeskom realizme"' (On Thomistic 'Epistemological Realism'). *VF* 1962, 11, 115–126. B. E. Byxovskij: 'Neotomistskij obskurantizm' (Neo-Thomist Obscurantism). *Sovremennye religiozno-filosofskie tečenija v kapitalističeskix stranax*. Moskva. 1962. pp. 52–111. B. E. Byxovskij: 'Neotomistskaja kriteriologija' (Neo-Thomist Criteriology). *Praktika – kriterij istiny v nauke*. Moskva. 1960. pp. 444–462.

30. Cf. Chapter VII, note 23.

31. Cf. Chapter VII, note 10.

32. Aseev and Kon: *op.cit.*, pp. 44–54. M. Čalin: *Filosofija otčanija i straxa* (A Philosophy of Despair and Fear). Moskva. 1962. A. I. Vladimirova: 'Protiv idealističeskoj fal'sifikacii dialektiki' (Against Idealist Falsification of the Dialectic). *VF* 1957, 1, 162–173. N. V. Motrošilova: 'Fenomenologija E. Gusserlja i osnovnoj vopros filosofii' (The Phenomenology of Husserl and the Basic Question of Philosophy). *VF* 1961, 12, 66–79.

33. B. S. Černyšev: 'Benedetto Kroče i dialektika' (Benedetto Croce and the Dialectic). *VF* 1958, 8, 63–73.

34. B. V. Birjukov: 'Teorija smysla Gotloba Frege' (The Theory of Sense of Gottlob Frege). In *Primenenie logiki v nauke i texnike*. Moskva. 1960. pp. 502–555. and 'O rabotax Frege po filosofskim voprosam matematiki' (On Frege's Works on Philosophic Questions of Mathematics). In *Filosofskie voprosy estestvoznanija*. Moskva. 1959. pp. 134–177. (English translation of both by I. Angelelli now in print). M. V. Popovič: 'Filosofskij aspekt problemy značenija i smysla' (The Philosophical Side of the Problem of Meaning and Sense). *VF* 1962, 12, 34–46.

35. S. A. Efirov: 'Teorija dialektiki Ferdinanda Gonseta i dialektičeskij materializm' (The Theory of Dialectic of Ferdinand Gonseth and Dialectical Materialism). *VF* 1958, 8, 51–62.

36. B. E. Byxovskij: 'Operacionalizm Bridžmena' (Bridgeman's Operationalism). *VF* 1958, 2, 75–89. and 'Nauka i zdravyj smysl' (Science and Common Sense). *FN* 1958, 3, 163–170.

37. Bodnar: *op.cit.*, p. 172ff.

38. V. A. Lektorskij: 'O kategorijax sub"ekta i ob"ekta v teorii poznanija' (On the Categories of Subject and Object in Theory of Knowledge). *Voprosy dialektičeskogo materializma*. Moskva. 1960. pp. 286–309.

39. A. S. Bogomolov: 'Roj Vud Sellars o materialističeskoj teorij poznanija' (Roy Wood Sellars on the Materialist Theory of Knowledge). *VF* 1962, 8, 140–142.

40. A. A. Jakušev: 'Sub"ektivno-idealističeskij smysl teorii simvolizma A. Uajtxeda' (The Subjective-Idealist Sense of Whitehead's Theory of Symbols). *VF* 1962, 12, 116–128.

CHAPTER IX

EVALUATION

A thoroughgoing criticism of contemporary Soviet theory of knowledge will have to await competent expositions of dialectical-materialism's ontological and logical doctrines[1], since it is subservient thereto. Our comments are limited to outlining the positive (36) and negative (37) elements in this doctrine, and to indicating the nonsense it contains (38). Finally, we shall point out the directions in which we think it could profitably be further developed (39).

36. POSITIVE ELEMENTS IN DIAMAT'S THEORY OF KNOWLEDGE

A philosophic doctrine which takes the immediate given of common sense as its point of departure has the advantage that even its opponents have to concede that this given does not admit of further justification (as does, for example, a point of departure such as sense-data). In spite of its being bound to a dogmatic tradition, contemporary Soviet philosophy does firmly maintain such a point of departure for its theory of knowledge, and this is consistently preserved throughout most of the development of this theory.

Further, Soviet theory of knowledge is based on a fundamentalist type of rationalism which is also that of the common-sense man. All that is is basically intelligible; what is not known is merely not yet known.

On the more immediately philosophic level, contemporary Soviet philosophers are to be commended for their systematic approach to philosophy, principally expressed in their refusal to let epistemology be artificially isolated from the other parts of philosophy – especially ontology (dialectics) and logic. In this, they distinguish themselves from the horde of incomplete philosophies which mark the current period.

A specifically Soviet doctrine which could be a positive contribution to philosophy in general is the notion of reflection as a general property of all matter. Of course, it would have to be cleansed of its distinctly anthropomorphic character but the resemblance to certain views of Teilhard de Chardin is already quite significant.

The Soviet effort to retain the notion of truth both as a correspondence and a process – though as yet incompletely developed – offers possibilities for the overcoming of one of the main speculative difficulties of our era – i.e. the enormous distance between the coherence-theory truth of the logician and the quasi-correspondence pragmatics of the rest of us.

The fact that contemporary Soviet philosophers, when discussing problems of knowledge, are more and more conscious of the necessity of an analytic approach is a most heartening sign. The fact that Alekseev has arrived – in the context of dialectical logic – at a distinction (between dialectical thought and the dialectic of thought) which is very close to a scholastic logical pair *(conceptus subjectivus* and *conceptus objectivus)* and not the least resembling the doctrine of the 'classics of Marxism' is, to our mind, highly significant.

Finally, the fact that contemporary Soviet philosophers are widely commenting and refuting Western views on knowledge is both a healthy sign and, perhaps, a new and rich possibility of dialogue. More and more problems are being faced by the Soviet philosopher (e.g., those of semantics) in much the same way as they are faced in the West. An effort of understanding and standardization of vocabulary may open up vast new vistas of East-West philosophical contact. That is, if Western philosophers are willing to take the trouble to familiarize themselves with Soviet doctrines.

37. NEGATIVE ELEMENTS IN DIAMAT'S THEORY OF KNOWLEDGE

Because it has begun to develop only recently and because it is essentially tributary to other areas of contemporary Soviet philosophic activity, theory of knowledge is probably the most dogmatically bound of contemporary Soviet philosophic disciplines. The use of innumerable quotations from and references to the classics – though it may be the cross of the non-Marxist-Leninist reader of Soviet philosophic texts – is not the main weakness. This lies in the restriction of problems discussed. As we have seen, the main problems which are still discussed by contemporary Soviet philosophers are those which were proposed by the classics. It is only very recently – and very hesitantly – that dialectical materialism's adherents have begun to take up other and more timely problems.

There is in all of contemporary Soviet philosophy – but especially in its theory of knowledge – an almost hopeless confusion as to terminology. We have indicated some of the difficulties of this nature in the body of our work. We would point out here only the fact that this confusion will persist as long as the 'basic question of all philosophy' is posed with the use of four terms, three of which are maintained in a state of systematic ambiguity. Matter: does it mean 'substance', or simply 'everything'? Spirit: is it a correlative of matter, or an epi-phenomenon thereof? Being: is it 'essence' (i.e. matter), or 'existence'. It seems that, once these terms are clarified, the rest of the diamat philosophic structure will fall into place and many of the problems so hotly discussed at present will be much easier to deal with.

A closely related difficulty – which, seemingly, could be cleared up by the above reform – is the chronic confusion of the physiological and psychological domains. Nerves seem, without a doubt, to have something or other to do with thinking; but, the nature and activity of the nerves is a physiological question, that on thought is a psychological-philosophical one. Here we touch on one of the weaknesses of contemporary Soviet philosophy in general which are responsible for the disrepute which it enjoys among the majority of Western philosophers. No philosopher interested in thought wants to waste time wading through descriptions of clinical cases of purely neurological interest; it is to be supposed, on the other hand, that the neurologist is just as repulsed by the random philosophical interpretations given these phenomena.

The entire *sovpadenie*-question serves as a further justification for the title of our previous disquisition on contemporary Soviet philosophy. For, this is scholasticism at its very worst, though one must add in defense of the scholastics that the aridity of their arguments was often due to their pedagogical intentions. That the *sovpadenie*-problem is a problem at all is due to the fact that contemporary Soviet philosophers continue to let a word for word – one might even say: letter for letter – interpretation of a few random quotes stand in the way of a perfectly obvious solution, the empirical one. Are there logicians in the Soviet Union? Yes. Are there ontologists in the Soviet Union? Yes. Are there epistemologists in the Soviet Union? Yes. Therefore, there are three distinct sciences. That there remains a serious question on the relations between the objects of these philosophic sciences, no one will care to deny. But, that Marxism-Leninism has not overcome the traditional partition of philosophy into three main compartments, is patent. All the words in the numerous Soviet publications on the subject will not change this state of affairs.

The reader will have noticed that the Soviet doctrine on the cognitive functions and modes is incredibly naive in more than one respect. Perhaps its gravest deficiency, however, is its inimitably eclectic character. It would be vain to try to list all the diverse sources at work therein, but already the combination of Engel's latter-day positivism and Lenin's neo-Hegelianism goes a long way toward explaining the innumerable derailments.

Finally, the 'Marxist dialectical method' suffers from all of the above-mentioned flaws. It, however, possesses them in the pre-eminent degree because it is meant to be the apex of the dialectical-materialist philosophic edifice. Its definitely *a priori* character makes it the esoteric possession of the initiated few: it is touted as the correct method for all science while, as a matter of fact, it is only available to those who admit an entire series of ontological, psychological and moral postulates – none of which are immediately acceptable to the non-Marxist-Leninist.[2]

38. NONSENSE IN DIAMAT'S THEORY OF KNOWLEDGE

The epistemology of dialectical materialism is governed – as is any portion of Marxism-Leninism – by the dogma of *partijnost'* (party-mindedness), according to which philosophical questions are decided on a purely subjectivist basis, i.e. according to the class-bias of the philosopher in question. That this is nonsense is evident from the fact that – consequently applied, which it is not even by Mitin himself – it means the end of science.

Lenin left to contemporary Soviet philosophy – along with other emotional prejudices of the nineteenth century – an overriding fear of a surreptitious introduction of God through philosophical arguments. That this is nonsense can be shown in the following way: the philosopher's God is not the God of revelation. A philosopher who has reasoned his way from concrete reality to the necessity of a 'prime mover', 'first cause', 'omniscient providence', etc., is by no means bound to the recognition of a personal God, much less to the recognition or practice of a religion. The most pertinent example is contemporary Soviet philosophy itself: the recognition of a supreme being, self-moving matter, does not lead either to a personal God or to religious practices.

The putting of logical functions (abstraction, generalization, etc.) on the sense-level is simply absurd. That contemporary Soviet philosophers do this is due to their unreasonable continuation of discussion of the *sovpadenie*-question. It is in direct contradiction with the basically common-sense point of departure of their philosophizing.

Practice as basis of knowledge and criterion of truth is worse than nonsense; it is a mystification. If practice means *pragma*, then the Soviets are bound to the consequences drawn from this doctrine by the pragmatists. If it means sense-contact with an external world, then nothing original is affirmed and a clarification of terminology is in order.

The contemporary Soviet epistemological doctrine on absolute and relative truth would not be worthy of special mention were it not for the fact that an effort is made to present them both as approximations to an ideal limit and, at the same time, as whole and part. Here the absurdity of a materialist marriage between Hegelianism and traditional realism appears in all its nakedness. The whole and part conception of truth has sense only within the limits of a structured system (the unlimited has, by definition, no parts). Truth as an ideal limit is precisely conceived only in function of a dynamic system. One or the other, but not both.

Finally, dialectical logic – as least as it has been so far conceived in contemporary Soviet philosophy – is the ultimate in absurdity. Of the many considerations which can be adduced to support this contention, we will retain three.

(a) *Dialectical logic is not logic*. Logic is made up of rules which deal with certain objective structures. If dialectical logic were a logic, it would have to contain at least one rule which formal logic does not contain. Contemporary Soviet philosophers have failed to present even one such rule.

(b) *Dialectical logic is not a calculus within general logic*. And this by definition for it is universally held by contemporary Soviet philosophers that formal logic is either subsidiary or parallel to dialectical logic. Dialectical logic cannot, therefore, be a discipline subject to formal logic and its laws.

(c) *Dialectical logic is a theory of knowledge.* In other words, it deals exclusively with the relations between knower and known.

39. POSSIBILITIES OF FURTHER DEVELOPMENT

It is a bit risky for a non-Marxist-Leninist to hazard suggestions on how some portion of dialectical materialism might be best developed in the future. There are, nevertheless, three points in the contemporary Soviet theory of knowledge which are obviously ripe for further exploitation.

(a) There is an already begun evolution – the most evident sign being Alekseev's distinction, pointed out above – toward what we would call a genuine concept of analogy. Reflection as a property of all matter and as the proper of thought could best be conceived analogically. This is even more the case with reality and thought as distinct modes of being: conceiving them analogically would render unnecessary the verbal leger-de-main one now meets in Soviet texts.

(b) In the effort to develop a dialectical method from below – i.e. beginning from the procedures of the real scientists instead of from preconceived notions on the nature of the dialectic – Soviet theoreticians may come to see that they need only do negligible violence to the classics in order to work out a viable doctrine on method.

(c) The extensive criticism of Western theories of knowledge – which criticism is in continuous development – has already lead to improvements in Soviet philosophic style. Many works of Soviet philosophers show the beneficient effects of having been able to read the philosophers they criticize in the original instead of in a textbook presentation. Familiarity with the original has made evident that Western philosophers are neither as naive nor as class-bound as the standard Soviet image of them would lead one to believe.

REFERENCES

1. Such are in preparation by H. Fleischer and J. M. Bocheński of the Institute of East-European Studies.
2. Cf. T. J. Blakeley: *Soviet Scholasticism.* Dordrecht, Holland. 1961. pp. 1–12.

BIBLIOGRAPHY

Part One contains all available Soviet sources which are pertinent to the subject matter of this book. Part Two cites only those Western works which have been of direct use to us in the course of writing this book.
The following abbreviations have been used:

Ak.	Akademija	ob.	oblastnyj (-nogo)
AN	Akademija Nauk (USSR unless	ot.	otdelenie
	otherwise specified)	per.	perevod
AON	Akademija obščestvennyx nauk	Pg.	pedagogičeskij (-kogo)
	pri CK KPSS	pos.	posleslovie
B	Bol'ševik	r.	redaktor
č	čast'	s.	sbornik
(d)	dissertacija	Soč.	Sočinenija
dial.	dialektičeskij (-kogo)	Ss.	Sbornik statej
dr.	drugie	SSR	Sovetskaja Socialističeskaja
fil.	filosofii (-fskij)		Respublica
FN	Naučnye doklady vysšej skoly.	SSSR	USSR
	Filosofskie nauki	st.	stat'ja (-i, ej)
G	gosudarstvennyj	t.	tom
gorod.	gorodskoj	tex.	texnika (-ki)
Gt.	Gospolitizdat	tr.	trud (y)
IF	Institut filosofii AN USSR	U.	Universitet
In-t	Institut	Učz.	Učpedgiz
ist.	istorii (-riceskij, -kogo)	UZ	Učenye zapiski
Izd.	izdatel'stvo	V	Vestnik
Izv.	Izvestija	VF	Voprosy filosofii
K	Kiev (-skij)	VP	Voprosy psixologii
kaf.	kafedra	VPŠ	Vysšaja partijnaja škola pri
kn.	kniga		CK KPSS
Ko	Kommunist	vop.	vopros (y)
L.	Leningrad (-skij)	Vyp.	vypusk
M.	Moskva (-kovskij)		

SOVIET SOURCES

ABAŠEV-KONSTANTINOVSKIJ, A. P.: 'Problemy soznanija v svete kliničeskoj psixologii' (Problems of Consciousness in the Light of Clinical Psychology). *VP* 1958, 4, 30–42.
ABDIL'DIN, Z.: 'Gegel' o konkretnosti ponjatija' (Hegel on the Concreteness of the Concept). In *Nekotorye voprosy filosofii*. Alma-Ata. 1961. 146–166.
ABRAMJAN, L. A.: *Signal i uslovnyj refleks* (The Signal and the Conditioned Reflex). Erevan. 161 str.
AFANASEV, V. G.: *Osnovy marksistskoj filosofii*. Moskva. 1960. 351 str.
AKPEROV, M. S.: 'K voprosu o sootnošenii ob"ektivnoj, otnositel'noj i absoljutnoj

istiny v matematike' (On the Question of the Relationship of Objective, Relative and Absolute Truth in Mathematics). *V MGU* 1962, 2, 54–68.

ALEKSANDROV, G. F.:
   (1) *Marksizm-Leninizm o naučnom predvidenii* (Marxism-Leninism on Scientific Prediction). Moskva. 1939.
   (2) 'Razvitie I. V. Stalinym marksistsko-leninskoj teorii poznanija v trudax po voprosam jazykoznanija (The Development by I. V. Stalin of Marxist-Leninist Theory of Knowledge in his Works on Liguistics). V AN SSSR 1952, 6, 5.

ALEKSANDROV, G. F., GORBAČ, V. I., KOVALGIN, V. M.: *Razvitie V. I. Leninym marksistskogo ucenija o zakonax dialektiki* (The Development by V. I. Lenin of the Marxist Doctrine on the Laws of the Dialectic). Minsk. 1960. 442 str.

ALEKSANDROVA, S. E.:
   (1) 'Kritika reakcionnyx vozzrenij pragmatistov na prirodu ponjatija' (Criticism of the Reactionary Views of the Pragmatists on the Nature of the Concept). In *Voprosy logiki*. Leningrad. 1957. 149–156.
   (2) 'O nigilizme v teorii umozaključenij' (On Nihilism in the Theory of Reasoning). In *Učenye zapiski* (LGU 285). Leningrad. 1960. 142–155.
   (3) 'Sub"ektivno-idealističeskoe istolkovanie pragmatistami zakonov myšlenija' (Subjective-idealistic Interpretation of the Laws of Thought by the Pragmatists). *V LGU* 1957, 23, 89.
   (4) *Pragmatizma v logike i ego reakcionnaja suščnost'* (Pragmatism in Logic and its Reactionary Essence). LGU. 1953/54. (d)
   (5) 'Reakcionnyj xarakter pljuralizma v teorii dokazatel'stva' (Reactionary Character of Pluralism in the Theory of Proof). *V LGU* 1961, 3, 96–106.

ALEKSEEV, G. P.: 'V. I. Lenin ob utončennyx formax religii'. In *Kniga V. I. Lenina "Materializm i empiriokriticizm"* – *važnejšij etap v razvitii marksistskoj filosofii* (V. I. Lenin's Book "Materialism and Empirio-Criticism" as the most Important Stage in the Development of Marxist Philosophy). Moskva. 1959. 425–440.

ALEKSEEV, M. N.:
   (1) *Dialektika form myšlenija* (The Dialectic of the Forms of Thought). Moskva. 1959.
   (2) *Dialektičeskaja logika* (Dialectical Logic). Moskva. 1960. 150 str.
   (3) 'Marksizm ob ob"ektivnom xaraktere zakonov nauki i zakony logiki' (Marxism on the Objective Character of the Laws of Science and the Laws of Logic). In *Učenye zapiski* (MGU 169). Moskva. 1954. 113–126.
   (4) 'Čto takoe dialektičeskaja logika' (What is Dialectical Logic?). In *Problemy dialektičeskoj logiki*. Moskva. 1959. 47–72.
   (5) 'K voprosu o logike i ee izučenii' (On the Problem of Logic and its Study). *B* 1952, 11.
   (6) 'Dialektika umozaključenija' (The Dialectic of Reasoning). *FN* 1959, 3, 69–79.
   (7) 'O dialektike ponjatija' (On the Dialectic of Concept). *Izv. AN Armanskoj SSR* 1959, 3.
   (8) 'Značenie trudov I. V. Stalina po voprosam jazykoznanija dlja logiki' (The Importance of I. V. Stalin's Works on Linguistics for Logic). *V MGU* 1952, 1, 87.
   (9) 'F. Engel's i V. I. Lenin o dialektike suždenija' (Engels and Lenin on the Dialectic of Judgement). *V MGU* 1953, 4, 59.
   (10) 'Vosxoždenie ot abstraktnogo k konkretnomu v dialektičeskom metode issledovanija' (The Ascension from Abstract to Concrete in the Dialectical Method of Investigation). *V MGU* 1958, 2, 103.

(11) 'O dialektike, dialektičeskom metode i dialektičeskoj logike' (On the Dialectic, Dialectical Method and Dialectical Logic). *V MGU* 1959, 4, 127.

(12) 'O dialektičeskoj prirode suždenija' (On the Dialectical Nature of the Judgement). *VF* 1956, 2, 49–61.

(13) 'Logika naučnogo issledovanija' (The Logic of Scientific Investigation). *VF* 1962, 11, 76–85.

(14) *Suždenie i predloženie* (Judgement and Proposition). *MGU* 1950/51. (d)

ALEKSEEV, M. N., ČERKESOV, V. I.: 'Trudy I. V. Stalina po jazykoznaniju i voprosy logiki' (I. V. Stalin's Works on Linguistics and Questions of Logic). In *Filosofskie zapiski VI*. Moskva. 1953. 3–18.

ALEKSEEV, V. I.: *Razvitie F. Engel'som teorii poznanija dialektičeskogo materializma v period posle Parižskoj Kommuny*. (The Development by Engels of the Theory of Knowledge of Dialectical Materialism in the Period after the Paris Commune). *MGU*. 1953/54. (d)

ANAN'EV, B. G.:
(1) *Teorija oščuščenija* (Theory of Sensations). Leningrad. 1961. 455 str.

(2) 'Problema predstavlenija v sovetskoj psixologičeskoj nauki' (The Problem of the Representation in Soviet Psychology). In *Filosofskie zapiski V*. Moskva. 1950.

ANCIFEROVA, L. I.: *O zakonomernostjax elementarnoj poznavatel'noj dejatel'nosti* (On the Laws of Elementary Cognitive Activity). Moskva. 1961. 149 str.

ANDREEV, I. D.:
(1) *Dialektičeskij materializm o processe poznanija* (Dialectical Materialism on the Process of Knowledge). Moskva. 1954.

(2) *Osnovy teorii poznanija* (Principles of the Theory of Knowledge). Moskva. 1959. 351 str.

(3) *Dialektičeskij materializm* (Dialectical Materialism). Moskva. 1960.

(4) 'Nekotorye voprosy teorii poznanija v trude I. V. Stalina "Marksizm i jazykoznanija" ' (Some Questions of Theory of Knowledge in Stalin's *Marxism and Linguistics*). In *Voprosy dialektičeskogo i istoričeskogo materializma v trude I. V. Stalina "Marksizm i voprosy jazykoznanija"*. I. Moskva. 1951. 159–192.

(5) 'Mesto i rol' praktiki v logičeskom myšlenii' (The Place and Role of Practice in Logical Thought). In *Voprosy logiki*. Moskva. 1955. 120–155.

(6) 'Materialističeskaja dialektika kak teorija poznanija i dialektičeskaja logika' (The Materialist Dialectic as Theory of Knowledge and Dialectical Logic). In *Voprosy teorii poznanija i logiki*. Moskva. 1960. 3–91.

(7) *Praktika kak kriterij istiny v logike* (Practice as Criterion of Truth in Logic). IF. 1948–51. (d)

ANDRJUŠČENKO, M. N.:
(1) 'Leninskaja teorija otraženija i kibernetika' (The Leninist Theory of Reflection and Cybernetics). In *Naučnye trudy* (Leningradskij elektrotexničeskij Institut) Leningrad. 1960.

(2) 'Nekotorye filosofskie voprosy kibernetiki' (Some Philosophic Problems of Cybernetics). *FN* 1959, 3, 96–107.

(3) 'Deduktivnaja teorija i problema formalizacii (filosofskij aspekt)' (Deductive Theory and the Problem of Formalization – Philosophical Aspect). *V LGU* 1959, 5, 51.

ANISIMOV, S. F.: 'Immanenty – soratniki maxistov' (The Immanentists as Comrades in Arms of the Machists). In *Kniga V. I. Lenina "Materializm i empiriokriticizm – važnejsij etap v razvitii marksistskoj filosofii*. Moskva. 1959. 359–385.

BIBLIOGRAPHY

ANOXIN, P. K.: 'Operežajuščee otraženie dejstvitel'nosti' (The Outstripping Reflection of Reality). *VF* 1962, 7, 97–111.

ANTONOV, M. P.: *Razvitie abstraktnogo myšlenija v ontogeneze* (The Development of Abstract Thought in Ontogenesis). *AON.* 1948/51. (d)

ANTONOV, N. P.:
  (1) *Proisxoždenie i suščnost' soznanija* (The Origin and Essence of Consciousness). Ivanovo. 1959. 372 str.
  (2) 'O nerazryvnoj svjazi myšlenija i jazyka' (On the Inseparable Bonds of Thought and Language). *B* 1952, 15, 19.
  (3) 'Specifika individual'nogo soznanija čeloveka kak vysšaja stupen' razvitija psixiki' (The Specific Character of Man's Individual Consciousness as the Highest Level of the Development of the Psychic). *VP* 1958, 79–88.

ARISJAN, L.: *Iz istorii teorii poznanija* (From the History of the Theory of Knowledge). Erevan. 1957.

ARTANOVSKIJ, S. N.: 'Protiv semantičeskogo idealizma' (Against Semantic Idealism). *V LGU* 1958, 11, 68.

ARTEMOV, V. A.: 'K voprosu o jazyke i mysli' (On the Question of Language and Thought). In *Materialy soveščanija po psixologii.* Moskva. 1957. 266–272.

ARXANGEL'SKIJ, L. M.:
  (1) 'K voprosu o roli jazyka v formirovanii ponjatij' (On the Role of Language in the Formation of Concepts). In *Učenye zapiski* (Ural'skij GU). Sverdlovsk. 1955.
  (2) 'Kriterij praktiki v logike' (The Criterion of Practice in Logic). In *Praktika – kriterij istiny v nauke.* Moskva. 1960. 340–366.
  (3) 'O edinstve i osobennostjax dialektiki, logiki i teorii poznanija' (On the Unity and Peculiarities of Dialectic, Logic and Theory of Knowledge). *FN* 1958, 3, 191–192.
  (4) 'Obščestvennaja praktika i cel' poznanija' (Social Practice and the Goal of Knowledge). *FN* 1960, 2, 59–69.
  (5) *Marksizm-leninizm o edinstve jazyka i myšlenija* (Marxism-Leninism on the Unity of Language and Thought). Ural'skij GU. 1953/54. (d)

ARXIPCEV, F. T.: 'Ponjatie materii i osnovnoj vopros filosofii' (The Concept of Matter and the Basic Question of Philosophy). *VF* 1959, 12, 143–152.

ARZAMAZOV, V. P.:
  (1) 'K voprosu o ponjatii i slove' (On the Question of the Concept and Word). In *Nekotorye voprosy teorii poznanija* (Some Questions of Theory of Knowledge). Irkutsk. 1960. 207–243.
  (2) *Obrazovanie ponjatija* (The Formation of the Concept). Irkutskij GU. 1953/54. (d)

ASATIANI, G. M.: *Nekotorye voprosy teorii poznanija v knige V. I. Lenina "Materializm i empiriokriticizm"* (Some Questions of Theory of Knowledge in V. I. Lenin's *Materialism and Empiriocriticism*). Tbilisi GU. 1950/51. (d)

ASEEV, JU. A.:
  (1) 'Neopozitivizm i matematičeskaja logika' (Neo-positivism and Mathematical Logic). *Voprosy logiki* (Učenye zapiski LGU 263) 80–92.
  (2) 'Nekotorye osobennosti sovremennogo idealizma i metodologičeskie problemy ego kritiki' (Some Peculiarities of Contemporary Idealism and Methodological Problems of its Criticism). *FN* 1963, 5, 107–115.

ASEEV, JU. A., KON, I. S.: *Osnovnye napravlenija buržuaznoj filosofii i sociologii XX veka*

(Basic Tendencies of Twentieth Century Bourgeois Philosophy and Sociology). Leningrad. 1961. 107 str.

ASKINADZE, JA. F.: *I. V. Stalin o marksistskoj dialektike kak posledovatel'no naučnom metode* (Stalin on the Marxist Dialectic as a Consequent Scientific Method). MGU. 1953/54. (d)

ASMUS, V. F.:
   (1) *Dialektičeskij materializm i logika* (Dialectical Materialism and Logic). Kiev.1924.
   (2) *Očerki istorii dialektiki v novoj filosofii* (Essay on the History of the Dialectic in Modern Philosophy). Moskva. 1930.
   (3) *Dialektika Kanta* (The Dialectic of Kant). Moskva. 1930.
   (4) *Učenye logiki o dokazatel'stvo i oproverženii* (Logical Doctrine on Proof and Refutation). Moskva. 1954. 87 str.
   (5) *Dekart* (Descartes). Moskva. 369 str.
   (6) *Problema intuicii v filosofii i matematike* (The Problem of Intuition in Philosophy and Mathematics). Moskva. 1963. 312 str.
   (7) 'Kritika buržuaznyx idealističeskix učenij logiki epoxi imperializma' (Critique of Bourgeois Idealist Teaching on Logic in the Era of Imperialism). In *Voprosy logiki*. Moskva. 1955. 192–284.
   (8) 'Immanuil Kant' (Immanuel Kant). *VF* 1954, 5, 192–284.
   (9) 'Učenie o neposredstvennom znanii v istorii filosofii novogo vremeni' (Doctrines on Direct Knowing in the History of Modern Philosophy). *VF* 1955, 5, 43–56. (followed up with slight variations in the wording of the titles in: *VF* 1957, 6, 59–61; 1959, 11, 128–140; 1962, 9, 112–120).
   (10) 'Nekotorye voprosy dialektiki istoriko-filosofskogo processa i ego poznanija' (Some Questions on the Dialectic of the Historical-Philosophical Process and of Knowledge of it). *VF* 1961, 4, 111–123.

ASRATJAN, E. A.:
   (1) 'O dialektiko-materialističeskom xaraktere učenija I. P. Pavlova' (On the Dialectical-Materialist Character of the Doctrine of I. P. Pavlov). *VF* 1949, 1, 147–164.
   (2) 'Marksistsko-leninskaja teorija otraženija i učenie I. P. Pavlova o vysšej nervnoj dejatel'nosti' (The Marxist-Leninist Theory of Reflection and I. P. Pavlov's Doctrine on Higher Nervous Activity). *VF* 1955, 5, 31–42.
   (3) 'Vysšie formy processa otraženija i učenie I. P. Pavlova o vysšej nervnoj dejatel'nosti' (Higher Forms of the Process of Reflection and I. P. Pavlov's Doctrine on Higher Nervous Activity). *VF* 1956, 3, 98–115.
   (4) 'Uslovnyj refleks i rodstvennye emu javlenija' (The Conditioned Reflex and Similar Phenomena). *VF* 1962, 8, 66–77.

AXMANOV, A. S.:
   (1) *Logičeskoe učenie Aristotelja* (The Logical Doctrine of Aristotle). Moskva. 1960. 315 str.
   (2) 'Formy mysli i zakony formal'noj logiki' (Forms of Thought and Laws of Formal Logic). In *Voprosy logiki*. Moskva. 1955. 32–102.
   (3) 'Logičeskie formy i ix vyraženie v jazyke' (Logical Forms and their Expression in Language). In *Myšlenie i jazyk*. Moskva. 1957. 166–212.
   (4) 'Formy mysli i pravila logiki' (Forms of Thought and Rules of Logic). In *Učenye zapiski* (M. ob. Pg. In-t Tr. kaf. fil. Vyp. 1). Moskva. 1954. 193–212.

AXMEDOV, E. K.: *Gipoteza i ee rol' v razvitii nauki* (The Hypothesis and its Role in the Development of Science). Azerbajdžanskij GU. 1950/51. (d)

AXMEDOV, M. M.: 'Klassiki marksizma-leninizma ob umozaključenijax' (The Classics of Marxism-Leninism on Reasonings). In *Naučnye trudy* (Uzbekskij GU 98). Samarkand. 1960.

AXUNDOV, M. A.: *Vidy dokazatel'stv* (Types of Proof). Azerbajdžanskij GU. 1953/54. (d)

BABAJANC, M. S.: 'Formal'no-logičeskie i dialektičeskie zakony myšlenija' (Formal-Logical and Dialectical Laws of Thought). In *Učenye zapiski* (Azerbajdžanskij GPgIn-t jazykov VIII). Baku. 1960.

BABOSOV, E. M.: *Dialektika analiza i sinteza v naučnom poznanii* (The Dialectic of Analysis and Synthesis in Scientific Knowledge). Minsk. 1963. 349 str.

BAČMANOV, V. S.:
(1) 'Javljaetsja li formal'naja logika filosofskoj naukoj' (Is Formal Logic a Philosophic Science?). In *Voprosy logiki.* Leningrad. 1957. 15–28.
(2) 'Suščestvuet li v dejstvitel'nosti myšlenija zakon obratnogo otnošenija ob'ema i soderžanija ponjatij' (Is There in the Actuality of Thought a Law of the Inverse Relation of the Extension and Content of Concepts?). In *Voprosy logiki.* Leningrad. 1960. 66–86.
(3) 'Formal'naja logika kak učenie o metode' (Formal Logic as a Doctrine on Method). In *Voprosy logiki.* Leningrad. 1959. 93–118.
(4) 'Otnositel'no dialektičeskix suždenij i dialektičeskoj logiki' (Concerning the Dialectical Judgement and Dialectical Logic). *V LGU* 1957, 5, 160.
(5) 'Kniga o zakonomernostjax logičeskogo processa' (A Book on the Laws of the Logical Process). *V LGU* 1957, 17, 167.

BAKRADZE, K. S.:
(1) *Sub"ektivnyj idealizm – ideologija imperialističeskoj burzuazii. Kritika pragmatizma i logičeskogo empirizma* (Subjective Idealism as the Ideology of the Imperialistic Bourgeoisie. A Critique of Pragmatism and Logical Empiricism). Tbilisi. 1955.
(2) *Sistema i metod filosofii Gegelja* (The System and Method of the Philosophy of Hegel). Tbilisi. 1958. 463 str.
(3) 'K voprosu o sootnošenii logiki i dialektiki' (On the Relationship of Logic and Dialectic). *VF* 1950, 2, 198–209.
(4) 'Logičeskij empirizm – oružie imperialističeskoj reakcii' (Logical Empiricism as a Weapon of the Imperialist Reaction). *VF* 1953, 3, 137–144.
(5) 'Protiv nenaučnoj i nedobrožodatel'noj kritiki' (Against Unscientific and Evil-Minded Criticism). *VF* 1956, 2, 218–224.

BASKIN, M. P., BAXITOV, M. S.: 'O nekotoryx osobennostjax sovremennogo sub"ektivnogo idealizma' (On Some Peculiarities of Contemporary Subjective Idealism). In *Sovremennyj sub"ektivnyj idealizm* (Contemporary Subjective Idealism). Moskva. 1957. 3–37.

BATIŠČEV, G. S.: *Protivorečie kak kategorija dialektičeskoj logiki* (Contradiction as a Category of Dialectical Logic). Moskva. 1963. 118 str.

BATIŠČEV, G. S., DAVYDOV, JU. N.: 'Problema abstraktnogo i trudnosti ee issledovanija' (The Problem of the Abstract and the Difficulties in Investigating it). *VF* 1961, 8, 161–165.

BAŽENOV, L. B.:
(1) *Osnovnye voprosy teorii gipotezy* (Basic Questions of the Theory of Hypothesis). Moskva. 1961. 68 str.
(2) 'O prirode logičeskoj pravil'nosti' (On the Nature of Logical Correctness). In *Voprosy logiki.* Moskva. 1955. 103–119.

(3) 'O gipoteze v estestvoznanii' (On the Hypothesis in Natural Science). *VF* 1962, 9, 154–164.

BEGIAŠVILI, A. F.:
(1) *Metod analiza v sovremennoj buržuaznoj filosofii* (The Analytic Method in Contemporary Bourgeois Philosophy). Tbilisi. 1960. 198 str.
(2) 'K voprosu ob osnovanii empirizma v neopozitivistskoj filosofii' (On the Problem of the Establishing of Empiricism in Neopositivist Philosophy). In *Naučnye trudy* (AN Gruzinskoj SSR). Tbilisi. 1960.
(3) 'Kritičeskij analiz sovremennoj anglijskoj lingvističeskoj filosofii' (Critical Analysis of Contemporary English Linguistic Philosophy). *VF* 1963, 10, 111–122.
(4) 'Ob odnom protivorečii v neopozitivistskoj filosofii' (On one Contradiction in Neopositivist Philosophy). *FN* 1959, 2, 164–170.

BELAVIN, K. I.: 'O vzaimosvjazi indukcii i dedukcii' (On the Interconnections of Induction and Deduction). In *Voprosy logiki*. Leningrad 1957. 106–116.

BELOV, P. T.:
(1) *O proizvedenii V. I. Lenina "Materializm i empiriokriticizm"* (On Lenin's *Materialism and Empiriocriticism*). Moskva. 1952.
(2) 'K itogam diskussii po knige M. Rozentalja "Marksistskij dialektičeskij metod"' (Conclusion to the Discussion of M. Rozental''s *Marxist Dialectical Method*). *B* 1948, 4, 68–72.

BERG, A. I.: 'O nekotoryx problemax kibernetiki' (On Some Problems of Cybernetics). *VF* 1960, 5, 51–62.

BIBLER, V. S., MOROČNIK, S. B.: 'V. I. Lenin o probleme istiny' (Lenin on the Problem of Truth). In *Naučnye trudy* (Stalinabadskij G medicinskij In-t). Stalinabad. 1960.

BIRJUKOV, B. V.:
(1) 'Teorija smysla Gotloba Frege' (The Theory of Sense of Gottlob Frege). In *Primenenie logiki v nauke i texnike*. Moskva. 1960. 502–555.
(2) 'O rabotax Frege po filosofskim voprosam matematiki' (On Frege's Works on Philosophic Questions of Mathematics). In *Filosofskie voprosy estestvoznanija*. Moskva. 1959. str. 134–177.

BIRJUKOV, B. V., GETMANOVA, A. D., KARPINSKAJA, R. S.: 'Kniga o kriterii praktiki v nauke' (A Book on the Criterion of Practice in Science). *FN* 1962, 5, 155–159.

BIRJUKOV, D. A.: *Mif o duše* (The Myth on the Soul). Moskva. 1952. 395 str.

BJALIK, B.: 'Terminy i ponjatija' (Terms and Concepts). In *Problemy realizma*. Moskva. 1959. 546–551.

BODNAR, J.: *O sovremennoj filosofii SŠA* (On Contemporary U.S. Philosophy). Moskva. 1959. 246 str.

BOGDANOV, G. N.: *O konkretnosti istiny i putjax istinnogo poznanija* (On the Concreteness of Truth and the Paths to true Knowledge). M. Ob. Pg. In-t. 1953/54. (d)

BOGOMOLOV, A. S.: 'Roj Vud Sellars o materialističeskoj teorii poznanija' (Roy Wood Sellars on the Materialist Theory of Knowledge). *VF* 1962, 8, 140–142.

BOGUSLAVSKIJ, V. M.:
(1) 'K voprosu o nerazryvnoj svjazi jazyka i myšlenija' (On the Questions of the Inseparable Bond of Language and Thought). In *Učenye zapiski* (M. gorodskoj Pg. In-t). Moskva. 1957.
(2) 'Slovo i ponjatie' (Word and Concept). In *Myšlenie i jazyk*. Moskva. 1957. 213–275.

(3) 'Issledovanie po teorii suždenija' (Investigation on the Theory of Judgement). *VF* 1957, 1, 198–202.

(4) 'K voprosu ob obrazovanii ponjatija' (On the Formation of the Concept). *VF* 1958, 8, 14–24.

(5) 'Ob"ektivnoe i sub"ektivnoe v dialektike myšlenija' (Objective and Subjective in the Dialectic of Thought). *VF* 1960, 10, 52–63.

BOGUSLAVSKIJ, V. M., BORISOVA, I. S.: 'Problema istiny i ee kriterija v neopozitivizme' (The Problem of Truth and its Criterion in Neo-positivism). In *Praktika – kriterij istiny v nauke*. Moskva. 1960. 393–418.

BOJARINCEV, A. L.: 'V. I. Lenin i I. V. Stalin o gibkosti ponjatij' (Lenin and Stalin on Plasticity of Concepts). KGU. 1953/54. (d)

BOKAREV, V. A.: 'Možet li mašina myslit'?' (Can the Machine Think?). *VF* 1961, 10, 173–177.

Bolšaja sovetskaja encyklopedija (Great Soviet Encyclopedia). Moskva. 1956. Tom 42, str. 236–245: 'teorija poznanija' (Theory of Knowledge).

BOL'ŠUNOV, JA. V., SAFROŠIN, V. G.: 'Ob osveščenii problemy sootnošenija material'-nogo i psixičeskogo v sovetskoj filosofskoj literature' (On the Clarification of the Problem of the Relationship of the Material and Psychic in Soviet Philosophical Literature). *FN* 1962, 6, 101–105.

BOL'SUXIN, A., KISELEV, V.: 'O social'nyx i gnoseologičeskix kornjax religii' (On the Social and Epistemological Roots of Religion). In *Naučnye trudy* (Gor'kovskij GPg. In-t). Gorkij. 1960.

BORISOV, V. N.: *O logičeskoj forme ponjatija* (On the Logical Form of the Concept). LGU. 1953/54. (d)

BRANSKIJ, V. P.: 'K voprosu ob osobennostjax sovremennogo fizičeskogo idealizma i metafiziki' (On Peculiarities of Contemporary Physical Idealism and Meta-physics). *V LGU* 1961, 23, 120–130.

BRODSKIJ, I. N.:
(1) 'K voprosu o processe obrazovanija ponjatij' (On the Process of Formation of Concepts). In *Voprosy logiki*. Leningrad. 1957. 45–60.

(2) 'O prirode otricatel'nogo suždenija' (On the Nature of the Negative Judgement). In *Voprosy logiki*. Leningrad. 1959. 37–50.

(3) 'Otricatel'noe ponjatie' (The Negative Concept). In *Voprosy logiki*. Leningrad. 1960.

(4) 'Otraženie dialektiki obščego i otdel'nogo v suždenii' (The Reflection of the Dialectic of General and Particular in the Judgement). *V LGU* 1956, 17, 86.

(5) *Otraženie dialektiki obščego i otdel'nogo v ponjatii i suždenii* (The Reflection of the Dialectic of General and Particular in the Concept and Judgement). LGU. 1951/52. (d)

BRUDNYJ, A. A.: 'Znak i signal' (Sign and Signal). *VF* 1961, 4, 124–133.

BRUTJAN, G. A.:
(1) *Teorija poznanija obščej semantiki* (The Theory of Knowledge of General Semantics). Erevan. 1959. 305 str.

(2) 'Irracionalizm i sofistika – oružie podžigatelej vojny' (Irrationalism and Sophistry as Tools of the Preparers of War). *VF* 1952, 4, 138–151.

(3) 'Interesnaja kniga po teorii poznanija' (Interesting Book on Theory of Knowledge). *VF* 1956, 6, 201–205.

(4) 'Paralogizm, sofizm i paradoks' (Paralogism, Sophism and Paradox). *VF* 1959, 1, 56–66.

153

(5) 'Filosofskaja suščnost' teorii lingvističeskoj otnositel'nosti' (The Philosophic Essence of the Theory of Linguistic Relativity). *FN* 1963, 4, 107–115.

BUEVA, L. P.: 'Individual'noe soznanie i uslovija ego formirovanija' (Individual Consciousness and the Conditions of its Formation). *FN* 1963, 5, 67–79.

BUROV, A. I.: 'O gnoseologičeskoj prirode xudožestvennogo obobščenija' (On the Epistemological Nature of Artistic Generalization). *VF* 1951, 4, 101–112.

BUXALOV, JU. F.:

(1) 'K voprosu ob opredelenii istiny' (On the Question of the Definition of Truth). In *Sbornik rabot prepodavatelej filosofii vuzov g. Xar'kovskogo Gosudarstvennogo Universiteta.* Charkov. 1959.

(2) 'O sootnošenii sub"ektivnogo i ob"ektivnogo v poznavatel'nom obraze' (On the Relation of Subjective and Objective in the Cognitive Image). *VF* 1961, 5, 124–132.

(3) 'Sootnošenie sub"ektivnogo i ob"ektivnogo v praktike' (The Relation of Subjective and Objective in Practice). *FN* 1961, 1, 59–67.

(4) BUXALOV, J. F., VEL'CMAN, V. N., SYČEV, N. I.: 'Nekotorye zamečanija na knigu P. Čerkašina "Gnoseologičeskie korni idealizma" ' (Some Remarks on P. Čerkašin's Book *The 'Epistemological Roots of Idealism*). *FN* 1963, 3, 109–112.

BYXOVSKIJ, B. E.:

(1) *Očerk filosofii dialektičeskogo materializma* (Sketch of the Philosophy of Dialectical Materialism). Moskva-Leningrad. 1930.

(2) *Metod i sistema Gegelja* (Hegel's Method and System). Moskva. 1941.

(3) 'Neotomistskaja kriteriologija' (Neo-Thomist Criteriology). In *Praktika – kriterija istiny v nauke.* Moskva. 1960. 444–462.

(4) 'Marazm sovremennoj buržuaznoj filosofii (Ob anglo-amerikanskom semanti-českom idealizme)' (The Mess of Contemporary Bourgeois Philosophy: On Anglo-American Semantic Idealism). *B* 1947, 16, 50–64.

(5) 'Filosofstvujuščie mrakobesy' (Philosophizing Obscurantism). *B* 1948, 8, 51–65.

(6) 'Operacionalizm Bridžmena' (Bridgeman's Operationalism). *VF* 1958, 2, 75–89.

(7) 'Nauka i zdravyj smysl' (Science and Common Sense). *FN* 1958, 3, 163–170.

(8) 'Neotomistskij obskurantizm' (Neo-Thomist Obscurantism). In *Sovremennye religiozno-filosofskie tečenija v kapitalističeskix stranax.* Moskva. 1962. str. 52–111.

CELIŠČEV, V. I.: 'Voprosy teorii naučnogo predvidenija' (Questions of the Theory of Scientific Prediction). *V LGU* 1960, 17, 41.

CERETELI, S. B.:

(1) 'K leninskomu ponimanija dialektičeskoj prirody istiny' (On the Leninist Conception of the Dialectical Nature of Truth). *VF* 1960, 4, 73–84.

(2) *O dialektičeskoj prirode logičeskoj svjazi* (On the Dialectical Nature of the Logical Bond). *V AN SSSR* 1957, 12, 127. (d)

CHE WEN: 'Matter and Consciousness'. In *Jen-min Jih-pao.* Peking. Nov. 1, 1961 (Translation in *Survey of China Mainland Press.* Hong Kong. Nov. 17, 1961, No. 2621, pp. 2–12).

CIMINTIJA, A. B.: *K marksistsko-leninskomu ponimaniju prirody soznanija* (On the Marxist-Leninist Conception of the Nature of Consciousness). Tbilisi GU. 1953/54. (d)

COCONAVA, B. S.: *Nekotorye voprosy marksistsko-leninskogo učenija o ponjatii* (Some Aspects of the Marxist-Leninist Doctrine on Concepts). M. gorodskoj Pg. In-t. 1953/54. (d)

CORNFORTH, M.: *Dialectical Materialism*. Vol. 3: *The Theory of Knowledge*. London. 1954.

CUPROV, P. A.: 'V. I. Lenin o poznanii kak otraženii ob"ektivnogo mira' (Lenin on Knowledge as Reflection of the Objective World). In *Naučnye trudy* (M. avtomobil'-no-dorožnyj In-t). Moskva. 1960.

ČALIN, M.: *Filosofija otčajanija i straxa* (A Philosophy of Despair and Fear). Moskva. 1962. 128 str.

ČEČIN, M. N.: 'Kritika V. I. Leninym maxistskoj teorii "elementov mira" i "opyta" ' (Lenin's Critique of the Machist Theory of 'Elements of the World' and 'Experience'). In *Kniga* . . . (s. Alekseev, G. P.) 326–336.

ČERKAŠIN, P. P.:
  (1) *Gnoseologičeskie korni idealizma* (Epistemological Roots of Idealism). Moskva. 1961. 238 str.
  (2) 'V.I.Lenin o gnoseologičeskix kornjax idealizma' (Lenin on the Epistemological Cores of Idealism). *VF* 1954, 1, 59–77.

ČERKESOV, V. I.:
  (1) *Materialističeskaja dialektika kak logika i teorija poznanija* (The Materialist Dialectic as Logic and Theory of Knowledge). Moskva. 1962. 476 str.
  (2) 'O predmete marksistskoj dialektičeskoj logiki' (On the Object of Marxist Dialectical Logic). In *Problemy dialektičeskoj logiki*. Moskva. 1959. 27–46.
  (3) 'O logike i marksistskoj dialektičeskoj logike' (On Logic and Marxist Dialectical Logic). *VF* 1950, 2, 209–222.
  (4) 'Nekotorye voprosy teorii ponjatija v dialektičeskoj logike' (Some Questions of Theory of Concept in Dialectical Logic). *VF* 1956, 2, 62–76.
  (5) 'Udačnyj kritičeskij očerk kantianskoj filosofii' (A Well-Done Critical Outline of Kantian Philosophy). *FN* 1962, 1, 162–165.

ČERNYŠEV, B. S.: 'Benedetto Kroče i dialektika' (Benedetto Croce and the Dialectic). *VF* 1958, 8, 63–73.

ČIKNAVEROVA, A. A.: 'Osnovnye formal'no-logičeskie zakony myšlenija i ix rol' v poznanii' (The Basic Formal-Logical Laws of Thought and Their Role in Knowledge). *FN* 1960, 1, 73–81.

ČILINGARJAN, A. S.: *Obščestvennaja praktika i ee rol' v processe poznanija* (Social Practice and its Role in the Process of Knowledge). MGU. 1953/54. (d)

ČUDOV, A. A.: 'Umozaključenie zameščenija' (Reasoning by Substitution). *Izvestija AN SSSR* 1948, 3, 270–280.

ČUEVA, I. P.: 'Kritika teorii poznanija "russkogo" intuitivizma' (Critique of the Theory of Knowledge of 'Russian' Intuitionism). *V LGU* 1958, 11, 57.

ČUPAXIN, I. JA.:
  (1) *Voprosy teorii ponjatija* (Questions of the Theory of Concept). Moskva. 1961. 139 str.
  (2) 'K voprosu o sootnošenii ponjatij i suždenija' (On the Question of the Relationship of Concepts and the Judgement). In *Filosofija*. Leningrad. 1956. 75–97.
  (3) 'Trebovanija formal'noj logiki i dialektiki k opredeleniju ponjatij' (Requirements of Formal Logic and Dialectics in the Defining of Concepts). In *Voprosy logiki*. Leningrad. 1957. 61–76.

(4) 'O faktax neposledovatel'nosti v učenii o ponjatii' (On the Facts of Inconsequence in the Doctrine on Concepts). In *Voprosy logiki.* Leningrad. 1959. 3–17.

(5) 'K voprosu o sootnošenii ponjatija i umozaključenija' (On the Question of the Relation of the Concept and Reasoning). In *Voprosy logiki.* Leningrad. 1960. 3–27.

(6) *Teorija ponjatija v dialektičeskom materializme* (The Theory of Concept in Dialectical Materialism). AON. 1948/51. (d)

ČUPIN, P. P.: 'Dialektika obščego i otdel'nogo v kategorii "praktika"' (The Dialectic of General and Particular in the Category 'Practice'). *FN* 1962, 1, 80–87.

ČURAKOV, JU. D.: 'Leninskoe učenie o korennoj protivopoložnosti dialektiki sofistike i ego značenie dlja bor'by s sofistikoj sovremennogo revizionizma' (The Leninist Doctrine on the Fundamental Opposition of Dialectic to Sophistry and its Importance for the Fight with the Sophistry of Contemporary Revisionism). In *Gnoseologičeskoe soderžanie logičeskix form i metodov.* Kiev. 1960. 62–72.

DEBORIN, A. M.: *Filosofija i politika* (Philosophy and Politics). Moskva. 1961. 745 str.

DEDOV, K. M.: 'K voprosu ob otnošenijax meždu psixologiej i fiziologiej vysšej nervnoj dejatel'nosti' (On the Relationships between Psychology and the Physiology of Higher Nervous Activity). *VF* 1954, 1, 216–218.

DEMAEV, D. I.: *Teorija sillogističeskix umozaključenij* (The Theory of Syllogistic Reasonings). IF. 1948/51. (d)

DEMIDOV, M. P.: *Klassiki marksizma-leninizma o edinstve myšlenija i jazyka* (The Classics of Marxism-Leninism on the Unity of Thought and Language). Voenno-političeskaja Akademija. 1953/54. (d)

Dialektičeskij materializm. R. G. F. Aleksandrov. Moskva. 1953. 439 str.

Dialektičeskij materializm. Učebnoe posobie. R. A. D. Makarov i dr. Moskva. 1960. 471 str.

Dialektičeskij materializm. Sokraščennye stenogrammy lekcij, pročitannyx v ZVPS, s priloženiem metodičeskix sovetov (v pomošč' zaočnikam). R. D. I. Danilenko i dr. Moskva. 1961. 310 str.

Dialektičeskij i istoričeskij materializm. C.1. (Dialectical and Historical Materialism. Part 1). Moskva. 1933.

Dialektika i logika. Formy myšlenija (Dialectic and Logic. The Forms of Thought). Moskva. 1962. 310 str.

Dialektika i logika. Zakony myšlenija (Dialectic and Logic. The Laws of Thought). Moskva. 1962. 336 str.

DMITRIEV, A. T., MAN'KOVSKIJ, L. A.: 'Obščaja forma suždenija v klassičeskoj logike' (The General Form of Judgement in Classical Logic). *V LGU* 1948, 6, 140–142.

DOLGOV, K. M.: 'Leninskoe ponimanie sootnošenie logiki, dialektiki i teorii poznanija i ego razrabotka' (The Leninist Conception of the Relation of Logic, Dialectic and Theory of Knowledge and its Elaborations). *VF* 1962, 5, 157–160.

DOSEV, P. (T. PAVLOV): *Teorija otraženija* (The Theory of Reflection). Moskva-Leningrad. 1936.

DROZDOV, A. V.:

(1) *Voprosy klassifikacii suždenij* (Questions of the Classification of Judgements). Leningrad. 1956. (d)

(2) 'Formal'naja logika i dialektičeskie suždenie' (Formal Logic and the

156

Dialectical Judgement). In *Voprosy logiki*. Leningrad. 1957. 77–93.

(3) 'Za tvorčeskuju razrabotku voprosov logiki' (Toward a Creative Elaboration of Logical Questions). In *ibid.* 164 175.

(4) 'O suščnosti i sostave sub'ekta i predikata suždenija' (On the Essence and Distribution of the Subject and Predicate of the Judgement). *Voprosi logiki*. Leningrad. 1959. 28–36.

DUBROVSKIJ, D. I.: 'K voprosu o kritike V. I. Leninym pragmatizma' (On Lenin's Criticism of Pragmatism). *VF* 1962, 4, 24–31.

DUDEL', S. P.: 'Poznavaemost' mira i ego zakonomernostej' (The Knowability of the World and its Laws). *VF* 1952, 3, 168–190.

DZJADIK, L. K.: *Ob"ektivnyj xarakter logičeskogo zakona protivorečija* (The Objective Character of the Logical Law of Contradiction). M. oblastnoj Pg. In-t. 1953/54. (d)

DŽAFARLI, T. M.: *O nekotoryx voprosax teorii induckii* (On Some Questions of the Theory of Induction). Tbilisi GU. 1953/54. (d)

DŽIBUTI, G. A.: *Nekotorye voprosy teorii i klassifikacii suždenij* (Some Questions of the Theory and Classification of Judgements). Tbilisi GU. 1953/54. (d)

EFIMOV, S. F.: 'Konkretnoe ponjatie i čuvtsvennoe znanie' (The Concrete Concept and Sensible Knowledge). *VF* 1956, 3, 59–73.

EFIROV, S. A.:

(1) 'Problemy dialektiki v sovremennoj buržuaznoj filosofii' (Problems of Dialectic in Contemporary Bourgeois Philosophy). *VF* 1956, 5, 120–131.

(2) 'Teorija dialektiki Ferdinanda Gonseta i dialektičeskij materializm' (The Theory of Dialectic of Ferdinand Gonseth and Dialectical Materialism). *VF* 1958, 8, 51–62.

EMDIN, M. V.: 'Po povodu odnoj monografii' (On the Publication of One Study). *V LGU* 1962, 23, 140–142.

ENGELS, F.:

(1) *Herrn Eugen Dührings Umwälzung der Wissenschaft*. Leipzig. 1878. (MEGA Sonderausgabe: Moscow. 1935). English: *Herr Eugen Dührings Revolution in Science (Anti-Dühring)*. Chicago. 1935.

(2) *Ludwig Feuerbach und der Ausgang der klassischen deutschen Philosophie*. (Articles published in *Neue Zeit*. 1886) Stuttgart. 1888. English in: K. Marx, F. Engels: *Selected Works*, I–II. Moscow–London. 1950/1951.

(3) *Dialektik der Natur*. (MEGA Sonderausgabe). Moscow. 1935. English: London. 1934 and Moscow/London. 1954/1955.

ESENIN-VOL'PIN, A. S.: 'Ob aksiomatičeskom metode' (On the Axiomatic Method). *VF* 1959, 7, 121–126.

EVČUK, V. I.:

(1) 'Konkretnost' istiny i ee značenie v processe poznanija' (The Concreteness of Truth and its Importance in the Process of Knowledge). In *Voprosy marksistsko-leninskoj filosofii*. Moskva. 1956. 122–150.

(2) *V. I. Lenin i I. V. Stalin o konkretnosti istiny* (Lenin and Stalin on the Concreteness of Truth). AON. 1953/54. (d)

EVDOMIKOV, V. I.: 'Problema analiza i sinteza v istorii logiki' (The Problem of Analysis and Synthesis in the History of Logic). In *Voprosy dialektičeskogo i istoričeskogo materializma*. Moskva. 1957.

FARBER, V. G.: *Marks i Engels o suždenii kak edinstvo toždestva i ražlicija* (Marx and Engels on the Judgement as the Unity of Identity and Difference). M. G. Pg. In-t. 1951/52. (d)

FATALIEV, X. M.:
(1) 'Neopozitivizm i nekotorye problemy sovremennogo estestvoznanija' (Neo-positivism and Some Problems of Contemporary Natural Science). *FN* 1958, 1, 156–167.
(2) 'Vraždebnost' neopozitivizma sovremennoj nauke' (Inimity of Neo-positivism to Contemporary Science). In *Materialy vsesojuznogo soveščanija zavedujuščix kafedrami obščestvennyx nauk*. Moskva. 1958. 318–334.
FILATOVA, A. N.: *Nekotorye voprosy teorii ponjatija* (Some Questions of Theory of Concept). Moskva. 1962. 109 str.
FILIMONOV, N. P.: 'Čelovek i mašina' (Man and the Machine). *VF* 1960, 10, 118–128.
FILIMONOV, V. V.: 'Princip reljativizma – odna iz gnoseologičeskix princip "fizičeskogo" idealizma' (The Principle of Relativism as one of the Epistemological Principles of 'Physical' Idealism). In *Učenye zapiski* (Komi G. Pg. In-t) Syktyvkar. 1960.
FILIPPOVA, M. M.: *Značenie učenija I. P. Pavlova o vysšej nervnoj dejatel'nosti kak estestvenno-naučnogo obosnovanija leninskoj teorii otraženija* (The Importance of the Doctrine of I. P. Pavlov on Higher Nervous Activity as the Natural-Science Foundation of the Leninist Theory of Reflection). AON. 1948/51. (d)
Filosofija marksizma i neopozitivizm (The Philosophy of Marxism and Neo-positivism). Moskva. 1963. 542 str.
Filosofskaja enciklopedija (Philosophical Encyclopedia). Moskva. 1960ff.
Filosofskie voprosy učenija o vysšej nervnoj dejatel'nosti (Philosophic Questions of the Doctrine on Higher Nervous Activity). Moskva. 1954. 276 str.
FINN, V. K., LAXUTI, D. G.: 'Ob odnom podxode k logičeskoj semantike' (On one Approach to Logical Semantics). In *Tezisy konferencii po masinnomu perevodu*. Moskva. 1958. 62–63.
FIŠER, E. G.: 'Mao Cze-dun o stupenjax poznanija mira i o roli praktiki v processe poznanija' (Mao Tse-tung on the Levels of Knowledge of the World and on Practice in Knowledge). In *Naučnye trudy*. (Xabarovskij In-t inženerov železnodorožnogo transporty). Xabarovsk. 1960.
FOMIN, V. I.: *Problema istiny v "Materializme i empiriokriticizme"* (The Problem of Truth in *Materialism and Empirio-Criticism*). AON. 1948/51. (d)
FROLOV, I. T.: 'Gnoseologičeskie problemy modelirovanija biologičeskix sistem' (Epistemological Problems of the Modelling of Biological Systems). *VF* 1961, 2, 39–51.
FROLOV, JU. P.:
(1) 'Materialističeskaja dialektika i zakony protivorečija v učenii o pervoj i vtoroj signal'nyx sistemax dejstvitel'nosti' (The Materialist Dialectic and Laws of Contradiction in the Doctrine on the First and Second Signal Systems of Reality). In *Konferencija po teme "Problema protivorečij v svete sovremennoj nauki i praktiki"*. Moskva. 1958. 184–203.
(2) 'Sovremennaja kibernetika i mozg čeloveka' (Contemporary Cybernetics and Man's Brain). *VF* 1956, 3, 116–122.
FURMAN, A. A.:
(1) 'Leninskaja teorija otraženija i sovremennaja fizika' (The Leninist Theory of Reflection and Contemporary Physics). In *Naučnye trudy* (Tomskij GU). Tomsk. 1960.
(2) 'Nekotorye voprosy leninskoj teorii otraženija v svete sovremennoj fiziki' (Some Questions of the Leninist Theory of Reflection in the Light of Contemporary Physics). In *Velikoe proizvedenie marksistskoj filosofii*. Novosibirsk. 1960.

FURMAN, A. E.: 'Materialističeskaja dialektika kak metod poznanija i praktičeskoj dejatel'nosti' (The Materialist Dialectic as a Method of Thought and of Practical Activity). In *Kniga dlja čtenija po marksistskoj filosofii*. Moskva. 1960. 135–200.

G. S.: 'O roli praktiki v processe poznanija' (On the Role of Practice in the Process of Knowledge). *VF* 1955, 1, 139–144.

GABRIEL'JAN, G. G.: *Marksistskaja logika kak dialektika i teorija poznanija* (Marxist Logic as Dialectic and Theory of Knowledge). Erevan. 1963. 436 str.

GAGARIN, A. P.: *Pragmatizm SŠA* (U.S. Pragmatism). Moskva. 1963. 64 str.

GAJDUKOV, JU. G.:

(1) 'Poznavaemost' mira i ego zakonomernostej' (The Knowability of the World and its Laws). In *O dialektičeskom materializme*. Moskva. 1952. 357–419.

(2) 'K voprosu o specifike projavlenija praktiki v različnyx naukax' (On the Specific Forms of Practice in Different Sciences). In *Voprosy teorii poznanija i logiki*. Moskva. 1960. 195–224.

(3) 'Rol' praktiki v processe poznanija' (The Role of Practice in the Process of Knowledge). *B* 1955, 3, 103.

(4) 'K voprosu o kriterii praktiki' (On the Question of the Criterion of Practice). *VF* 1959, 6, 101–110.

(5) *Dialektičeskij materializm o roli praktiki v processe poznanija* (Dialectical Materialism on the Role of Practice in the Process of Knowledge). *V AN SSSR* 1955, 8, 111. (d)

GAK, G. M.:

(1) *Učenie ob obščestvennom soznanii v svete teorii poznanija* (Doctrine on Social Consciousness in the Light of Theory of Knowledge). Moskva. 1960.

(2) 'O sootnošenii dialektiki, logiki i teorii poznanija' (On the Relation of Dialectic, Logic and Theory of Knowledge). In *Učenye zapiski* (M. oblastnoj Pg. In-t). Moskva. 1956.

GALKINA-FEDORUK, E. M.:

(1) *Suždenie i predloženie* (Judgement and Proposition). Moskva. 1956. 74 str.

(2) *Slovo i ponjatie* (Word and Concept). Moskva. 1956.

(3) 'Slovo i ponjatie v svete učenija klassikov marksizma-leninizma' (Word and Concept in the Light of the Doctrine of the Classics of Marxism-Leninism). *V MGU* 1951, 9, 105.

GAL'PERIN, S. I.: 'O edinstve fiziologičeskogo i psixičeskogo' (On the Unity of the Physiological and Psychic). *VF* 1958, 12, 124–132.

GARADŽA, V. I.: 'Problemy very i znanija v tomizme' (The Problem of Faith and Knowledge in Thomism). *VF* 1963, 9, 89–98.

GARAUDY, R.: *La théorie matérialiste de la connaissance* (The Materialist Theory of Knowledge). Paris. 1953. (Russian: *Voprosy marksistsko-leninskoj teorii poznanija*. Moskva. 1951).

GAZENKO, V. I.: 'V. I. Lenin o reakcionnoj suščnosti agnosticizma' (Lenin on the Reactionary Essence of Agnosticism). In *Učenye zapiski* (M. gorodskoj Pg. In-t). Moskva. 1957.

GELASVILI, A. A.: *K voprosu o zakonax myšlenija* (On the Laws of Thought). Tbilisi GU. 1953/54. (d)

GEORGIEV, F. I.:

(1) *Poznavaemost' mira i ego zakonomernostej* (Knowability of the World and its Laws). Moskva. 1955.

(2) *Protivopoložnost' marksistskogo i gegelevskogo učenija o soznanii* (Opposition

159

of the Marxist and Hegelian Doctrines on Consciousness). Moskva. 1961.
158 str.

(3) 'Problema čuvstvennogo i racional'nogo v poznanii' (The Problem of the
Sensible and Rational in Knowledge). *VF* 1955, 1, 28–41.

(4) 'V. I. Lenin o vzaimootnošenii psixičeskogo i fiziologičeskogo' (Lenin on the
Interrelation of the Psychic and the Physiological). *FN* 1959, 1, 17–24.

(5) 'Princip otraženija; reflektornaja teorija' (The Principle of Reflection and the
Reflectoral Theory). *FN* 1963. 5, 52–57.

(6) 'Oščuščenija i myšlenija – sub"ektivnyk obraz ob"ektivnogo mira' (Sensation
and Thought as Subjective Image of the Objective World). *V MGU* 1948, 6, 3.

(7) 'O marksistskom dialektičeskom metode' (On the Marxist Dialectical Method).
V MGU 1949, 4, 3.

(8) 'Marksistskij filosofskij materializm – edinstvenno naučnaja teorija poznanija'
(Marxist Philosophical Materialism as the Unique Scientific Theory of
Knowledge). *V MGU* 1954, 1.

GERASIMOV, I. G.: *Dialektičeskij materializm ob ob"ektivnoj istine* (Dialectical
Materialism on Objective Truth). *IF.* 1953/54. (d)

GEVORKJAN, G. A.: *O roli abstrakcii v poznanii* (On the Role of Abstraction in
Knowledge). Erevan. 1957.

GIMEL'ŠTEJB, E. X.: 'Nekotorye dostiženija kibernetiki v svete marksistsko-leninskogo
učenija o prirode soznanija (Mašina i soznanie)' (Some Achievements of Cybernetics in the Light of Marxist-Leninist Doctrine on the Nature of Consciousness:
The Machine and Consciousness). *FN* 1962, 3, 68–74.

GLAGOLEV, V. F.:

(1) 'Induktivnye umozaključenija' (Inductive Reasonings). In *Logika*. Moskva.
1956. 168–181.

(2) 'Indukcija i dedukcija' (Induction and Deduction). In *Voprosy dialektičeskogo
materializma*. Moskva. 1960. 344–360.

(3) 'O roli myšlenija v poznanii' (On the Role of Thought in Knowledge). In
Voprosy teorii poznanija i logiki. Moskva. 1960. 169–194.

(4) *Teorija induktivnyx umozaključenij* (The Theory of Inductive Reasonings).
IF. 1948/51. (d)

Gnoseologičeskoe soderžanie logičeskix form i metodov (The Epistemological Content
of Logical Forms and Methods). Kiev. 1960. 126 str.

GLEZERMAN, G. E.: 'Naučnye osnovy predvidenija' (Scientific Bases of Prediction).
Pod znamenem marksizma 1940, 7.

GODER, M. N.: *Opredelenie kak problema logiki* (Definition as a Problem of Logic).
1953/54. (d)

GOKIELI, L. P.:

(1) *K probleme aksiomatizacii logike*. Tbilisi. 1947.

(2) *O ponjatii čisla*. Tbilisi. 1951.

(3) *O prirode logičeskogo*. (On the Nature of the Logical). Tbilisi. 1958. 466 str.

GORSKIJ, D. P.:

(1) *Voprosy abstrakcii i obrazovanie ponjatij* (Problems of Abstraction and the
Formation of Concepts). Moskva. 1961. 351 str.

(2) 'Nekotorye voprosy ob'ema ponjatija' (Some Questions on the Extention of
the Concept). In *Voprosy Logiki*. Moskva. 1955. 285–326.

(3) 'Rol' jazyka v poznanii' (The Role of Language in Knowledge). In *Myšlenie
i jazyk*. Moskva. 1957. 73–116.

(4) 'Izvraščenie neopozitivizmom voprosov logiki' (The Distortion by Neo-positivism of Logical Questions). In *Sovremennyj sub'ektivnyj idealizm*. Moskva. 1957. 219–286.

(5) 'Dialektika endiničnogo i obščego' (The Dialectic of Singular and General). In *Voprosy dialektičeskogo materializma*. Moskva. 1960. 209–234.

(6) 'Otnošenija, ix logičeskie svojstva i ix značenie v logike' (Relations. Their Logical Properties and their Importance in Logic). In *Učenye zapiski* (MGU 169). Moskva. 1954. 127–160.

(7) 'K voprosu ob obrazovanii i razvitii ponjatij' (On the Question of the Formation and Development of Concepts). *VF* 1952, 4, 64–77.

(8) 'O roli jazyka v poznanii' (On the Role of Language in Knowledge). *VF* 1953, 2, 75–92.

(9) 'O kategorijax materialističeskoj dialektiki' (On the Categories of the Materialist Dialectic). *VF* 1955, 3, 17–31.

(10) 'O sposobax obobščenija' (On Methods of Generalization). *VF* 1958, 5, 51–63.

(11) 'Ponjatie kak predmet izučenija dialektičeskoj logiki' (The Concept as Object of Dialectical Logic). *VF* 1959, 10, 35–47.

(12) 'Problema formal'no-logičeskogo i dialektičeskogo toždestva' (The Problem of Formal-Logical and Dialectical Identity). *VF* 1960, 8, 46–57.

(14) 'O vidax naučnyx abstrakcij i sposobax ix obosnovanija' (On Types of Scientific Abstractions and Modes of Their Establishment). *VF* 1961, 9, 65–78.

(15) 'Istina i ee kriterij' (Truth and its Criterion). *VF* 1962, 2, 121–133.

(16) 'O processe idealizacii i ego značenii v naučnom poznanii' (On the Process of Idealization and its Importance in Scientific Knowledge) .*VF* 1963, 2, 50–60.

(17) *Ob ob'eme v logike* (On Extension in Logic) MGU. 1951/52. (d)

GORSKIJ, D. P., BURXARD, A. I.: 'Rešenie neopozitivizmom osnovnogo voprosa filosofii' (Neo-positivism's Solution of the Basic Question of Philosophy). *VF* 1956, 3, 123–136.

GORSKIJ, D. P., IVANOV, M. A.: 'Novaja kniga po teorii poznanija' (A New Book on the Theory of Knowledge). *VF* 1953, 3, 192–198.

GORSKIJ, D. P., KOMLEV, M. G.: 'K voprosu o sootnošenii logiki i grammatyki' (On the Relationship of Logic and Grammar). *VF* 1953, 6, 63–82.

GRAŠČENKO, N. I.: 'Leninskaja teorija otraženija i sovremennaja fiziologija organov čuvstv' (The Leninist Theory of Reflection and Contemporary Physiology of the Sense-Organs). In *Filosofskie problemy sovremennogo estestvoznanija*. Moskva. 1959. 341–364.

Idem. *VF* 1959, 6, 88–100.

GREKOVA, A. JA.: 'Obsuždenie knigi M. Leonova i M. Rozentalja o marksistskom dialektičeskom metode' (Discussion of the Books of M. Leonov and M. Rozental' on the Marxist Dialectical Method). *VF* 1948, 1, 301–305.

GRICENKO, I. I.: 'O sovpadenii logiki i istorii poznanija' (On the Coincidence of the Logic and History of Knowledge). In *Bor'ba V. I. Lenina za voinstvujuščij materializm i revoljucionnuju dialektiku* (Lenin's Fight for Militant Materialism and a Revolutionary Dialectic). Moskva. 1960.

GRIGOR'EV, G. S.: 'Teorija poznanija dialektičeskogo materializma o edinstve myšlenija i bytija' (The Theory of Knowledge of Dialectical Materialism on the Unity of Thought and Being). In *Voprosy teorii poznanija*. Perm'. 1960. 23–47.

GRIGOR'JAN, B. T.: 'O sovremennom neokantianstve' (On Contemporary Neo-Kantianism). *VF* 1957, 4, 125–131.

GRAZNOV, B. S.: 'O gnoseologičeskoj prirode abstraktny ob"ektov matematiki' (On the Epistemological Nature of the Abstract Objects of Mathematics). *FN* 1963, 5, 58–65.

GRUŠIN, B. A.: 'Logičeskie i istoričeskie priemy issledovanija v "Kapitale" K. Marksa' (Logical and Historical Methods of Investigation in Marx' *Capital*). *VF* 1955, 4, 41–53.

GULIAN, K. I.: *Metod i sistema Gegelja* (The Method and System of Hegel). Moskva. 1962. 445 str.

IL'ENKOV, É. V.:

(1) *Dialektika abstraktnogo i konkretnogo v "Kapitale" Marksa* (The Dialectic of Abstract and Concrete in the *Capital* of Marx). Moskva. 1960. 285 str.

(2) 'Logičeskoe i istoričeskoe' (The Logical and the Historical). In *Voprosy dialektičeskogo materializma*. Moskva. 1960. 310–343.

(3) 'O roli protivorečija v poznanii' (On the Role of Contradiction in Knowledge). In *Konferencija po teme "Problema protivorečij v sovremennoj nauki i praktiki"*. Moskva. 1958. 269–290.

(4) 'K voprosu o protivorečii v myšlenii' (On Contradictions in Thought). *VF* 1957, 4, 63–72.

(5) *Nekotorye voprosy materialističeskoj dialektiki v rabote K. Marksa "K kritike političeskoj ekonomii"* (Some Questions of the Materialist Dialectic in Marx' *Critique of Political Economy*). MGU. 1953/54. (d)

IL'ENKOV, F. I.: 'O dialektike abstraktnogo i konkretnogo v naučno-teoretičeskom poznanii' (On the Dialectic of Abstract and Concrete in Scientific-Theoretical Knowledge). *VF* 1955, 1, 42–56.

ILIADI, A. N.: *Praktičeskaja priroda čelovečeskogo poznanija* (The Practical Nature of Human Knowledge). Moskva. 1962. 167 str.

IL'IN, V. V.: 'O strukture umozaključenij' (On the Structure of Reasonings). In *Naučnye trudy* (Kazanskij aviacionnyj In-t). Kazan'. 1960.

Istorija filosofii (History of Philosophy). Pod red. M. A. Dynnika, M. T. Iovčuka, B. M. Kedrova, M. B. Mitina, O. V. Traxtenberga. Moskva. 1957–1963 (five volumes).

Istorija i teorija ateizma (History and Theory of Atheism). Moskva. 1962. 485 str.

IVANOV, E. A.: *O sootnošenii zakonov formal'noj i dialektičeskoj logiki v processe operirovanija ponjatijami* (On the Relation of Formal and Dialectical Logic in the Process of Operating with Concepts). Moskva. 1963. 98 str.

IVANOV, G. M.:

(1) 'Gnoseologičeskie korni idealizma sovremennoj buržuaznoj metodologii istorii v svete leninskoj kritiki maxizma' (The Epistemological Core of the Idealism of Contemporary Bourgeois Methodology of History in the Light of the Leninist Critique of Machism). In *Naučnye trudy* (Tomskij GU) Tomsk. 1960.

(2) 'Sovremennaja buržuaznaja metodologija istorii o specifike predmeta istoričeskogo poznanija' (Contemporary Bourgeois Methodology of History on the Specific Object of Historical Knowledge). In *Učenye zapiski* (Tomskij GU). Tomsk. 1960.

JAKUŠEV, A. A.: 'Sub'ektivno-idealističeskij smysl teorii simvolizma A. Uajtxeda' (The Subjective-Idealist Sense of Whitehead's Theory of Symbolism). *VF* 1962, 12, 116–128.

JAKUŠEVSKIJ, I. T.:

BIBLIOGRAPHY

(1) 'Ob osnovnyx formax praktiki' (On the Basic Forms of Practice). In *Učenye zapiski* (VPŠ). Moskva. 1960.

(2) 'O dialektiko-materialističeskom ponimanii praktiki' (On the Dialectical-Materialist Conception of Practice). *FN* 1958, 4, 113–121.

JANOVSKAJA, S. A.:

(1) 'O tak nazyvaemyx opredelenijax čerez abstrakciju' (On the So-Called Definitions Through Abstraction). In *Sbornik statej po filosofii matematiki*. Moskva. 1936.

(2) 'Problemy analiza ponjatij nauki i novejšij neopozitivizm' (Problems of the Analysis of the Concepts of Science and Modern Neopositivism). *VF* 1961, 6, 47–53.

JAROSLAVSKIJ, E. I.:

(1) 'K voprosu o razvitii myšlenija v svete leninskoj teorii otraženija' (On the Development of Thought in the Light of the Leninist Theory of Reflection). In *Naučnye trudy* (Omskij medicinskij In-t). Omsk. 1960.

JAROŠEVSKIJ, T. M.: 'O tomistskom "gnoseologičeskom realizme" ' (On Thomistic 'Epistemological Realism'). *VF* 1962, 11, 115–126.

JUDANOV, A. A.: *Bor'ba Lenina s izvraščenijami marksistskogo učenija o roli praktiki v poznanii* (Lenin's Fight with Perversions of the Marxist Doctrine on the Role of Practice in Knowledge). M. G. Pg. In-t. 1947. (d)

JUROVSKIJ, S. V.: 'K voprosu o gnoseologičeskix kornjax religii' (On the Epistemological Cores of Religion). *V LGU* 1958, 23, 53.

JUSUPOV, E.: *Logičeskie zakony i formy myšlenija v svete dialektičeskogo materializma* (Logical Laws and Forms of Thought in the Light of Dialectical Materialism). M. oblastnoj Pg. In-t. 1953/54. (d)

K voprosu o sootnošenii logiki i dialektiki (On the Relation of Logic and Dialectic). (Učenye zapiski Komi G. Pg. In-t). 1950.

KAKABADZE, Z. M.: *Problemy logičeskogo v svete leninskoj teorii otraženija* (Problems of the Logical in the Light of the Leninist Theory of Reflection). Tbilisi GU. 1953/54. (d)

KAL'SIN, F. F.: *Osnovnye voprosy teorii poznanija* (Basic Questions of Theory of Knowledge). Gor'kij. 1957.

KAMMARI, M. D.:

(1) 'V. I. Lenin o roli sub"ektivnogo faktora v istorii' (Lenin on the Role of the Subjective Factor in History). *VF* 1955, 2, 16–32.

(2) 'Revizionistskij mif ob "osvoboždenii" nauki ot ideologii' (The Revisionist Myth on the 'Liberation' of Science from Ideology). *VF* 1958, 7, 3–19.

KANTOROVIČ, S. G.: *Logika dokazatel'stva i oproverženija* (The Logic of Proof and Refutation). IF. 1948/51. (d)

KARABANOV, N. V., RUZAVIN, G. I.: 'Dialektičeskoe otricanie' (Dialectical Negation). In *Voprosy dialektičeskogo materializma*. Moskva. 1960. 66–84.

KARAPETJAN, A.: *Kritičeskij analiz filosofii Kanta* (Critical Analysis of the Philosophy of Kant). Erevan. 1958. 566 str.

KARAPETJAN, R. O.: 'V. I. Lenin ob ob"ektivnoj istine' (Lenin on Objective Truth). In *Kniga . . .* (s. Alekseev, G. P.). 232–245.

KARASEV, B. A.: 'Voprosy edinstva dialektiki, teorii poznanija i logiki v knige V. I. Lenina "Materializm i empiriokriticizm" ' (Questions of the Unity of Dialectic, Theory of Knowledge and Logic in Lenin's *Materialism and Empiriocriticism*). In *Kniga . . .* (s. Alekseev, G. P.). 199–213.

KARDAŠ, A. D.:
(1) 'K voprosu o sootnošenii suždenija i predloženija' (On the Relationship of Judgement and Proposition). In *Gnoseologičeskoe soderžanie logičeskix form i metodov*. Kiev. 1960. 50–61.
(2) *Suždenie i predloženie* (Judgement and Proposition). KGU. 1953/54. (d)

KARLJUK, A. S.: *Reakcionnaja suščnost' "fizičeskogo" idealizma* (The Reactionary Essence of 'Physical' Idealism). Minsk. 1954.

KARYMŽANOV, A. X.:
(1) *Problema sovpadenija dialektiki, logiki i teorii poznanija* (The Problem of the Coincidence of Dialectic, Logic and Theory of Knowledge). Alma-Ata. 1962. 199 str.
(2) 'K voprosu o sootnošenii logiki, dialektiki i teorii poznanija v učenii I. Kanta' (On the Relationship of Logic, Dialectic and Theory of Knowledge in the Doctrine of Kant). In *Naučnye trudy* (AN Kazaxskoj SSR). Alma-Ata. 1960.
(3) 'O myšlenii kak predmete logiki i psixologii' (On Thought as the Object of Logic and Psychology). *VF* 1961, 7, 132–140.
(4) *Razrabotka V. I. Leninym problem sovpadenija dialektiki, logiki i teorii poznanija v "Filosofskix tetradjax"* (The Elaboration by Lenin of Problems of the Coincidence of Dialectic, Logic and Theory of Knowledge in the *Philosophic Notebooks*). IF. 1960. (d)

KAZAKOV, A. P., ELMEEV, V. JA.: 'Ob absoljutnosti i otnositel'nosti praktiki kak kriterija istiny' (On the Absoluteness and Relativity of Practice as Criterion of Truth). In *Dialektičeskij materializm*. Leningrad. 1958. 180–189.

KAZAKOVCEV, V. S.: 'Kibernetika i nekotorye voprosy vzaimosvjazi nauk' (Cybernetics and Some Questions of the Interrelation of Sciences). *VF* 1962, 3, 79–93.

KEBURIJA, D. M.: 'K voprosu o konkretnosti ponjatija' (On the Concreteness of the Concept). *VF* 1957, 2, 28–38.

KEDROV, B. M.:
(1) *Engel's i estestvoznanie* (Engels and Natural Science). Moskva. 1947.
(2) *Klassifikacija nauk* (Classification of Sciences). Moskva. 1961. 471 str.
(3) *Kak izučat' knigu V. I. Lenina "Materializm i empiriokriticizm"* (How to Study Lenin's *Materialism and Empirio-Criticism*). Moskva. 1961. 167 str.
(4) *Predmet i vzaimosvjaz' estestvennyx nauk* (The Object and Interconnection of the Natural Sciences). Moskva. 1962. 409 str.
(5) *Edinstvo dialektiki, logiki i teorii poznanija* (The Unity of Dialectic, Logic and Theory of Knowledge). Moskva. 1963. 294 str.
(6) 'O soderžanii i ob'eme izmenjajuščegosja ponjatija' (On the Content and Extension of the Changing Concept). In *Filosofskie zapiski VI*. Moskva. 1953. 188–254.
(7) 'Klassiki marksizma-leninizma o logike' (The Classics of Marxism-Leninism on Logic). In *Voprosy dialektičeskogo i istoričeskogo materializma*. Moskva. 1956. 283–298.
(8) 'O klassifikacii nauk' (On Classification of Sciences). In *Filosofskie voprosy sovremennoj fiziki*. Moskva. 1958.
(9) 'Opredlenie naučnyx ponjatij čerez zakon' (Definition of Scientific Concepts Through the Law). In *Doklady i vystuplenija predstavitelej sovetskoj filosofskoj nauki na XII meždunarodnom filosofskom kongresse*. Moskva. 1958. 93–101.
(10) ' "Fazovyj sposob" v formal'noj logike' ('Phase Method' in Formal Logic). In *Primenenie logiki v nauke i texnike*. Moskva. 1960. 421–501.

(11) 'Ob otnošenii logiki k marksizmu' (On the Relation of Logic to Marxism). *VF* 1951, 4, 212–227.

(12) 'O klassifikacii nauk' (On Classification of Sciences). *VF* 1955, 2, 49–68.

(13) ' "Estestvennoe" i "iskusstvennoe" v poznanii i v dejstvitel'nosti čeloveka ('Natural' and 'Artificial' in Knowledge and in Man's Actuality). *VF* 1958, 11, 18–31.

(14) 'O dialektiko-logičeskom obobščenii istorii estestvoznanija' (On the Dialectical-Logical Generalization of the History of Natural Science). *VF* 1960, 1, 61–74.

(15) 'Opyt metodologičeskogo analiza naučnyx otkrytij' (Experience of Methodological Analysis of Scientific Discoveries). *VF* 1960, 5, 63–78.

(16) 'Vzaimosvjaz dvux stupenej poznanija' (Relation of the two Steps of Knowledge). *FN* 1962, 5, 50–58.

KEŠELAVA, V. V.: 'Kritika K. Marksom gegelevskogo metoda spekuljativnoj konstrukcii (1844–1845 gg.)' (Marx' Critique in 1844–1845 of the Hegelian Method of Speculative Construction). *VF* 1958, 4, 111–121.

KIČANOVA, I. M.: 'Filosofija Fomy Akvinskogo' (The Philosophy of Thomas Aquinas). *VF* 1958, 3, 104–117.

KIRILLOVA, E. G.: 'L. Fejerbax o proisxoždenii i gnoseologičeskix kornjax religii' (Feuerbach on the Origin and Epistemological Core of Religion). In *Iz istorii filosofii*. Moskva. 1957.

KIR'JANOV, G. F.: 'Obsuždenie knigi M. M. Rozentalja "Marksistskij dialektičeskij metod" ' (Discussion of M. M. Rozental' 's *Marxist Dialectical Method*). *VF* 1947, 2, 374–375.

KISELEVA, N. A.:
(1) 'Kniga V. I. Lenina "Materializm i empiriokriticizm" – ostrejšee oružie v bor'be protiv "fizičeskogo" idealizma' (Lenin's *Materialism and Empirio-Criticism* as Sharpest Arm in the Fight with 'Physical' Idealism). In *Kniga* . . . (s. Alekseev, G. P.). 103–128.

(2) 'Matematičeskie abstrakcii kak otraženie zakonomernostej ob"ektivnogo mira' (Mathematical Abstraction as a Reflection of the Laws of the Objective World). *FN* 1960, 2, 94–104.

KISELINČEV, A.: *Marksistsko-leninskaja teorija otraženija i učenie I. P. Pavlova o vysšej nervnoj dejatel'nosti* (The Marxist-Leninist Theory of Reflection and I. P. Pavlov's Doctrine on Higher Nervous Activity). Moskva. 1956.

KLEMENT'EV, E. D.: 'Kritika nominalističeskix tendencij v sovremennoj buržuaznoj filosofii v svete raboty V. I. Lenina "Materializm i empiriokriticizm" ' (Critique of the Nominalist Tendencies of Contemporary Bourgeois Philosophy in the Light of Lenin's *Materialism and Empirio-Criticism*). In *Naučnye trudy* (Tomskij GU). Tomsk. 1960.

KNIGIN, A. N.: •
(1) 'O mnogoznačnyx isčislenijax i zakone isključennogo tret'ego' (On Polyvalent Calculi and the Law of Excluded Middle). In *Voprosy logiki*. Leningrad. 1957. 29–44.

(2) 'Značenie raboty V. I. Lenina "Materializm i empiriokriticizm" dlja kritiki neopozitivistskoj koncepcii istiny' (The Importance of Lenin's *Materialism and Empirio-Criticism* in Criticizing the Neo-positivist Conception of Truth). In *Velikoe proizvedenie marksistskoj filosofii*. Novosibirsk. 1960.

(3) 'K voprosu o sootnošenii logiki matematičeskoj i logiki tradicionnoj' (On the Relationship of Mathematical and Traditional Logics). *V LGU* 1958, 5, 65.

KOEMETS, E. X.: *Reakcionnaja suščnost' neokantianskoj logiki* (The Reactionary Essence of Neo-Kantian Logic). Tartuškij GU. 1951/52. (d)

KOGAN, L. A.: 'Obsuždenie knig M. Leonova i M. Rozentalja o marksistskom dialektičeskom metode' (Discussion of the Books of M. Leonov and M. Rozental' on the Marxist Dialectical Method). *VF* 1948, 1, 297–301.

KOLBANOVSKIJ, V. N.: 'Pravil'no li utverždat', čto soznanie material'no?' (Is it Correct to Affirm that Consciousness is Material?). *VF* 1954, 4, 236–238.

KON, I. S.: 'Nauka kak forma obščestvennogo soznanija' (Science as a Form of Social Consciousness). *VF* 1951, 1, 41–58.

KONDAKOV, N. I.:
(1) 'O formal'noj logike' (On Formal Logic). *VF* 1956, 2, 224–228.
(2) 'Po povodu odnoj neudačnoj popytki rešit problemu svjazi suždenija i predloženija' (On Another Unsuccessful Attempt to Solve the Problem of the Bonds between Judgement and Proposition). *VF* 1957, 5, 201–205.

KOPNIN, P. V.:
(1) *Dialektika kak logika* (Dialectic as Logic). Kiev. 1961. 446 str.
(2) *Gipoteza i poznanie dejstvitel'nosti* (The Hypothesis and Knowledge of Reality). Kiev. 1962. 180 str.
(3) 'Dialektika i protivorečija v myšlenii' (The Dialectic and Contradiction in Thought). In *Konferencija . . .* (s. Frolov, Ju. P.). 77–98.
(4) 'O nekotoryx voprosax teorii umozaključenija' (On some Questions of Theory Reasoning). In *Voprosy logiki*. Moskva. 1955.
(5) 'Abstraktnoe i konkretnoe' (Abstract and Concrete). In *Kategorii materialističeskoj dialektiki*. Moskva. 1957. 324–351.
(6) 'Priroda suždenija i formy vyraženija ego v jazyke' (The Nature of Judgement and Forms of its Expression in Language). In *Myšlenie i jazyk*. Moskva. 1957. 276–351.
(7) 'Kategorii kak vyraženie elementov dialektiki' (Categories as Expressions of the Elements of the Dialectic). In *Voprosy dialektičeskogo materializma*. Moskva. 1960. 361–381.
(8) 'Gipoteza kak forma razvitija nauki' (The Hypothesis as a Form of the Development of Science). In *Naučnye trudy* (Tomskij GU). Tomsk. 1954.
(9) 'Novaja kniga po logike' (A new Book on Logic). *VF* 1953, 6, 205–208.
(10) 'Mesto i značenie gipotezy v poznanii' (The Place and Importance of the Hypothesis in Knowledge). *VF* 1954, 4, 48–59.
(11) 'Eksperiment i ego rol' v poznanii' (The Experiment and its Role in Knowledge). *VF* 1955, 4, 29–40.
(12) 'Formy myšlenija i ix vzaimosvjaz' (The Forms of Thought and their Interrelation). *VF* 1956, 3, 44–58.
(13) 'Dialektika form myšlenija v filosofii Gegelja' (The Dialectic of Forms of Thought in the Philosophy of Hegel). *VF* 1957, 4, 51–62.
(14) 'Dialektika i protivorečija v myšlenii' (The Dialectic and Contradiction in Thought). *VF* 1958, 7, 89–96.
(15) 'Ideja i ee rol' v poznanii' (The Idea and its Role in Knowledge). *VF* 1959, 9, 53–64.
(16) 'Marksistskaja filosofija kak metod naučnogo poznanija' (Marxist Philosophy as a Method of Scientific Knowledge). *VF* 1960, 5, 135–144.
(17) 'Ponjatie myšlenija i kibernetika' (The Concept of Thought and Cybernetics). *VF* 1961, 2, 103–112.

(18) 'Dialektičeskaja logika i naučnoe issledovanie' (Dialectical Logic and Scientific Investigation). *VF* 1962, 10, 3–9.

(19) 'O xaraktere znanija, soderžaščegosja v gipoteze' (On the Character of Knowledge Contained in the Hypothesis). *FN* 1958, 2, 106–120.

(20) 'K voprosu o dialektičeskom materializme kak naučnoj sisteme' (On Dialectical Materialism as a Scientific System). *FN* 1960, 1, 38–50.

(21) 'Materialističeskaja dialektika – logika razvitija sovremennoj nauki' (The Materialist Dialectic as the Logic of the Development of Contemporary Science). *FN* 1963, 4, 66–73.

(22) 'Rassudok i razum i ix funkcii v poznanii' (Understanding and Reason and their Function in Knowledge). *VF* 1963, 4, 64–75.

(23) *Formy myšlenija i ix rol' v poznanii* (The Forms of Thought and their Role in Knowledge). *V AN SSSR.* 1956, 10, 128. (d)

(24) *Bor'ba materializma i idealizma v razvitii učenija o suščnosti suždenija* (The Conflict of Materialism and Idealism in the Development of the Doctrine on the Essence of the Judgement). M. gorodskoj Pg. In-t. 1947. (d)

KORČAGIN, A. A.:
(1) 'Suždenie i formy vyraženija ego v jazyke' (Judgement and the Forms of its Expression in Language). In *Voprosy teorii poznanija.* Perm'. 1960. 137–158.

(2) *Suždenie i predloženie v svete stalinskogo učenie o edinstve myšlenija i jazyke* (Judgement and Proposition in the Light of the Stalinist Teaching on the Unity of Thought and Language). MGU. 1951/52. (d)

KORNEEVA, A. I.: *Kritika neopozitivistskix vzgljadov na prirodu poznanija* (Critique of Neo-Positivist Views on the Nature of Knowledge). Moskva. 1962. 226 str.

KORŠUNOV, A. M.:
(1) 'Elementy obobščennosti obraza v čuvstvennom poznanii' (Elements of Generality of the Image in Sense-Knowledge). *FN* 1962, 2, 83–90.

(2) 'Obraz i znak' (Image and Sign). *V MGU* 1962, 1, 60–70.

KORŽEVA, T. S.: *Dialektičeskoe edinstve dedukcii i indukcii* (The Dialectical Unity of Deduction and Induction). M. gorodskoj Pg. In-t. 1953/54. (d)

KOSTJUK, G. S.:
(1) 'Voprosy psixologii myšlenija' (Questions of the Psychology of Thought). In *Psixologičeskaja nauka v SSSR.* Moskva. 1959. 357–440.

(2) 'Voprosy myšlenija v sovetskoj psixologii' (Questions of Thought in Soviet Psychology). *VP* 1957, 5, 66.

KOŠEVOJ, K. K.:
(1) 'Kategorii ediničnogo i obščego, časti i celogo v processe poznanija' (The Categories of Singular and General and Part and Whole in the Process of Knowledge). In *Naučnye trudy* (Permskij G. medicinskij In-t.) Perm'. 1960.

(2) 'Kategorii suščnosti i javlenija v suždenii i predloženii' (The Categories of Essence and Appearance in the Judgement and Proposition). In *ibid.*

(3) 'Zakon perexoda količestva v kačestvo v processe poznanija' (The Law of the Transition of Quantity into Quality in the Process of Knowledge). In *ibid.*

(4) *Edinstvo suždenija i predlozenija v processe poznanija* (The Unity of Judgement and Proposition in the Process of Knowledge). LGU. 1953/54. (d)

KOŠEVOJ, K. K., DOLININA, I. G.: 'Kategorii formy i soderžanija v suždenii i predloženii' (The Categories of Form and Content in the Judgement and Proposition). In *Naučnye trudy* (Permsky G. medicinsky In-t). Perm'. 1960.

KOŠIN, A. G.: *Problema ob"ektivnoj istiny v dialektičeskom materializma* (The

Problem of Objective Truth in Dialectical Materialism). AON. 1947. (d)

KOVALGIN, V. M.:
(1) *Problema oščuščenij i reflektornaja teorija* (The Problem of Sensation and the Theory of Reflectors). Minsk. 1959. 230 str.
(2) *Marksistskaja filosofija protiv idealizma i metafiziki* (Marxist Philosophy Against Idealism and Metaphysics). Minsk. 1961. 132 str.
(3) 'V. I. Lenin ob osnovax teorii otraženija' (Lenin on the Bases of the Theory of Reflection). In *Voprosy marksistskoj filosofii v trudax V. I. Lenin* (Questions of Marxist Philosophy in the Works of Lenin). Minsk. 1958. 41–74.

KOZEVA, T. A.: 'Protiv projavlenij dualizma v fiziologii i psixologii' (Against Signs of Dualism in Physiology and Psychology). *VF* 1952, 5, 248–249.

KOZLOVA, M. S.: 'Lejbnic i neopozitivizm' (Leibniz and Neo-positivism). *VLGU* 1962, 17, 83–94.

KREMJANSKIJ, V. I.: 'Tipy otraženija kak svojstva materii' (Types of Reflection as a Property of Matter). *VF* 1963, 8, 131–142.

KRISTOSTUR'JAN, N. G.:
(1) 'Eksperiment i ego značenie kak kriterija istiny' (The Experiment and Its Importance as a Criterion of Truth). In *Praktika – kriterij istiny v nauke*. Moskva. 1960. 55–90.
(2) 'V. I. Lenin o konkretnosti istiny' (Lenin on the Concreteness of Truth). *B* 1955, 9, 11.
(3) 'O sootnošenii obščego i otdel'nogo v poznanii' (On the Relation of General and Particular in Knowledge). *VF* 1954, 6, 34–46.
(4) *K voprosu o predmete logiki* (On the Object of Logic). IF. 1951/52. (d) (s. *V AN SSSR* 1953, 1, 103).

KRYVELEV, I. A.: 'Gnoseologičeskie korni religii' (The Epistemological Roots of Religion). In *Voprosy istorii religii i ateizma VI* (Questions of the History of Religion and Atheism). Moskva. 1958. 36–74.

KUBLANOV, B. G.: *Gnoseologičeskaja priroda literatury i iskusstva* (The Epistemological Nature of Literature and Art). L'vov. 1958. 289 str.

KUFTYREV, A. I.: 'V. I. Lenin o sootnošenii obščestvennogo bytija i obščestvennogo soznanija' (Lenin on the Relations of Social Being and Social Consciousness). In *Kniga*... (s. Alekseev, G. P.). 404–415.

KULAGIN, P. V.: *Lenin o dialektičeskom puti poznanija istiny* (Lenin on the Dialectical Path of the Knowledge of Truth). AON. 1948/51. (d)

KULJABIN, G. A.: *Marks i Engel's o roli praktiki v teorii poznanija* (Marx and Engels on the Role of Practice in Theory of Knowledge). AON. 1948/51. (d)

KUPRIKOV, T. K.: *Rol' čuvstvennyx vosprijatij v poznanii ob"ektivnogo mira* (The Role of Sense Perception in the Knowledge of the Objective World). AON. 1948/51. (d)

KURAŽKOVSKAJA, E. A.:
(1) 'V. I. Lenin o dialektike processa poznanija' (Lenin on the Dialectic of the Process of Knowledge). In *Kniga*... (s. Alekseev, G. P.). 184–198.
(2) 'Sootnošenie čuvstvennogo i racional'nogo v teorii poznanija' (The Relation of Sense and Rational in Theory of Knowledge). *V MGU* 1947, 12, 185.
(3) 'V. I. Lenin o roli oščuščenij v processe poznanija i dannye sovremennogo estestvoznanija' (Lenin on the Role of Sensation in the Process of Knowledge and Facts of Contemporary Natural Science). *V MGU* 1959, 2, 37.

KURSANOV, G. A.:
(1) *Logičeskie zakony myšlenija* (The Logical Laws of Thought). Lenizdat. 1947.

(2) *Gnoseologija sovremennogo pragmatizma* (The Epistemology of Contemporary Pragmatism). Moskva. 1958.

(3) *Dialektičeskij materializm o ponjatii* (Dialectical Materialism on the Concept). Moskva. 1963. 383 str.

(4) 'Učenie V. I. Lenina ob istine i sovremennaja nauka' (Lenin's Doctrine on Truth and Contemporary Science). In *Velikoe proizvedenie voinstvujuščego materializma*. Moskva. 1959. 217–232.

(5) 'Reakcionnaja gnoseologija i "teorii" ponjatija neopozitivizma' (Reactionary Epistemology and 'Theories' of the Concept of Neo-positivism). *Izvestija AN SSSR* 1948, 5, 422–436.

(6) 'Nekotorye novejšie "otkrovenija" buržuaznyx gnoseologov' (Some Recent 'Revelations' of Bourgeois Epistemologists). *V AN SSSR* 1954, 10, 72.

(7) 'O nekotoryx koncepcijax istiny v sovremennoj idealističeskoj gnoseologii' (On Some Conceptions of Truth in Contemporary Idealist Epistemology). *VF* 1957, 2, 188–193.

KUZ'MIN, A. F.: *Osnovnye voprosy sovetskoj nauki logiki* (Basic Questions of Soviet Logic). AON. 1948/51. (d)

KUZ'MIN, V. S.: *Naučnye opredelenija u klassikov marksizma-leninizma* (Scientific Definitions in the Works of the Classics of Marxism-Leninism). AON. 1948/51. (d)

KUZNECOV, O. P.: 'Osveščenie voprosov sovremennoj induktivnoj logiki v žurnale "Filosofi of sajens" ' (Clarification of Questions of Contemporary Inductive Logic in the Journal *Philosophy of Science*). *VF* 1958, 6, 179–181.

KVIZINADZE, R. E.: *O marksistsko-leninskom ponimanii istiny* (On the Marxist-Leninist Conception of Truth). Tbilisi GU. 1953/54. (d)

LADENKO, I. S.: 'Značenie raboty V. I. Lenina "Materializm i empiriokriticizm" dlja kritiki formalističeskogo napravlenija v sovremennoj logike' (The Importance of Lenin's *Materialism and Empiriocriticism* in Criticizing the Formalist School in Contemporary Logic). In *Naučnye trudy* (Tomskij GU). Tomsk. 1960.

LADYGINA-KOTS, N. N.: 'Razvitie form otraženija v processe evoljucii organizmov' (Development of the Forms of Reflection in the Process of the Evolution of Organisms). *VF* 1956, 4, 94–103.

LAPŠIN, O. V.: 'Materialističeskaja teorija otraženija i učenie o razvitii živoj materii' (The Materialist Theory of Reflection and the Doctrine on the Development of Living Matter). *VF* 1958, 4, 78–87.

LAZARENKO, T. M.: 'O traktovke ponjatija v dialektičeskoj logike' (On the Treatment of the Concept in Dialectical Logic). In *Voprosy marksistsko-leninskoj filosofii*. Moskva. 1959. 306–339.

LAZAREV, F., ONUŠČENKO, V.: 'Mežvuzovskaja konferencija po dialektičeskoj logike' (Inter-School Conference on Dialectical Logic). *V MGU* 1960, 4, 81.

LEBEDEV, L. P.: *Problema emocii v svete marksistsko-leninskoj teorii otraženija* (The Problem of Emotions in the Light of the Marxist-Leninist Theory of Reflection). IF. 1953/54. (d)

LEBEDEV, M. P.:

(1) 'V. I. Lenin ob aktivnosti i tvorčeskix vozmožnostjax soznanija' (Lenin on the Active and Creative Potentialities of Consciousness). In *Naučnye trudy* (M. G. Pg. In-t). Moskva. 1960.

(2) 'Materija i soznanie' (Matter and Consciousness). *VF* 1956, 5, 70–84.

LEKTORSKIJ, V. A.: 'O kategorijax sub"ekta i ob"ekta v teorii poznanija' (On the

Categories of Subject and Object in Theory of Knowledge). In *Voprosy dialektičeskogo materializma*. Moskva. 1960. 286–309.

LENIN, V. I.:
(1) *Sočinenija* (Complete Works). 4th edition. Moskva. 194ff.
(2) *Materializm i empiriokriticizm*. In *Sočinenija* t. 14. English: *Materialism and Empirio-Criticism*. Moscow-London. 1952.
(3) *Filosofskie tetrady*. Moskva. 1933. English: V. I. Lenin: *Collected Works*. Moscow. 1960ff. Vol. 39.

(LENIN):
(1) *50 let knigi V. I. Lenina "Materializm i empiriokriticizm"* (Fiftieth Anniversary of Lenin's *Materialism and Empirio-Criticism*). Perm'. 1958.
(2) *V. I. Lenin i nektorye voprosy teorii poznanija* (Lenin and some Questions of Theory of Knowledge). Gorkij. 1959.

LEONOV, M. A.:
(1) *Marksistskoj dialektičeskij metod* (The Marxist Dialectical Method). Moskva. 1947.
(2) *Očerk dialektičeskogo materializma* (Essay on Dialectical Materialism). Moskva. 1948. 655 str.
(3) 'Osnovnye čerty marksistskogo dialektičeskogo metoda' (Basic Traits of the Marxist Dialectical Method). In *Dialektičeskij materializm*. Moskva. 1947. 32–89.
(4) 'Edinstvo dialektičeskogo metoda i materialističeskoj teorii v marksistsko-leninskoj filosofii' (The Unity of the Dialectical Method and Materialist Theory in Marxist-Leninist Philosophy). *B* 1947, 14, 29–40.
(5) 'Lenin i Stalin o konkretnosti marksistskogo dialektičeskogo metoda' (Lenin and Stalin on the Concreteness of the Marxist Dialectical Method). *Izvestija AN SSSR* 1949, 1, 3–19.
(6) 'Voprosy marksistskoj teorii poznanija v svete truda I. V. Stalina po jazykoznaniju' (Questions of Marxist Theory of Knowledge in the Light of Stalin's Work on Linguistics). *VF* 1952, 5, 115–131.

LEVI, S. S.: *Dialektičeskij materializm ob ob"ektivnoj istine* (Dialectical Materialism on Objective Truth). LGU. 1953/54. (d)

LEVIN, G. A.:
(1) *Voprosy teorii poznanija v proizvedenii V. I. Lenina "Materializm i empiriokriticizm"* (Questions of Theory of Knowledge in Lenin's *Materialism and Empirio-Criticism*). Minsk. 1960.
(2) 'Obosnovanie i tvorčeskoe razvitie V. I. Leninym teorii poznanija dialektičeskogo materializma' (Establishment and Creative Development by Lenin of the Theory of Knowledge of Dialectical Materialism). In *Voprosy marksistskoj filosofii v trudax V. I. Lenina*. Minsk. 1958. 3–40.
(3) *Razvitie V. I. Leninym teorii poznanija dialektičeskogo materializma v rabote "Materializm i empiriokriticizm"* (Development by Lenin of the Theory of Knowledge of Dialectical Materialism in *Materialism and Empirio-Criticism*). LGU. 1951/52. (d)

LEŽEBOKOV, P. A.: *Logičeskij zakon protivorečija* (The Logical Law of Contradiction). MGU. 1953/54. (d)

LINGART, I.: *Amerikanskij pragmatizm* (American Pragmatism). Moskva. 1954. 254 str.

LJUBIMOV, V. V.: *Voprosy dokazatel'stva v logike* (Problems of Proof in Logic). IF. 1951/52. (d) (s. *V AN SSSR* 1953, 1, 103).

LOGVIN, M. A.: 'O fiziologičeskoj osnove soznanija v svete novejšix issledovanij dejatel'nosti mozga' (On the Physiological Foundations of Consciousness in the Light of Recent Investigations of Cerebral Activity). *FN* 1962, 5, 42–49.

LOZOVSKIJ, B. I.: 'O logike formal'noj i logike dialektičeskoj' (On Formal and Dialectical Logic). *VF* 1951, 4, 232–238.

LYSENKO, N. F.: *Priroda logičeskix form v svete truda V. I. Lenina "Materializm i empiriokriticizm"* (The Nature of Logical Forms in the Light of Lenin's *Materialism and Empirio-Criticism*). AON. 1953/54. (d)

MAJSTROV, L. E.: 'Ob abstrakcijax i aksiomatičeskom metode v matematike' (On Abstractions and Axiomatic Method in Mathematics). In *Nekotorye filosofskie voprosy estestvoznanija*. Moskva. 1957. 75–91.

MAJSTROVA, T. L.: *Uslovnye suždenija* (Conditional Judgements). IF. 1948/51. (d)

MAKAROV, V. T.: *Klassiki marksizm-leninizma o zakonax myšlenija* (The Classics of Marxism-Leninism on the Laws of Thought). AON. 1948/51. (d)

MAKOVEL'SKIJ, A. O.:
(1) 'Formal'naja logika i dialektika' (Formal Logic and Dialectics). *Izvestija AN Azerbajdžanskoj SSR* 1950, 2.
(2) 'Čem dolžna byt' logika kak nauka?' (What Should Logic as a Science be like?). *VF* 1951, 2, 179–181.

MAKSIMOV, A. A.: 'O značenii abstrakcii v mexanike i fizike' (On the Importance of Abstraction in Mechanics and Physics). *VF* 1951, 5, 34–50.

Malaja sovetskaja enciklopedija. Moskva. 1960. 'Teorija poznanija'. (vol. 9) str. 222–223.

MAL'CEV, V. I.:
(1) 'O nekotoryx čertax dialektičeskoj logiki' (On some Traits of Dialectical Logic). In *Učenye zapiski* (MGU). Moskva. 1958. 3–26.
(2) 'Problema opredelenija ponjatij v dialektičeskoj logike' (The Problem of Defining Concepts in Dialectical Logic). In *Problemy dialektičeskoj logiki*. Moskva. 1959. 3–26.
(3) 'Propoved' alogizma v buržuaznoj filosofii' (Propagation of Illogicality in Bourgeois Philosophy). *V MGU* 1953, 1, 73.
(4) 'O edinstve dialektiki, teorii poznanija i logiki v marksistsko-leninskoj filosofii' (On the Unity of Dialectic, Theory of Knowledge and Logic in Marxist-Leninist Philosophy). *V MGU* 1957, 2, 75.
(5) 'Mozno li metod K. Marksa nazyvat' analitičeskim?' (Can Marx' Method be Called Analytic?). *FN* 1961, 4, 147–151.

MAL'CEV, V. I., UVAROV, A. I.: 'Kak osveščat problemu edinstva dialektiki, teorii poznanija i logiki?' (How to Clarify the Problem of the Unity of Dialectic, Theory of Knowledge and Logic?) *FN* 1963, 3, 77–82.

MAMARDAŠVILI, M. K.:
(1) 'Otnošenie logičeskix protivorečij, antinomij, protivorečij mysli i real'nyx svazej protivopoložnostej, vyražaemyx v myšlenii' (Relationship of Logical Contradictions, Antinomies, Conceptual Contradictions and Real Bonds of Opposition Expressed in Thought). In *Konferencija* . . . (s. Frolov, Ju. P.). 306–311 (319).
(2) 'K ponjatiju formy i soderžanija myšlenija v "Logike" Gegelja' (On the Concept of Form and Content of Thought in the *Logic* of Hegel). *V MGU* 1958, 4, 87.
(3) 'Processy analiza i sinteza' (Processes of Analysis and Synthesis). *VF* 1958, 2, 50–63.

171

(4) 'K kritike eksistencialistskogo ponimanija dialektiki' (Critique of the Existentialist Conception of the Dialectic). *VF* 1963, 6, 108–120.

MANGUŠEV, T. D.: 'Edinstvo jazyka i myšlenija' (Unity of Language and Thought). MGU. 1953/54. (d)

MANSUROV, N. S.: Oščuščenie – sub"ektivnyj obraz ob"ektivnogo mira (Sensation as Subjective Image of the Objective World). Moskva. 1963. 118 str.

MARMIČEV, E. A.: 'K kritike "matematičeskogo" idealizma' (Critique of 'Mathematical' Idealism). *V LGU* 1962, 11, 83–93.

MARKOV, M. A.: 'O prirode fizičeskogo znanija' (On the Nature of Physical Knowledge). *VF* 1947, 2, 140–176.

MARTIROSJAN, G. A.: *O roli abstraktnogo myšlenija v processe poznanija* (On the Role of Abstract Thought in the Process of Knowledge). M. G. Pg. In-t. 1953/54. (d)

MARX, K.:
(1) 'Thesen über Feuerbach' (Theses on Feuerbach). In F. Engels: *Ludwig Feuerbach* ... Stuttgart. 1888, pp. 69–72.
(2) *Die Frühschriften.* Herausgegeben von Siegfried Landshut. Stuttgart. 1953.

MASLENNIKOV, M. M.: *Sravnenie i ego rol' v naučnom poznanii* (Comparison and its Role in Scientific Knowledge). MGU. 1953/54. (d)

MATJUŠKIN, A. M.: 'Analiz i obobščenie otnošenij' (Analysis and Generalization of Relations). In *Process myšlenija i zakonomernosti analiza, sinteza i obobščenija* (The Process of Thought and the Laws of Analysis, Synthesis and Generalization). Moskva. 1960. 122–152.

MEDVEDEV, N. V.: *Marksistsko-leninskaja teorija otraženija i učenie I. P. Pavlova o vysšej nervnoj dejatel'nosti* (The Marxist-Leninist Theory of Reflection and the Doctrine of I. P. Pavlov on Higher Nervous Activity). Moskva. 1954. 112 str.

MEGRABJAN, A. A.: *O prirode individual'nogo soznanija* (On the Nature of Individual Knowledge). Erevan. 1959.

MEL'NIKOV, K. F.: *Gipoteza i ee rol' v nauke* (The Hypothesis and its Role in Science). AON. 1948/51. (d)

MEL'NIKOV, V. V.: 'Razrabotka V. I. Leninym voprosa o sootnošenii dialektiki, logiki i teorii poznanija v "Filosofskix tetradjax"' (Elaboration by Lenin of the Question on the Relationship of Dialectic, Logic and Theory of Knowledge in the *Philosophic Notebooks*). In *Naučnye trudy* (Samarkandskij GU) Samarkand. 1960.

MEL'VIL', JU. K.: 'Pragmatizm – filosofija imperialističeskoj reakcii' (Pragmatism as the Philosophy of the Imperialist Reaction). *VF* 1950, 2, 306–330.

MEL'VIL', JU. K., MITROXIN, L. N.: '"Nigilizm Džona D'jui"' (The Nihilism of John Dewey). *VF* 1956, 3, 235–240.

MEŠČERJAKOVA, I. N.: 'V. I. Lenin of poznavaemosti mira i ego zakonomernostej' (Lenin on the Knowability of the World and its Laws). In *Naučnye trudy* (Vsesojuznyj zaočnyj energetičeskij In-t). Moskva. 1960.

MEŽUEV, V. M.: 'Osnovnye principy gegelevskoj kritiki formal'noj logiki' (Basic Principles of the Hegelian Critique of Formal Logic). *VF* 1957, 1, 80–91.

MIROŠXINA, N. M.:
(1) 'Voprosy teorii poznanija dialektičeskogo materializma' (Problems of the Theory of Knowledge of Dialectical Materialism). In *Voprosy dialektičeskogo materializma.* Moskva. 1951. 171–189.
(2) 'V. I. Lenin o edinstve dialektiki, logiki i teorii poznanija' (Lenin on the

Unity of the Dialectic, Logic and Theory of Knowledge). In *Naučnye trudy* (Taškentskij GU) Taškent. 1960.

(3) 'K voprosu o ponjatii v svete marksistsko-leninskogo učenija o processe poznanija' (On Concepts in the Light of the Marxist-Leninist Doctrine on the Process of Knowledge). In *Filosofija*. Taškent. 1957. 5–37.

Mirovozzrenčeskie i metodologičeskie problemy naučnoj abstrakcii (World-Outlook and Methodological Problems of Scientific Abstraction). Moskva. 1960.

MITIN, M. B.:

(1) *Gegel' i teorija materialističeskoj dialektiki* (Hegel and the Theory of the Materialist Dialectic). Moskva. 1932.

(2) ' "Materializm i empiriokriticizm" V. I. Lenina i bor'ba protiv sovremennoj idealističeskoj reakcii' (Lenin's *Materialism and Empirio-Criticism* and the Fight against Contemporary Idealist Reaction). *VF* 1949, 1, 60–84.

(3) 'Material'noe i ideal'noe' (Material and Ideal). *VF* 1962, 7, 74–87.

(4) 'Marksistsko-leninskaja gnoseologija i problema znaka i značenija (Marxist-Leninist Epistemology and the Problem of Sign and Sense). *VF* 1963, 6, 13–21.

MITROXIN, L. N.:

(1) 'Kriterij istiny v filosofii pragmatizma' (The Criterion of Truth in the Philosophy of Pragmatism). In *Praktika – kriterij istiny v nauke*. Moskva. 1960. 367–392.

(2) 'Problema ponjatija v logike pragmatizma' (The Problem of the Concept in the Logic of Pragmatism). *V MGU* 1957, 1, 90.

MIXAILOVA, I. B.: 'Xaraktere obobščenija v predstavlenijax' (On the Character of Generalization in Representations), *VF* 1963, 7, 74–84.

MIXAILOVSKIJ, G. V.: *Značenie učenija I. P. Pavlova o vysšej nervnoj dejatel'nosti dlja marksistsko-leninskogo rešenija voprosy o vzaimootnošenii čuvstvennogo i racional'-nogo v processe poznanija* (Importance of the Doctrine of I. P. Pavlov on Higher Nervous Activity for the Solution of the Question on the Mutual Relationship of Sensible and Rational in the Process of Knowledge). MGU. 1953/54. (d)

MIXALENKO, JU. P.:

(1) *Filosofia D. Juma – teoretičeskaja osnova anglijskogo pozitivizma XX veka* (Hume's Philosophy as Theoretical Base of Twentieth Century English Positivism). Moskva. 1962. 150 str.

(2) 'O nepravil'noj ocenke filosofii Juma' (On an Incorrect Evaluation of Hume's Philosophy). *VF* 1958, 11, 177–178.

MKRTYČEV, G. G.: *Marksizm-leninizm o roli praktiki v poznanii* (Marxism-Leninism on the Role of Practice in Knowledge). AON. 1948/51. (d)

MOGENDOVIČ, M. R.: 'O nevrologičeskoj osnove psixičeskogo' (On the Neurological Basis of the Psychic). *VF* 1961, 10, 120–139.

MOLODCOV, V. S.: 'Klassovye i gnoseologičeskie osnovy revizionizma' (The Class and Epistemological Bases of Revisionism). *VF* 1958, 12, 14–24.

MOROČNIK, S. B.: 'Korennaja protivopoložnost' dialektiki i sofistiki' (Basic Opposition Between Dialectic and Sophistry). *VF* 1950, 3, 295–308.

MOROZOV, E. I.:

(1) 'O sootnošenii indukcii i dedukcii' (On the Relationship of Induction and Deduction). In *Gnoseologičeskoe soderžanie logičeskix form i metodov*. Kiev. 1960. 86–104.

(2) 'Kritika Engel'som vseinduktivizma' (Engels' Critique of Omni-Inductionism). In *Nekotorye voprosy teorii poznanija*. Irkutsk. 1960. 169–206.

(3) *O sootnošenii indukcii i dedukcii* (On the Relationship of Induction and Deduction). Irkutskij GU. 1953/54. (d)

MOSKALENKO, F. JA.: 'V. I. Lenin o poznavatel'nom značenii indukcii i induktivnyx vyvodov' (Lenin on the Cognitive Importance of Induction and Inductive Conclusions). In *Gnoseologičeskoe soderžanie logičeskix form i metodov*. Kiev. 1960. 73–85.

MOTROŠILOVA, N. V.:
   (1) 'O knige E. Al'brexta "Otnošenie teorii poznanija, logiki i jazyka"' (On E. Albrecht's *Relationship of Theory of Knowledge, Logic and Language*). *VF* 1958, 7, 133–135.
   (2) 'Fenomenologija E. Gusserlja i osnovnoj vopros filosofii' (The Phenomenology of Husserl and the Basic Question of Philosophy). *VF* 1961, 12, 66–79.

MŠVENIERADZE, V. V.:
   (1) 'Filosofija neopozitivizma' (The Philosophy of Neopositivism). *VF* 1957, 2, 39–50.
   (2) 'O filosofskoj suščnosti "semantičeskij koncepcii istiny"' (On the Philosophic Essence of the 'Semantic Conception of Truth'). In *Logičeskie issledovanija* (Logical Investigations). Moskva. 1959. 48–68.

Myšlenie i jazyk (Thought and Language). Moskva. 1957.

NABIN, T.: 'K voprosu o roli truda v formirovanii izmenenii soznanii' (On the Role of Work in the Formation and Modification of Consciousness). In *Nekotorye voprosy filosofii*. Alma-Ata. 1961. 118–130.

NARSKIJ, I. S.:
   (1) *Očerki po istorii pozitivizma* (Essays on the History of Positivism). Moskva. 1960. 199 str.
   (2) *Sovremennyj pozitivizm* (Contemporary Positivism). Moskva. 1961. 422 str.
   (3) 'Filosofskaja suščnost' neopozitivizma' (The Philosophic Essence of Neo-positivism). In *Sovremennyj sub"ektivnyj idealizm*. Moskva. 1957. 140–218.
   (4) 'Kritika neopozitivizma po voprosu o vzaimootnošenii ponjatija istiny i kriterija istiny' (Critique of Neo-positivism on the Relationship of the Concept of Truth and the Criterion of Truth). In *Kritika sovremennoj buržuaznoj filosofii i revizionizma*. Moskva. 1959. 254–275.
   (5) ' "Materializm i empiriokriticizm" V. I. Lenina i logičeskij pozitivizm' (Lenin's *Materialism and Empirio-Criticism* and Logical Positivism). In *Velikoe proizvedenie voinstvujuščego materializma*. Moskva. 1959. 331–359.
   (6) 'Kritika koncepcii jazyka v teorii poznanija "obščej semantiki"' (Critique of the Conception of Language in the Theory of Knowledge of 'General Semantics'). In *Kritika sovremennoj buržuaznoj filosofii i sociologii*. Moskva. 1961. 59–109.
   (7) ' "Materializm i empiriokriticizm" V. I. Lenina i sovremennyj pozitivizm' (Lenin's *Materialism and Empirio-Criticism* and Contemporary Positivism). *V MGU* 1959, 2, 15.
   (8) 'K voprosy o sootnošenii formal'noj logiki i dialektiki' (On the Relationship of Formal Logic and Dialectic). *V MGU* 1960, 3, 51–63.
   (9) 'Kritika konvencionalizma kak metodologičeskoj osnovy sovremennogo pozitivizma' (Critique of Conventionalism as Methodological Basis of Contemporary Positivism). *V MGU* 1961, 1, 84–97.
   (10) 'Cennoe issledovanie o marksistskoj dialektike' (Valuable Investigation on the Marxist Dialectic). *VF* 1957, 4, 185–188.

(11) 'Kritika učenija neopozitivizma o kriterii istiny' (Critique of the Doctrine of Neo-positivism on the Criterion of Truth:. *VF* 1959, 9, 87–98.

(12) Filosofskie problemy obščej semantiki' (Philosophic Problems of General Semantics). *VF* 1961, 3, 164–169.

(13) 'Kritika osnovnyx principov teorii poznanija neopozitivizma' (Critique of the Basic Principles of the Theory of Knowledge of Neo-positivism). *VF* 1962, 1, 62–70.

(14) 'Problema značenija i kritika ee neopozitivistskix vešenij' (The Problem of Meaning and Critique of Neopositivist Solutions). *VF* 1963, 6, 22–33.

(15) 'Neopozitivisty v roli "kritikov" dialektičeskogo materializma' (Neo-positivists as 'Critics' of Dialectical Materialism). *FN* 1962, 4, 57–64.

NASEDKIN, A. D.: *O svjazi slova i ponjatija* (On the Bonds of Word and Concept). M. G. Pg. In-t. 1953/54. (d)

NATADZE, R.: 'Genezis obrazovanija ponjatij' (Genesis of the Formation of Concepts). In *Naučnye trudy* (Tbilisskij GU) Tbilisi. 1946.

Naučnaja sessija, posvjaščennaja problemam fiziologičeskogo učenija akademika I. P. Pavlova (Scientific Session, Devoted to Problems of the Physiological Doctrine of the Academician I. P. Pavlov). Stenografičeskij otčet. Moskva. 1950.

NAUMENKO, L. K.:

(1) 'Nekotorye gnoseologičeskie aspekty problemy obosnovanija matematiki' (Some Epistemological Aspects of the Problem of the Foundations of Mathematics). In *Nekotorye voprosy filosofii*. Alma-Ata. 1961. 77–117.

(2) 'Aktivnosti' poznajuščego sub"ekta v processe otraženija' (The Active Character of the Knowing Subject in the Process of Reflection). *Izvestija AN Kazaxskoj SSR* 1960, 1.

NAZAROV, I. N.: 'Proizvodstvennyj eksperiment i ego rol' v poznanii' (The Experiment of Production and its Role in Knowledge). In *Bor'ba* ... (s. Gricenko, I. I.)

Nekotorye voprosy dialektičeskogo materializma (Some Questions of Dialectical Materialism). Leningrad. 1962. 194 str.

Nekotorye voprosy teorii poznanija (Some Questions of Theory of Knowledge). Irkutsk. 1960. 259 str.

NELEP, A. T.: 'Ob ob"ektivnyx osnovax analiza i sinteza' (On the Objective Bases of Analysis and Synthesis). In *Naučnye trudy* (Doneckij politexničeskij In-t). Stalino. 1960.

NESTEROVA, N. P.: *Problema modal'nosti suždenij* (The Problem of Modality of Judgements). MGU. 1953/54. (d)

NIKITIN, E. P.:

(1) 'Priroda naučnogo ob'jasnenija i sovremennyj pozitivizm' (The Nature of Scientific Explanation and Contemporary Positivism). *VF* 1962, 8, 96–107.

(2) 'Tipy naučnogo ob'jasnenija' (Types of Scientific Explanation). *VF* 1963, 10, 30–39.

(3) 'V čem že specifika svojstva otraženija?' (Wherein lies the Specific Trait of Reflection?). *FN* 1961, 3, 171–174.

(4) 'Pragmatistskaja interpretacija principa naučnogo ob'jasnenija' (The Pragmatist Interpretation of the Principle of Scientific Explanation). *FN* 1962, 3, 120.

NIKITIN, N. I.: 'O zakonax myšlenija' (On the Laws of Thought). *V MGU* 1956, 2, 69–84.

NIKITIN, P. I.:

(1) 'O dialektike form myšlenija' (On the Dialectic of the Forms of Thought). *V MGU* 1960, 6, 59.

(2) *Logika, ee predmet i značenie* (Logic: its Object and Importance). MGU. 1950/51. (d)

NIKITINA, V. P.:

    (1) 'Aristotel' o neobxodimosti vyvoda v prostom kategoričeskom sillogizme' (Aristotle on the Necessary Conclusion in the Simple Categorical Syllogism). In *Voprosy logiki.* Leningrad. 1957. 131–148.

    (2) *Učenie Aristotelja o formax myšlenija* (Aristotle's Doctrine on the Forms of Thought). Leningrad. 1956. (d)

NIKOLAEV, I. V.: 'Učenie o ponjatii v dialektičeskoj logike' (Doctrine on Concept in Dialectical Logic). In *Filosofija.* Leningrad. 1961. 254–273.

NIKOLAEV, JA. I.: 'Nekotorye voprosy teorii poznanija v knige V. I. Lenina "Materializm i empiriokriticizm" ' (Some Questions of Theory of Knowledge in Lenin's *Materialism and Empirio-Criticism*). In *Naučnye trudy* (M. kooperativnyj In-t). Moskva. 1960.

NOVIK, I. B.: 'O specifičeskix osobennostjax soznanija čeloveka' (On the Specific Peculiarities of Human Consciousness). *VF* 1956, 6, 229–231.

NOVINSKIJ, I. I.: 'O ponjatii svjazi i svjazi ponjatii v marksistskoj filosofii' (On the Concept of Bond and the Bonds of Concepts in Marxist Philosophy). *FN* 1959, 2, 106–115.

O "Filosofskix tetradjax" V. I. Lenina (On the *Philosophic Notebooks* of Lenin). Moskva. 1959.

O religii. Xrestomatija (On Religion. A Reader). Moskva. 1963. 598 str.

ODUEVA, N. K.: 'O perexode ot oščuščenija k mysli' (On the Transition from Sensation to Thought). In *Voprosy marksistsko-leninskoj filosofii.* Moskva. 1959. 264–305.

OJZERMAN, T. I.:

    (1) *Filosofija Gegelja* (The Philosophy of Hegel). Moskva. 1956.

    (2) *Osnovnye stupeni processa poznanija* (The Basic Stages in the Process of Knowledge). Moskva. 1957.

    (3) *Osnovnye etapy razvitija domarksistskoj filosofii* (Basic Steps in the Development of Pre-Marxist Philosophy). Moskva. 1957.

    (4) 'Problema istiny i ee kriterija' (The Problem of Truth and its Criterion). *V MGU* 1956, 1, 45–66.

    (5) 'O materialističeskom rešenii vtoroj storony osnovnogo voprosa filosofii' (On the Materialist Solution of the Second Side of the Basic Question of Philosophy). *V MGU* 1959, 3, 147–155.

    (6) 'Dialektičeskij materializm i gegelevskaja koncepcija sovpadenija dialektiki, logiki i teorii poznanija' (Dialectical Materialism and the Hegelian Conception of the Coincidence of the Dialectic, Logic and Theory of Knowledge). *VF* 1958, 1, 105–113.

    (7) 'Osnovnoj filosofskij vopros i kritika sovremennogo idealizma' (The Basic Philosophic Question and Criticism of Contemporary Idealism). *VF* 1960, 8, 137–148.

    (8) 'Krizis sovremennoj buržuaznoj filosofii i fideizm' (The Crisis of Contemporary Bourgeois Philosophy and Fideism). In *Sovremennye religiozno-filosofskie tečenija v kapitalističeskix stranax.* Moskva. 1962. str. 3–51.

OJZERMAN, T. I., ASMUS, V. F.: 'Klassičeskaja nemeckaja filosofija. Idealističeskie učenija Kanta, Fixte, Šellinga, Gegelja' (Classical German Philosophy. The Idealist Doctrines of Kant, Fichte, Schelling, Hegel). In *Kratkij očerk istorii filosofii* (Short Outline of the History of Philosophy). Moskva. 1960. 247–297.

OKULOV, A. F.: 'Kniga o bor'be Lenina protiv neokantianstva' (Book on Lenin's Fight Against Neo-Kantianism). *B* 1949, 17, 67.

ORLOV, V. V.:

    (1) 'Ososbennosti čuvstvennogo poznanija' (Particularities of Sense-Knowledge). In *Dialektičeskij materializm*. Leningrad. 1958. 97–116.

    (2) 'Leninskaja teorija otraženija' (The Leninist Theory of Reflection). In *50 let knigi V. I. Lenina "Materializm i empiriokriticizm"*. Perm'. 1958.

    (3) 'Materializm kak metod poznanija i praktičeskoj dejatel'nosti' (Materialism as a Method of Knowledge and of Practical Activity). In *Voprosy teorii poznanija*. Peim'. 1960. 3–22.

OVUŽEJNIKOVA, S. V.: 'Logičeskaja funkcija kategorij dialektiki' (The Logical Function of the Categories of the Dialectic). *FN* 1963, 3, 32–38.

OS'MAKOV, I. I.: 'O zakone myšlenija i o nauke logika' (On the Law of Thought and the Science of Logic). *VF* 1950, 3, 317–330.

Osnovnye voprosy naučnogo ateizma (Basic Questions of Scientific Atheism). Moskva. 1962. 412 str.

Osnovy naučnogo ateizma (Principles of Scientific Atheism). Moskva. 1961. 454 str.

Osnovy marksistskoj filosofii (Principles of Marxist Philosophy). Moskva. 1958. 'Materija i soznanie' (Matter and Consciousness) 159–193. 'Dialektika processa poznanija' (Dialectic of the Process of Knowledge) 303–346.

OSTROUX, F. JA.: 'Protiv iskaženija marksizma v voprosax logiki' (Against Distortions of Marxism on Logic). *VF* 1951, 3, 164–173.

OVSJANNIKOV, M. F.:

    (1) *Filosofija Gegelja* (The Philosophy of Hegel). Moskva. 1959. 305 str.

    (2) 'V. I. Lenin o filosofskix istokax maxizma' (Lenin on the Philosophic Roots of Machism). In *Kniga . . .* (s. ALEKSEEV, G. P.). 289–310.

'Pamjati filosofa-vojna' (Memorial to a Philosopher-Soldier). *VF* 1962, 12, 177.

PANFILOV, V. Z.: 'K voprosu o sootnošenii jazyka i myšlenija' (On the Relationship of Language and Thought). In *Myšlenie i jazyk*. Moskva. 1957. 117–165.

PANTIN, I. K.: *Materialističeskoe mirovozzrenie i teorija poznanija russkix revoljucionnyx demokratov* (The Materialist World-Outlook and Theory of Knowledge of the Russian Revolutionary Democrats). Moskva. 1961. 116 str.

PARAMONOV, N. Z.: 'Abstraktnoe i konkretnoe kak momenty poznanija' (The Abstract and Concrete as Moments of Knowledge). In *Voprosy teorii poznanija i logiki*. Moskva. 1960. 142–168.

PAVLOV, T.:

    (1) *Osnovnoe v učenii I. P. Pavlova v svete dialektičeskogo materializma* (The Essence of the Doctrine of I. P. Pavlov in the Light of Dialectical Materialism). Moskva. 1958.

    (2) *Izbrannye filosofskie proizvedenija. Tom 1.* (Selected Philosophic Works. Vol. 1). Moskva. 1961.

    (3) 'Sxolastika i empirizm. Teorija otraženija i teorija ieroglifov' (Scholasticism and Empiricism. Theory of Reflection and Theory of Hieroglyphs). *VF* 1961, 7, 106–116.

PAVLOV, V. T.:

    (1) *Otnošenija meždu ponjatijami* (Relations Among Concepts). Kiev. 1961. 175 str.

(2) 'Otnošenie toždestva meždu ponjatijami' (The Relationship of Identity Between Concepts). In *Gnoseologičeskoe soderžanie logičeskix form i metodov.* Kiev. 1960. 26–49.

PAŽITNOV, L. N.: 'Kritika Marksom gegelevskoj koncepcii sub''ekta-ob''ekta' (Marx' Critique of the Hegelian Conception of Subject-Object). *VF* 1957, 6, 35–46.

PEREDERIJ, V. I.: 'Kritika neopozitivistskogo ponimanija predmeta filosofii' (Critique of the Neo-positivist Conception of the Object of Philosophy). *FN* 1962, 2, 98–105.

PETLENKO, V. P.: 'V. I. Lenin ob adekvatnosti otraženija i nekotorye voprosy kritiki fiziologičeskogo idealizma' (Lenin on the Adequacy of Reflection and Some Questions of the Critique of Physiological Idealism). *V LGU* 1957, 23, 57.

PETROV, I. G.: 'Leninskij analiz ponjatija "opyt" v filosofii i kritika sub''ektivizma v poznanii' (The Leninist Analysis of the Concept 'Experience' in Philosophy and Criticism of Subjectivism in Knowledge). *V MGU* 1960, 1, 51–66.

PETROV, V. V.: 'Predposylki vozniknovenija ponjatij' (Prerequisites for the Arising of Concepts). In *Gnoseologičeskoe soderžanie logičeskix form i metodov.* Kiev. 1960. 3–25.

PETROVSKIJ, A. V.: 'Ob ob''ektivnoj xaraktere psixologičeskix zakonomernostej' (On the Objective Character of Psychological Laws). *VF* 1953, 3, 173–177.

PLETNEV, D. V.: 'Ob''ektivnost' logičeskogo protivorečija' (The Objectivity of Logical Contradictions). *FN* 1959, 4, 82–92.

PLOTNIKOV, A. M.:
(1) 'Nekotorye voprosy dialektiki toždestva i različija v processe suždenija' (Some Questions on the Dialectic of Identity and Difference in the Process of Judgement). In *Voprosy logiki.* Leningrad. 1959. 18–27.
(2) 'O roli sravnenija v processe obrazovanija ponjatij' (On the Role of Comparison in the Process of the Formation of Concepts). In *Voprosy logiki.* Leningrad. 1960. 87–101.

PODKORYTOV, G. A.:
(1) 'Istoričeskij i logičeskij metody poznanija' (Historical and Logical Methods of Knowledge). In *Dialektičeskij materializm.* Leningrad. 1958. 190–205.
(2) 'O forme ponjatija i forme konkretnogo znanija' (On the Form of the Concept and the Form of Concrete Knowledge). In *Voprosy logiki.* Leningrad. 1960. 28–41.
(3) 'Rol' indukcii v poznanii' (The Role of Induction in Knowledge). *V LGU* 1956, 11, 54.
(4) 'O formax myšlenija v dialektičeskoj logike' (On the Forms of Thought in Dialectical Logic). *V LGU* 1960, 23, 69–79.
(5) 'O ponjatii naučnogo metoda' (On the Concept of Scientific Method). *V LGU* 1962, 11, 72–82.
(6) 'Sootnošenie dialektičeskogo metoda s častnonaučnymi metodami' (Relation of the Dialectical Method to the Methods of the Single Sciences). *VF* 1962, 6, 36–47.
(7) 'Sootnošenie istorii i teorii v poznanii' (Relation of History and Theory in Knowledge). *VF* 1958, 10, 48–55.
(8) 'Rol' dedukcii v poznanii' (The Role of Deduction in Knowledge). *FN* 1960, 4, 50–58.

PODOSETNIK, V. M.:
(1) 'K voprosu o stupenjax processa poznanija istiny' (On the Steps in the Process of the Knowledge of Truth). *VF* 1954, 5, 77–81.

(2) *Razvitie I. V. Stalinym marksistskoj teorii poznanija v trude "Marksizm i voprosy jazykoznanija"* (Stalin's Development of the Marxist Theory of Knowledge in *Marxism and Questions of Linguistics*). AON. 1951/52. (d)

POLIKAROV, A.: 'Obščaja xarakteristika sovremennogo idealizma i napravlenij ego kritiki' (General Characteristics of Contemporary Idealism and Directions of Criticism of it.) *FN* 1961, 3, 84–97.

PONOMAREV, JA. A.: 'K voprosu o prirode psixičeskogo' (On the Nature of the Psychic). *VF* 1960, 3, 88–99.

POPOV, N. P.: *Opredelenie ponjatij* (Definition of Concepts). Leningrad. 1954.

POPOV, P. S.:
(1) *Istorija logiki novogo vremeni* (History of Modern Logic). Moskva. 1960.
(2) 'Voprosy dialektičeskoj logiki v knige V. I. Lenina "Materializm i empirio-kriticizm" ' (Questions of Dialectical Logic in Lenin's *Materialism and Empirio-Criticism*). In *Kniga* . . . (s. Alekseev, G. P.). 214–231.
(3) 'Suždenie i ego stroenie' (Judgement and its Structure). In *Filosofskie zapiski VI*. Moskva. 1953. 71–93.
(4) 'Učenie I. V. Stalina o edinstve jazyka i myšlenija i zadači logiki' (Stalin's Doctrine on the Unity of Language and Thought and the Tasks of Logic). *V MGU* 1951, 9, 47.
(5) 'Predmet formal'noj logiki i dialektika' (The Object of Formal Logic and the Dialectic). *VF* 1951, 1, 210–218.
(6) 'Opyt naučnogo izloženija logiki' (Attempt at a Scientific Presentation of Logic). *VF* 1956, 5, 175–180.
(7) 'Ob izučenii filosofii Platona' (On the Study of the Philosophy of Plato). *FN* 1958, 3, 171–176.

POPOV, S. I.:
(1) *Kant i kantianstvo* (Kant and Kantianism). Moskva. 1961. 297 str.
(2) 'Bor'ba V. I. Lenina protiv neokantianskoj revizii marksistskoj filosofii i značenie etoj bor'by dlja sovremennosti' (Lenin's Fight with the Neo-Kantian Revision of Marxist Philosophy and its Importance for Today). In *Očerki po istorii filosofii v Rossii* (Essays on the History of Philosophy in Russia). Moskva. 1960. 224–249.
(3) 'K voprosu o roli zakona edinstva i bor'by protivopoložnostej v dialektičeskoj logike' (On the Role of the Law of Unity and Conflict of Opposites in Dialectical Logic). In *Problemy dialektičeskoj logiki*. Moskva. 1959. 90–108.
(4) 'Značenie knigi V. I. Lenina "Materializm i empiriokriticizm" dlja kritiki sovremennogo neokantianstva' (Importance of Lenin's *Materialism and Empirio-Criticism* for Critizing Contemporary Neo-Kantianism). In *Velikoe proizvedenie voinstvujuščego materializma*. Moskva. 1959. 392 410.
(5) 'Kategorija protivorečija v logike dialektičeskoj i logike formal'noj' (The Category of Contradiction in Dialectical and Formal Logic). *V MGU* 1956, 2, 85–98.

POPOVIČ, M. V.: 'Filosofskij aspekt problemy značenija i smysla' (The Philosophic Aspect of the Problem of Meaning and Sense). *VF* 1962, 12, 34–46.

POPOVIČ, M. V., SADOVSKIJ, V. N.: 'Konferencija po logike naučnogo issledovanija' (Conference on the Logic of Scientific Investigation). *VF* 1962, 10, 133–141.

Praktika – kriterij istiny v nauke (Practice as Criterion of Truth in Science). Moskva. 1960. 462 str.

PRESNJAKOV, P. V.: *O "pervičnyx i "vtoričnyx" kačestvax v marksistskoj teorii otraženija* (On 'Primary' and 'Secondary' Qualities in the Marxist Theory of Reflection). MGU. 1947. (d)

PRESNJAKOV, P. V., KANTEMIROV, D. S.: *Teorija poznanija dialektičeskogo materializma i učenie o pervičnyx i vtoričnyx kačestvax* (The Theory of Knowledge of Dialectical Materialism and the Doctrine on Primary and Secondary Qualities). Alma-Ata. 1959. 220 str.

Problema oščuščenija v svete marksistsko-leninskoj teorii poznanija (The Problem of Sensation in the Light of the Marxist-Leninist Theory of Knowledge). Leningrad. 1953.

Problemy dialektičeskoj logiki (Problems of Dialectical Logic). Moskva. 1959. 108 str.

Process myšlenija i zakonomernosti analiza, sinteza i obobščenija (The Process of Thought and the Laws of Analysis, Synthesis and Generalization). Moskva. 1960.

PROTASENIJA, P. F.: *Proisxoždenie soznanija* (Origin of Consciousness). Minsk. 1959.

PUGAČ, G. V.: 'K voprosu o dialektičeskom xaraktere ponjatija' (On the Dialectical Character of the Concept). In *Voprosy teorii poznanija*. Perm'. 1960. 127–136.

PUPUNYROV, P. N.: 'O roli analogii v processe poznanija' (On the Role of Analogy in the Process of Knowledge). In *Voprosy logiki*. Leningrad. 1957. 117–130.

RAXUBO, P. G.: 'Ob osobennostjax sensualizma Dž. Lokka' (On the Peculiarities of Locke's Sensualism). In *Iz istorii filosofii*. Moskva. 1958.

RAJKOVA, D. D.: *Ponjatie v svete teorii otrazenija* (The Concept in the Light of the Theory of Reflection). M. oblastnoj Pg. In-t. 1953/54. (d)

RAZMYSLOV, P. I.: 'Vopros o prirode psixičeskogo v svete trudov klassikov marksizma' (The Problem of the Nature of the Psychic in the Light of the Works of the Classics of Marxism). *FN* 1962, 4, 101–105.

Redakcija *VF*:
(1) 'K itogam obsuždenija voprosov logiki' (Conclusion of the Discussion of Questions of Logic). *VF* 1951, 6, 143–149.
(2) Ot redakcii. *VF* 1955, 1, 145–149.
(3) 'Protiv putanicy i vulgarizacii v voprosax logiki' (Against Obscurantism and Vulgarization in Logic). *VF* 1955, 3, 158–171.
(4) 'Prospekt problemy "Edinstvo materialističeskoj dialektiki, logiki i teorii poznanija" ' (Outline of the Problem 'The Unity of the Materialist Dialectic, Logic and Theory of Knowledge'). *VF* 1955, 6, 239–244.
(5) Ot redakcii. *VF* 1962, 5, 160–161.

Redakcija *V MGU*:
(1) 'Diskussija po voprosu sootnošenija formal'noj logiki i dialektiki' (Discussion on the Relationship of Formal logic to Dialectics). *V MGU* 1951, 4, 145.
(2) 'Diskussija o predmete dialektičeskoj logiki' (Discussion on the Object of Dialectical Logic). *V MGU* 1957, 1, 169.

REJKOVSKIJ, JA.: 'K voprosu o fiziologičeskoj osnove i specifike ponjatij' (On the Physiological Basis and Specific Character of Concepts). In *Mirovozzrenčeskie i metodologičeskie problemy naučnoj abstrakcii*. Moskva. 1960. 241–301.

REVZIN, I. I.: 'Formal'naja teorija predloženija' (The Formal Theory of Propositions). In *Tezisy konferencii po masinnomu perevodu*. Moskva. 1958. 50–51.

REZNIKOV, L. O.:
(1) 'Problema obrazovanija ponjatij v svete istorii jazyka' (The Problem of the Formation of Concepts in the Light of the History of Language). In *Filosofskie zapiski I*. Moskva. 1946.
(2) 'Gnoseologičeskie osnovy svjazi myšlenija i jazyka' (The Epistemological

Bases of the Bonds of Thought and Language). In *Dialektičeskij materializm.* Leningrad. 1958. 136–163.

(3) 'K voprosu ob istinnosti ponjatij' (On the Truth-Value of Concepts). In *Voprosy logiki.* Leningrad. 1960. 42–65.

(4) 'Kritika reljativistskogo ponimanija slova' (Critique of the Relativist Conception of the Word). *V LGU* 1958, 5, 40.

(5) 'K voprosu o sootnošenii jazyka i myšlenija' (On the Relation of Language to Thought). *VF* 1947, 2, 184–204.

(6) 'O roli znakov v processe poznanija' (On the Role of Signs in the Process of Knowledge). *VF* 1961, 8, 118–132.

(7) 'Neopozitivistskaja gnoseologija i znakovaja teorija jazyka' (The Neopositivist Epistemology and the Sign-Theory of Language). *VF* 1962, 2, 99–109.

(8) 'Gnoseologija pragmatizma i semiotika Č. Morris' (The Epistemology of Pragmatism and Morris' Semiotics). *VF* 1963, 1, 102–114.

(9) 'O roli slova v obrazovanii ponjatija' (The Role of the Word in the Formation of the Concept). *FN* 1958, 1, 108–119.

(10) 'O knige F. F. Kal'sina "Osnovy voprosy teorii poznanija" ' (On F. F. Kal'sins Book *Basic Questions of Theory of Knowledge*). *FN* 1960, 2, 173–180.

(11) 'Antinaučnyj xarakter pragmatistskogo ponimanija znaka, značenija i predmeta' (The Anti-Scientific Character of the Pragmatist Conception of Sign, Meaning and Object). *FN* 1963, 1, 74–82.

RJAKIN, A. N.: *Ob otraženii kak obščem svojstve vsej materii* (On Reflection as a General Property of All Matter). Kaluga. 1958. 287 str.

ROMANOV, A. V.: *Kritika teorii indukcii Dž. St. Millja i ee filosofskix predposylok* (Critique of the Theory of Induction of J. S. Mill and of its Philosophic Presuppositions). MGU. 1953/54. (d)

ROŠKA, D. D.: 'K voprosu o ponjatii v gegelevskoj filosofii' (On the Concept in Hegelian Philosophy). In *Problemy filosofii.* Moskva. 1960. 223–232.

ROVENSKIJ, Z., UEMOV, A., UEMOVA, E.: *Mašina i mysl'* (Machine and Thought). Moskva. 1960. 143 str.

ROZENTAL', M. M.:

(1) *Razvitie V. I. Leninym marksistskoj teorii poznanija* (Lenin's Development of the Marxist Theory of Knowledge). Moskva. 1950.

(2) *Marksistskij dialektičeskij metod* (Marxist Dialectical Method). Moskva. 1947 (ed. 2, 1951).

(3) *Voprosy dialektiki v "Kapitale" Marksa* (Questions of Dialectic in Marx' *Capital*). Moskva. 1955.

(4) *Principy dialektičeskoj logiki* (Principles of Dialectical Logic). Moskva. 1960. 478 str.

(5) *Lenin i dialektika* (Lenin and the Dialectic). Moskva. 1963. 522 str.

(6) 'Marksistskaja teorija poznanija' (Marxist Theory of Knowledge). In *Kniga dlja čtenija po marksistskoj filosofii. Moskva. 1960.* 201–256.

(7) 'O dialektičeskoj logike' (On Dialectical Logic). *Ko* 1960, 11, 27–38.

(8) 'Materialističeskaja dialektika kak tvorčeski razvivajuščajasja nauka' (The Materialist Dialectic as a Creatively Developping Science). *VF* 1953, 4, 18–39.

(9) 'O roli naučnoj abstrakcii v poznanii' (On the Role of Scientific Abstraction in Knowledge). *VF* 1954, 2, 33–49.

(10) 'V. I. Lenin o zadačax i principax razrabotki dialektičeskoj logiki' (Lenin on the Tasks and Principles of the Elaboration of Dialectical Logic). *VF* 1955, 2, 33–48.

181

(11) 'Velikij vklad v marksistskuju theoriju poznanija' (Great Advance in Marxist Theory of Knowledge). *VF* 1959, 5, 18–32.

Rožin, V. P.:

(1) 'Neskol'ko zamečanij po spornym voprosam logiki' (Remarks on Disputed Questions of Logic). *VF* 1951, 4, 238–241.

(2) 'O materialističeskoj dialektike kak logika i teorii poznanija' (On the Materialist Dialectic as Logic and Theory of Knowledge). *V LGU* 1956, 5, 29–37.

Rubin, A. I.: 'O logičeskom učenii Aristotelja' (On the Logical Doctrine of Aristotle). *VF* 1955, 2, 194–199.

Rubinov, I. G.: 'Problema istinnosti ponjatij v svete leninskoj teorii otraženija' (The Problem of the Truth-Value of Concepts in the Light of the Leninist Theory of Reflection). In *Naučnye trudy* (Tomskij GU) Tomsk. 1960.

Rubinštejn, S. L.:

(1) *Osnovy obščej psixologii* (Principles of General Psychology). Moskva. 1940.

(2) *Bytie i soznanie* (Being and Consciousness). Moskva. 1957.

(3) *O myšlenii i putjax ego issledovanija* (On Thought and Paths of its Investigation). Moskva. 1958.

(4) *Principy i puti razvitija psixologii* (Principles and Paths of the Development of Psychology). Moskva. 1959.

(5) 'Učenie I. P. Pavlova i nekotorye voprosy perestrojki psixologii' (The Doctrine of I. P. Pavlov and some Questions of the Reconstruction of Psychology). *VF* 1952, 3, 197–210.

(6) 'Princip determinizma i psixologičeskaja teorija myšlenija' (The Principle of Determinism and the Psychological Theory of Thought). In *Psixologičeskaja nauka v SSSR*. Moskva. 1959. 315–356.

(8) 'Filosofija i psixologija' (Philosophy and Psychology). *VF* 1957, 1, 114–127.

Rudov, A. G.: 'Protiv dogmatizma. K voprosu o fiziologičeskoj osnove oščuščenij' (Against Dogmatism. On the Question of the Physiological Basis of Sensation). *VF* 1956, 6, 216–218.

Rutkevič, M. N.:

(1) *Praktika – osnova poznanija i kriterij istiny* (Practice as Basis of Knowledge and Criterion of Truth). Moskva. 1952. 243 str.

(2) *Dialektičeskij materializm*. Moskva. 1959. 598 str.

(3) 'Marksizm-leninizm o roli praktiki v poznanii' (Marxism-Leninism on the Role of Practice in Knowledge). In *Voprosy dialektičeskogo materializma*. Moskva. 1951. 212–238.

(4) 'Praktika kak kriterij istinnosti znanij' (Practice as Criterion of the Truth-Value of Knowledge). In *Praktika – kriterij istiny v nauke*. Moskva. 1960. 5–54.

(5) 'Formy dviženija materii, soznanie i kibernetika' (The Forms of Movement of Matter, Consciousness and Cybernetics). In *Filosofskie voprosy fiziki i ximii* (Philosophical Questions of Physics and Chemistry). Sverdlovsk. 1959. 63–72.

(6) 'K voprosu o roli praktiki v processe poznanija' (On the Role of Practice in the Process of Knowledge). *VF* 1954, 3, 34–45.

(7) 'Dialektičeskij xarakter kriterija praktiki' (The Dialectical Character of the Criterion Practice). *VF* 1959, 9, 43–52.

Ruzavin, G. I.: 'O xaraktere matematičeskoj abstrakcii' (On the Character of Mathematical Abstraction). *VF* 1960, 9, 143–154.

Sadovskij, V. N.:

(1) 'Kritika filosofii analiza' (Critique of the Philosophy of Analysis). *VF* 1961, 11, 169–172.

(2) 'Problemy metodologii deduktivnyx teorij' (Problems of the Methodology of Deductive Theories). *VF* 1963, 3, 63–75.

SADOVSKIJ, V. N., SMIRNOV, V. A.: 'Soveščanie po problemam logiki i metodologii nauk' (Meeting on Problems of Logic and Methodology of Sciences). *VF* 1960, 11, 153–158.

SADYXOV, G. M.: *Učenie o suždenii* (On Judgements). Azerbajdžanskij GU. 1953/54. (d)

SAFONOV, JU. F.: 'Sootnošenie otnositel'noj i absoljutnoj istiny i nekotorye zakonomernosti razvitija fizičeskix teorij' (The Relation of Absolute and Relative Truth and some Laws of the Development of Physical Theory). *FN* 1960, 3, 129–139.

SAGATOVSKIJ, V. N.:

(1) 'Razvitie V. I. Leninym učenija o roli praktiki v processe poznanija' (Lenin's Development of the Doctrine on the Role of Practice in the Process of Knowledge). In *Naučnye trudy* (Tomskij GU) Tomsk. 1960.

(2) 'K voprosu sootnošenii soderžanija ponjatija i opredelenija' (On the Relationship Between the Content of the Concept and the Definition). *V LGU* 1961, 17, 85–93.

(3) 'Čuvstvennye osnovy ponjatija' (Sense Foundations of the Concept). *VF* 1962, 1, 123–133.

(4) 'Ponjatie kak element i forma logičeskogo myšlenija' (The Concept as Element and Form of Logical Thought). *FN* 1961, 4, 78–86.

SANAJA, K. D.: *K ponimaniju ponjatija v svete dialektičeskogo materializma* (On the Concept of Concept in the Light of Dialectical Materialism). Tbilisskij GU. 1951/52. (d)

SARADŽJAN, V. X.: 'O edinstve dialektiki, logiki i teorii poznanija' (On the Unity of Dialectic, Logic and Theory of Knowledge). In *Naučnye trudy* (AN Gruzinskoj SSR) Tbilisi. 1960.

SATYBALOV, A. A.: 'V. I. Lenin ob otnošenii empiriokritikov k "naivnomu realizmu"' (Lenin on the Relationship Between Empirio-Criticists and 'Naive Realism'). *V LGU* 1960, 11, 77–85.

SAVEL'EV, M. N.: *Mesto i rol' dokazatel'stvo v sisteme logiki* (The Place and Role of Proof in the Logical System). IF. 1953/54. (d)

SAVINA, T. B.: 'Kritika sub"ektivno-idealističeskogo istolkovanija čuvstvennogo poznanija' (Critique of the Subjective-Idealist Interpretation of Sense-Knowledge). *V MGU* 1959, 3, 157–172.

SAVINOV, A. V.: *Logičeskie zakony myšlenija* (Logical Laws of Thought). Moskva. 1958. 369 str. (d)

SAZONOV, JA. V.: 'O processe dialektičeskogo obobščenija' (On the Process of Dialectical Generalization). *V MGU* 1960, 1, 67–78.

SEDOV, B. M.: *Marksistsko-leninskoe učenie ob istine* (The Marxist-Leninist Doctrine on Truth). M. gorodskoj Pg. In-t. 1953/54. (d)

SELIVANOV, F. A.:

(1) 'Gnoseologičeskie kategorii istinnogo i ložnogo v svete raboty V. I. Lenina "Materializm i empiriokriticizm"' (The Epistemological Categories of True and False in the Light of Lenin's *Materializm and Empirio-Criticism*). In *Naučnye trudy* (Tomskij GU). Tomsk. 1960.

(2) 'Ob'em i soderžanie gnoseologičeskoj kategorii ložnogo' (Extension and

Content of the Epistemological Category False). In *Učenye zapiski* (Tomskij GU). Tomsk. 1960.

SEMENČEV, V. M.: *Gipoteza i ee rol' v naučnom poznanii* (Hypothesis and its Role in Scientific Knowledge). Kiev. 1954. (d)

SEMENOV, JU. I.: 'V. I. Lenin o tvorčeskom xaraktere čelovečeskogo poznanija' (Lenin on the Creative Character of Human Knowledge). In *Učenye zapiski* (Krasnojarskij G. Pg. In-t) Krasnojarsk. 1960.

SEREBRJANNIKOV, O. F.:

(1) 'Osnovnye otnošenija meždu suždenijami, obuslovlennye svojstvami ix vnutrennej struktury' (Basic Relations Between Judgements, Conditioning the Properties of their Internal Structure). In *Voprosy logiki*. Leningrad. 1960. 115–141.

(2) 'O ponjatii logičeskogo sledovanija' (On the Concept of Logical Consequence). *V LGU* 1960, 23, 80–90.

SERŽANTOV, V. F.:

(1) 'Materialističeskoe ponimanie oščuščenij' (The Materialist Conception of Sensation). In *Dialektičeskij materializm*. Leningrad. 1958. 79–96.

(2) *Soznanie kak svojstvo mozga* (Consciousness as a Property of the Brain). LGU. 1953/54. (d)

SIDOROV, M. M.: 'O kategorii "ob"ektivnaja istina" ' (On the Category 'Objective Truth'). *V MGU* 1958, 2, 93.

SIKORSKIJ, V. M.: *Soderžanie ponjatija i suščnost' opredelenija v logike* (Content of the Concept and Essence of the Definition in Logic). Belorusskij GU. 1953/54. (d)

SITKOVSKIJ, E. P.: 'Lenin o sovpadenii v dialektičeskom materializme dialektiki, logiki i teorii poznanija' (Lenin on the Coincidence in Dialectical Materialism of the Dialectic, Logic and Theory of Knowledge). *VF* 1956, 2, 77–90.

SIVOKON', P. E.: 'O proisxoždenii i značenii estestvennonaučnogo eksperimenta' (On the Origin and Importance of the Experiment in Natural Science). *V MGU* 1957, 4, 43.

SKAJSGIRIS, R. P.: 'Metafizičeskij otryv racional'nogo ot čuvstvennogo v teorii poznanija Bertrana Rassela' (The Metaphysical Separation of Rational and Sensible in the Theory of Knowledge of Bertrand Russell). In *Kritika sovremennoj buržuaznoj filosofii i sociologii*. Moskva. 1961. 3–58.

SKOČELJAS, V. P.: *O poznavaemosti mira i ego zakonomernostej* (On the Knowability of the World and its Laws). AON. 1948/51. (d)

SKRYPNIK, V. D.: *Marksizm-leninizm o nerazryvnoj svjazi jazyka i myšlenija* (Marxism-Leninism on the Unbreakable Bonds Between Language and Thought). AON. 1953/54. (d)

SKVORCOV, A. P.: 'O dissertacii P. S. Koz'jakova na temu "O sootnošenii formal'noj i dialektičeskoj logiki" ' (On P. S. Koz'jakov's Dissertation *On the Relation of Formal and Dialectical Logic*). *V MGU* 1947, 5, 137.

SKVORCOV, L. V.:

(1) 'Razvitie V. I. Leninym marksistskogo ponimanija roli praktiki v poznanii (1906–1909 gg.) i nekotorye voprosy kritiki buržuaznoj filosofii' (Lenin's Development of the Marxist Concept of the Role of Practice in Knowledge (1906–1909) and some Questions of the Critique of Bourgeois Philosophy). In *Očerki po istorii filosofii v Rossii*. Moskva. 1960. 274–298.

(2) 'Nekotorye problemy marksistsko-leninskogo ponimanija praktiki i ee roli v

poznanii' (Some Problems of the Marxist-Leninist Conception of Practice and its Role in Knowledge). *FN* 1958, 1, 99–107.

(3) 'Značenie raboty V. I. Lenina "Materializm i empiriokriticizm" dlja marksistskogo rešenija problemy sootnošenija sub"ekta i ob"ekta' (Importance of Lenin's *Materialism and Empirio-Criticism* for the Marxist Solution of the Problem of the Relationship of Subject and Object). *FN* 1959, 1, 25–38.

SLADKOV, B. S.: *Vzaimootnošenie indukcii i dedukcii* (The Interrelationship of Induction and Deduction). MGU. 1953/54. (d)

SLAVNOVA, L. V.: *V. I. Lenin i I. V. Stalin o roli naučnyx ponjatij v poznanii* (Lenin and Stalin on the Role of Scientific Concepts in Knowledge). IF. 1951/52. (d)

SLAVSKAJA, K. A.: 'Process myšlenija i ispol'zovanie znanij' (The Process of Thought and the Use of Knowledge). In *Process myšlenija...*(s. MATJUŠKIN, A. M.) 5–48.

SMARAGDOV, A. D.: 'Fiziologičeskie osnovy obraza u čeloveka' (The Physiological Basis of the Image in Man). *V MGU* 1958, 3, 117.

SMIRNOV, A. A.: 'Leninskaja teorija otraženija i psixologija' (The Leninist Theory of Reflection and Psychology). *VP* 1960, 2, 10.

SMIRNOV, L. V.: 'Ob odnoj raznovidnosti ponjatij' (On one Type of Concept). *V LGU* 1958, 23, 128.

SMIRNOV, V. A.:

(1) 'Rol' simvolizacii i formalizacii v naučnom poznanii' (The Role of Symbolization and Formalization in Scientific Knowledge). In *Naučnye trudy* (Tomskij GU) Tomsk. 1960.

(2) 'Ser'eznye ošibki v traktovke marksistskoj teorii poznanija' (Serious Errors in the Treatment of Marxist Theory of Knowledge). *VF* 1958, 9, 169–174.

(3) 'Kategorii kategoričeskogo sillogizma' (Categories of the Categorical Syllogism). *FN* 1959, 3, 80–83.

SMIRNOV, E. D.: 'Neopozitivistskaja koncepcija analitičeskogo i sintetičeskogo znanija v svete leninskoj kritiki maxizma' (The Neo-positivist Conception of Analytic and Synthetic Knowledge in the Light of the Leninist Critique of Machism). In *Naučnye trudy* (Tomskij GU). Tomsk. 1960.

SOBOLEV, S. L., KITOV, A. I., LJAPUNOV, A. A.: 'Osnovnye čerty kibernetiki' (Basic Traits of Cybernetics). *VF* 1955, 4, 136–148.

SOBOLEV, S. L., LJAPUNOV, A. A.: 'Kibernetika i estestvoznanie' (Cybernetics and Natural Science). *VF* 1958, 5, 127–138.

SOKOLOV, E. N.: *Vosprijatie i uslovnyj refleks* (Perception and the Conditioned Reflex). Moskva. 1958.

SOKOLOV, V. V.:

(1) 'Racionalizm XVII veka i teorija poznanija Spinozy' (Rationalism of the Seventeenth Century and Spinoza's Theory of Knowledge). *V MGU* 1962, 5, 64–74.

(2) 'Kniga, razoblačajuščaja amerikanskij pragmatizm' (A Book, Destroying American Pragmatism). *VF* 1955, 1, 180–184.

(3) 'Mifilogičeskoe i naučnoe myšlenie' (Mythological and Scientific Thought). *VF* 1958, 10, 158–163.

SOLGALOV, G. V.: 'O dialektičeskix protivorečijax v logičeskom poznanii' (On Dialectical Contradictions in Logical Thought). *V MGU* 1961, 3, 55–66.

Sovremennyj sub"ektivnyj idealizm (Contemporary Subjective Idealism). Moskva. 1957.

Sovremennye religiozno-filosofskie tečenija v kapitalističeskix stranax (Contemporary Religious-Philosophic Currents in Capitalist Countries). Moskva. 1962. 260 str.

SOXIN, F. A.: 'Soveščanie po voprosam psixologii poznanija' (Meeting on Questions of the Psychology of Knowledge). *VP* 1957, 3, 184.

SPASOV, D.: 'Dialektičeskuju logiku nado ne otricat', a razrabatyvat' (One Must not Deny Dialectical Logic but Develop it!). *VF* 1951, 2, 182–184.

SPIRKIN, A.:

(1) *Proisxoždenie soznanija* (The Origin of Consciousness). Moskva. 1960.

(2) 'Problema oščuščenija v leninskoj teorii otraženija' (The Problem of Sensation in the Leninist Theory of Reflection). In *Voprosy dialektičeskogo materializma* Moskva. 1951. 273–295.

(3) 'Proisxoždenie jazyka i ego rol' v formirovanii myšlenija' (The Origin of Language and its Role in the Formation of Thought). In *Myšlenie i jazyk.* Moskva. 1957. 3–72.

(4) 'K voprosu o zakonax jazyka' (On the Laws of Language). *VF* 1953, 5, 89–106.

(5) 'Formirovanie abstraktnogo myšlenija na rannix stupenjax razvitija čeloveka' (The Formation of Abstract Thought in the Earlier Stages of the Development of Man). *VF* 1954, 5, 62–76.

(6) 'O prirode soznanija' (On the Nature of Consciousness). *VF* 1961, 6, 118–127.

STARČENKO, A. A.: *Rol' analogii v poznanii* (The Role of Analogy in Knowledge). Moskva. 1961. 51 str.

STEMPKOVSKAJA, V. I.:

(1) *O roli abstrakcij v poznanii* (On the Role of Abstraction in Knowledge). Moskva. 1959. 110 str.

(2) 'O gibkosti i opredelennosti ponjatij' (On the Plasticity and Definiteness of Concepts). *VF* 1952, 5, 190–200.

(3) *Leninskaja kritika formal'noj logiki* (The Leninist Critique of Formal Logic). IF. 1948/51. (d)

STEMPKOVSKAJA, V. I., TAVANEC, P. V.: 'Razdelitel'noe i uslovnoe umozaključenija. Umozaključenija otnošenij' (Disjunctive and Conditional Reasonings. Reasonings of Relation). In *Logika.* Moskva. 1956. 154–167.

STJAŽKIN, N. I.:

(1) 'O dialektičeskoj prirode suščnosti i metodov ustranenija paradoksov logiki' (On the Dialectical Nature of the Essence and Methods of Elimination of the Paradoxes of Logic). *V MGU* 1957, 4, 87.

(2) 'O logičeskix paradoksax i ix otnošenii k dialektičeskim protivorečijam' (On Logical Paradoxes and Their Relation to Dialectical Contradictions). *VF* 1958, 1, 145–147.

STROGOVIČ, M. S.: 'O predmete formal'noj logiki' (On the Object of Formal Logic). *VF* 1950, 3, 309–317.

SUBBOTIN, A. L.:

(1) 'Principy gnoseologii Lokka' (Principles of Locke's Epistemology). *VF* 1955, 2, 105–117.

(2) 'O cepjax klassičeskix sillogizmov' (On the Bonds of the Classical Syllogisms). *FN* 1959, 3, 89–95.

(3) 'Matematičeskaja logika – stupen' v razvitii formal'noj logiki' (Mathematical Logic as a Stage in the Development of Formal Logic). *VF* 1960, 9, 93–99.

(4) *Priroda abstrakcii i obščestvennaja praktika* (The Nature of Abstraction and Social Practice). MGU. 1953/54. (d)

SUDARIKOV, A. A.: *Klassiki marksizma-leninizma o roli analogii v naučnom poznanii*

(The Classics of Marxism-Leninism on the Role of Analogy in Scientific Knowledge). MGU. 1953/54. (d)

SUL'ŽENKO, G. D.:
(1) 'Istina i kriterij istiny v fenomenologii' (Truth and the Criterion of Truth in Phenomenology). In *Praktika – kriterij istiny v nauke*. Moskva. 1960. 419–443.
(2) 'Marksistskij trud po teorii poznanija' (Marxist Work on Theory of Knowledge). *VF* 1956, 4, 205–209.

SUŠKO, N. JA.: 'Genial'nyj vklad v teoriju poznanija marksizma' (Tremendous Advance in the Theory of Knowledge of Marxism). In *Naučnye trudy* (Voenno-političeskaja akademija) Tom 29. Moskva. 1960.

SUVOROV, S. G.:
(1) 'Leninskaja teorija poznanija – filosofskaja osnova razvitija fiziki' (The Leninist Theory of Knowledge as the Philosophic Basis of the Development of Physics). *UFN* 39 (1949), 3.
(2) 'O roli eksperimenta i teorii v poznanii' (On the Role of the Experiment and Theory in Knowledge). *UFN* 66 (1958). 375–390.

SUXANOV, I. V.: 'Praktika – osnova poznanija i ob"ektivnyj kriterij istiny' (Practice as the Basis of Knowledge and the Objective Criterion of Truth). In *Naučnye trudy* (Kazanskij aviacionnyj In-t) Kazan'. 1960.

SUXOV, A. D.:
(1) 'Gnoseologičeskie korni religii' (The Epistemological Roots of Religion). *FN* 1958, 4, 102–112.
(2) *Social'nye i gnoseologičeskie korni religii* (The Social and Epistemological Roots of Religion). IF. 1959. (d)

SUXOV, G. S.: *O konkretnosti istiny* (On the Concreteness of Truth). *AN USSR*. 1953/54. (d)

SVINCOV, V. I.: *Dokazatel'stvo ego mesto i rol' v processe poznanija* (Proof: Its Place and Role in the Process of Knowledge). M. gorodskoj Pg. In-t. 1953/54. (d)

ŠAFF, A.: ' "Sociologija znanija" Manngejma i problema ob"ektivnoj istiny' (The 'Sociology of Knowledge' of Mannheim and the Problem of Objective Truth). *VF* 1956, 4, 118–128.

ŠAROVATOV, N. P.: *O marksistskoj dialektike kak edinstvenno naučnom metode poznanija* (On the Marxist Dialectic as the Unique Scientific Method of Knowledge). MGU. 1951/52. (d)

ŠAŠKEVIC, P. D.:
(1) *Teorija poznanija Immanuila Kanta* (Theory of Knowledge of Immanuel Kant). Moskva. 1960. 304 str.
(2) 'K voprosu o formirovanii gnoseologičeskix vzgljadov Kanta' (On the Formation of the Epistemological Views of Kant). In *Iz istorii filosofii*. Moskva. 1957.

ŠAULOV, D. D.: *Predstavlenie i ponjatie* (Representation and Concept). MGU. 1953/54. (d)

ŠAUMJAN, S. K.: 'Lingvističeskie problemy kinerbetiki i strukturnaja linguistics' (Linguistic Problems of Cybernetics and Structural Linguistics). *VF* 1960, 9, 120–131.

ŠČEDROVICKIJ, G. P.: 'O nekotoryx momentax v razvitii ponjatij' (On some Moments in the Development of Concepts). *VF* 1958, 6, 55–64.

ŠČURENKOVA, A. I.: 'O nekotoryx zakonomernostjax vozniknovenija i razvitija nervnoj sistemy v svete marksistsko-leninskoj teorii otraženija' (Some Laws of the Origin and Development of the Nervous System in the Light of the Marxist-Leninist Theory of Reflection). In *Naučnye trudy* (Stalinabadskij G. medicinskij In-t). Stalinabad. 1960.

ŠEJKO, A. N.:
(1) *Stroenie i pravila dokazatel'stva* (The Structure and Rules of Proof). KGU. 1953/54. (d)

(2) *Pravila logičeskogo dokazatel'stva* (Rules of Logical Proof). Kiev. 1956. 106 str.

ŠEPTULIN, A., ORGANOVA, L.: *Vzaimosvjaz' edinilnogo i obščego v naučnom i v xudožestvennom poznanii* (The Interrelation of Singular and General in Scientific and Artistic Knowledge). Krasnojarsk. 1957.

ŠOROXOVA, E. V.:
(1) *Problema soznanija v filosofii i estestvoznanii* (The Problem of Consciousness in Philosophy and Natural Science). Moskva. 1961. 363 str.

(2) 'Učenie I. P. Pavlova o signal'nyx sistemax v svete leninskoj teorii otraženija' (I. P. Pavlov's Doctrine on Signal Systems in the Light of the Leninist Theory of Reflection). *VF* 1952, 3, 104–116.

ŠTOFF, V. A.:
(1) 'K voprosu o roli model'nyx predstavlenij v naučnom poznanii' (On the Role of Modelling Representations in Scientific Knowledge). In *Dialektičeskij materializm*. Leningrad. 1958. 117–135.

(2) 'O roli modelej v kvantovoj mexanike' (On the Role of Models in Quantum Mechanics). *VF* 1958, 12, 67–79.

(3) 'Gnoseologičeskie funkcii modeli' (The Epistemological Functions of the Model). *VF* 1961, 12, 53–65.

ŠUBINA, G. P.: 'V. I. Lenin o sootnošenii ob"ektivnoj, absoljutnoj i otnositel'noj istiny v estestvoznanii' (Lenin on the Relationship of Objective, Absolute and Relative Truth in Natural Science). In *Naučnye trudy* (Xabarovskij In-t inženerov železnodorožnogo transporta). Xabarovsk. 1960.

ŠUR, E. B.: 'Učenie o ponjatii v formal'noj i dialektičeskoj logike' (Doctrine on Concept in Formal and Dialectical Logic). *VF* 1958, 3, 71–80.

ŠVYREV, V. S.:
(1) 'Kritika neo-pozitivistskoj koncepcii induktivnoj logiki' (Critique of the Neo-positivist Conception of Inductive Logic). *VF* 1961, 3, 74–85.

(2) 'Krušenie neopozitivistskoj koncepcii naučno-teoretičeskogo znanija' (Collapse of the Neo-positivist Conception of Scientific-Theoretical Knowledge). *VF* 1963, 7, 97–109.

(3) 'K voprosu o putjax logičeskogo issledovanija myšlenija' (On the Paths of Logical Investigation of Thought). *Doklady APN RSFSR* 1960, 2.

TARXOVA, M. A.:
(1) 'V. I. Lenin o roli praktiki v poznanii' (Lenin on the Role of Practice in Knowledge). In *Kniga* ... (s. Alekseev, G. P.) 246–272.

(2) *Razvitie I. V. Stalinym marksistsko-leninskogo učenija o praktike* (Stalin's Development of the Marxist-Leninist Doctrine on Practice). M. oblastnoj Pg. In-t. 1951/52. (d)

TATULOV, G.: *Vvedenie v teoriju poznanija dialektičeskogo materializma* (Introduction to Diamat's Epistemology). Moskva-Leningrad. 1930.

TAVADZE, I. K., KALANDARIŠVILI, G. M.: *V. I. Lenin o "Nauke logiki" Gegelja* (Lenin on Hegel's *Science of Logic*). Tbilisi. 1959. 313 str.

TAVANEC, P. V.:

(1) *Suždenie i ego vidy* (Judgement and its Types). Moskva. 1953. 176 str.
(2) *Voprosy teorii suždenija* (Questions of Theory of Judgement). Moskva. 1955. 194 str. (d)
(3) 'K voprosu o klassifikacii suždenij v istorii logiki' (On the Classification of Judgements in the History of Logic). In *Filosofskie zapiski VI*. Moskva. 1953. 38–70.
(4) 'Ob idealističeskoj kritike aristotelevskoj teorii suždenija' (On the Idealist Critique of the Aristotelian Theory of Judgement). *Izvestija AN SSSR* 1947, 4, 324–330.
(5) 'O vidax suždenija' (On Types of Judgement). *Izvestija AN SSSR* 1950, 1, 69–84.
(6) 'Kritika istolkovanija prirody suždenija logikoj otnošenij' (Critique of the Interpretation of the Nature of Judgement in the Logic of Relations). *Izvestija AN SSSR* 1950, 4, 360–372.
(7) 'Suždenie i predloženie' (Judgement and Proposition). *Izvestija AN SSSR* 1951, 2, 155–164.
(8) 'Uslovnoe suždenie' (Conditional Judgement). *Izvestija AN SSSR* 1952, 2, 165–176.
(9) 'Protiv idealističeskogo istolkovanija prirody suždenija' (Against the Idealist Interpretation of the Nature of the Judgement). *VF* 1948, 1, 150–171.
(10) 'Ob ob"ektivnom soderžanii zakonov formal'noj logiki' (On the Objective Content of the Laws of Formal Logic). *VF* 1953, 3, 34–45.
(11) 'O strukture dokazatel'stva' (On the Structure of Proof). *VF* 1956, 6, 69–75.
(12) 'Ob istinnosti ponjatij' (On the Truth-Value of Concepts). *VF* 1959, 12, 110–119.
TAVANEC, P. V., ŠVYREV, V. S.: 'Nekotorye problemy logiki naučnogo poznanija' (Some Problems of the Logic of Scientific Knowledge). *VF* 1962, 10, 10–21.
TERENT'EVA, Ju. A.: *Bor'ba Lenina protiv neokantianskoj revizii marksizma v Rossii* (Lenin's Fight Against the Neo-Kantian Revision of Marxism in Russia). AON. 1948/51. (d)
TEVOSJAN, A. M.: *Obrazovanie ponjatija kak problema logiki* (Formation of the Concept as a Logical Problem). MGU. 1953/54. (d)
TITARENKO, A. I.: 'Krivoe zerkalo pragmatistskoj fal'sifikacii' The Trick Mirror of Pragmatist Falsification). *V MGU* 1961, 1, 71–83.
TITARENKO, V. E.: *Materializm Demokrita* (The Materialism of Democritus). Moskva. 1953. 192 str. (d)
TJUXTIN, V. S.:
(1) *O prirode obraza* (On the Nature of the Image). Moskva. 1963. 122 str.
(2) 'K probleme obraza' (On the Problem of the Image). *VF* 1959, 6, 137–148.
(3) 'O suščnosti otraženija' (On the Essence of Reflection). *VF* 1962, 5, 59–71.
TONDL', L.: 'O poznavatel'noj roli abstrakcii' (On the Cognitive Role of Abstraction). In *Mirovozzrenčeskie i metodologičeskie problemy naučnoj abstrakcii*. Moskva. 1960. 119–152.
TONOJAN, G. A.: *Predmet logiki* (The Object of Logic). Tbilisskij GU. 1953/54. (d)
TOPČIEV, G. A.: *Edinstvo nauki i praktiki – mogučij istočnik progressa* (The Unity of Science and Practice as Mighty Stimulus of Progress). Moskva. 1950.
TOPORKOV, A. K.: *Elementy dialektičeskoj logiki* (Elements of Dialectical Logic). Moskva. 1928.
TRAXTENBERG, O. V.: *Očerki po istorii zapadnoevropejskoj srednovekovoj filosofii* (Essays on the History of West-European Medieval Philosophy). Moskva. 1957.

TROFIMOV, P. S.:
(1) 'Voprosy materialističeskoj dialektiki i teorii poznanija v "Kapitale" K. Marksa' (Questions of the Materialist Dialectic and Theory of Knowledge in Marx' *Capital*). In *Voprosy dialektičeskogo materializma*. Moskva. 1951. 81–116.
(2) 'Reakcionnaja suščnost' semantičeskoj filosofii' (The Reactionary Essence of Semantic Philosophy). *B* 1954, 5, 60.
(3) 'Obsuždenie knig M. Leonova i M. Rozentalja o marksistskom dialektičeskom metode' (Discussion of the Books by M. Leonov and M. Rozental' on the Marxist Dialectical Method). *VF* 1948, 1, 293–296.

TUGARINOV, V. P.:
(1) *Zakony ob"ektivnogo mira, ix poznanie i ispol'zovanie* (The Laws of the Objective World: Knowledge and Use of them). Leningrad. 1954.
(2) 'Marksizm-leninizm ob istine' (Marxism-Leninism on Truth). In *Voprosy dialektičeskogo materializma*. Moskva. 1951. 190–211.
(3) 'O edinstve dialektiki, logiki i teorii poznanija' (On the Unity of Dialectic, Logic and Theory of Knowledge). In *Materialy vsesojuznogo soveščanija zavedujuščix kafedrami obščestvennyx nauk*. Moskva. 1958. 302–317.
(4) 'O zakonax ob"ektivnogo mira i zakonax nauki' (On the Laws of the Objective World and the Laws of Science). *VF* 1952, 4, 78–92.

TUGARINOV, V. P., MAJSTROV, L. E.: 'Protiv idealizma v matematičeskoj logike' (Against Idealism in Mathematical Logic). *VF* 1950, 3, 331–339.

Učenie I. P. Pavlova i filosofskie voprosy psixologii (The Doctrine of I. P. Pavlov and Philosophic Questions of Psychology). R. S. A. Petruševskij, N. N. Ladygina-Kots, F. N. Šemjakin, E. V. Šoroxova. Ss. (IF). Moskva. 1952. 474 str.

UEMOV, A. I.: *Logičeskie ošibki* (Logical Errors). Moskva. 1958.

UKRAINCEV, B. S.:
(1) 'O suščnosti elementarnogo otobraženija' (On the Essence of Elementary Reflection). *VF* 1960, 2, 63–76.
(2) 'Informacija i otraženie' (Information and Reflection), *VF* 1963, 2, 26–38.

UVAROV, A. I.:
(1) 'K voprosu o prirode logičeskoj posledovatel'nosti' (On the Nature of Logical Consequence). In *Učenye zapiski* (Tomskij GU). Tomsk. 1960.
(2) 'O gnoseologičeskoj suščnosti sofistiki' (On the Epistemological Essence of Sophistry). *FN* 1958, 4, 135–144.

VAL'D, G.: 'Fal'sifikacija kategorii istiny v sovremennoj buržuaznoj filosofii' (Falsification of the Category Truth in Contemporary Bourgeois Philosophy). In *Problemy filosofii*. Moskva. 1960. 155–171.

VAR'JAŠ, A. I.: *Logika i dialektika* (Logic and Dialectic). Moskva-Leningrad. 1928.

VARTANJAN, G. M.: *Razvitie V. I. Leninym marksistskoj teorii otraženija* (Lenin's Development of the Marxist Theory of Reflection). Erevan. 1960.

VARTAPETJAN, K. B.: *O nekotoryx osnovnyx voprosax marksistsko-leninskoj gnoseologii* (On some Basic Questions of Marxist-Leninist Epistemology). Erevan. 1963. 331 str.

VASECKIJ, G. S.: *O knige V. I. Lenina "Materializm i empiriokriticizm"* (On Lenin's *Materialism and Empirio-Criticism*). Moskva. 1953.

VEKKER, L. M., LOMOV, B. F.: 'O čuvstvennoj obraze kak izobraženii' (On the Sense-Image as a Reflection). *VF* 1961, 4, 47–59.

VESELOVSKAJA, L. D.: *Nekotorye voprosy teorii suždenija* (Some Questions of Theory of Judgement). IF. 1951/52. (d)

VETROV, A. A.:
(1) 'Rasčlennost' formy kak osnovnoe svojstvo ponjatija' (Distributability of the Form as the Basic Property of the Concept). *VF* 1958, 1, 39–46.
(2) 'O semantičeskom ponjatii istiny' (On the Semantic Concept of Truth). *VF* 1962, 9, 63–74.

VETROV, A. A., ORLOV, V. V.: 'Protiv diskreditacii metoda materialističeskoj dialektiki' (Against Discrediting the Method of the Materialist Dialectic). *VF* 1961, 12, 151–155.

VIEVSKIJ, A. F.: *Voprosy istiny v rabote V. I. Lenina "Materializm i empiriokriticizm"* (Questions of Truth in Lenin's *Materialism and Empirio-Criticism*). Kiev. 1951/52. (d)

VJAKKEREV, F. F.: 'K voprosu o stupenjax poznanija ob''ektivnogo protivorečija' (On the Steps in the Knowledge of Objective Contradiction). In *Voprosy teorii poznanija*. Perm'. 1960. 48–57.

VLADIMIROVA, A. I.: 'Protiv idealističeskoj fal'sifikacii dialektiki' (Against Idealist Falsification of the Dialectic). *VF* 1957, 1, 162–173.

VOJŠVILLO, E. K.:
(1) 'K voprosu o predmete logiki' (On the Object of Logic). In *Voprosy logiki*. Moskva. 1955. 3–31.
(2) 'Kritika logiki otnošenij kak reljativistskogo napravlenija v logike' (Critique of the Logic of Relations as a Relativist Tendency in Logic). In *Filosofskie zapiski VI*. Moskva. 1953. 133–187.
(3) *Idem*. AON. 1948/51. (d)

VOJTONIS, N.: *Predistorija intellekta* (Pre-History of the Intellect). Moskva-Leningrad. 1949.

VOLČKOV, M. I.: 'K voprosu ob analize i sinteze' (On Analysis and Synthesis). In *Učenye zapiski* (Kujbyševskij G. Pg. In-t.) Kujbyšev. 1960.

VOLOVIK, L. A.: 'V. I. Lenin ob istine i ee konkretnosti' (Lenin on Truth and its Concreteness). In *Velikoe proizvedenie marksistskoj filosofii*. Novosibirsk. 1960.

Voprosy dialektičeskogo i istoričeskogo materializma v trude I. V. Stalina "Marksizm i voprosy jazykoznanija" (Questions of Dialectical and Historical Materialism in I. V. Stalin's Work *Marxism and Questions of Linguistics*). Ss. (IF). Moskva. Vyp. 1: 1951. 256 str. Vyp. 2: 1952. 318 str.

Voprosy logiki (Problems of Logic). Leningrad. 1957.
Voprosy logiki (Problems of Logic). Leningrad. 1959.
Voprosy logiki (Problems of Logic). Leningrad. 1960.
Voprosy teorii poznanija (Problems of Theory of Knowledge). Perm'. 1960.
Voprosy teorii poznanija i logiki (Problems of Theory of Knowledge and Logic). Moskva. 1960.

VOROB'EV, M. F.: 'Zakon perexoda količestva i kačestvo v logike Gegelja' (The Law of Transition from Quantity to Quality in Hegel's Logic). *V LGU* 1959, 11, 52–60.

VOSTRIKOV, A. V.:
(1) 'Voprosy teorii poznanija v trudax I. V. Stalina' (Questions of Theory of Knowledge in Stalin's Works). In *Voprosy marksistsko-leninskoj filosofii*. Moskva. 1950. 148–185.
(2) *Idem*. *VF* 1949, 2, 184–204.
(3) 'Materija i soznanie' (Matter and Consciousness). In *Dialektičeskij materializm*. Moskva. 1960. 87–138.
(4) 'Teorija poznanija dialektičeskogo materializma' (The Theory of Knowledge of Dialectical Materialism). In *Ibid*. 296–365.

(5) 'Razvitie Leninym marksistskoj teorii poznanija' (Lenin's Development of the Marxist Theory of Knowledge). In *Velikaja sila leninskix idej* (The Great Power of Leninist Ideas). Moskva. 1960. 145–177.

(6) 'Klassiki marksizma-leninizma o svjazi jazyka i myšlenija' (The Classics of Marxism-Leninism on the Bonds Between Language and Thought. *VF* 1952, 3, 47–64.

XAČATURJAN, A. B.: 'V. I. Lenin o dialektike ponjatij' (Lenin on the Dialectic of Concepts). In *Naučnye trudy* (M. G. Pg. In-t). Moskva. 1960.

XASXAČIX, F. I.:

(1) *O poznavaemosti mira* (On the Knowability of the World). Moskva. 1946. (second edition: Moskva. 1950).

(2) *Materija i soznanie* (Matter and Consciousness). Moskva. 1951.

XOREV, N. V.: 'K voprosu o dialektike processa poznanija' (On the Dialectic of the Process of Knowledge). In *Učenye zapiski* (M. gorodskoj Pg. In-t). Moskva. 1957.

XVAN DJAN EN: *Marksizm-leninizm o roli praktiki v processe poznanija* (Marxism-Leninism on the Role of Practice in the Process of Knowledge). MGU. 1953/53. (d)

ZABOTIN, V. V.: 'Problema voprosa i otveta v logike' (The Problem of Question and Answer in Logic). *FN* 1961, 1, 68–76.

ZAIČENKO, G. A.: 'K voprosu o skepticizme v teorii poznanija D. Lokka' (On Scepticism in Locke's Theory of Knowledge). *FN* 1959, 4, 123–131.

ZAKARŽEVSKIJ, L. K.: *K voprosu o roli čuvstvennyx vosprijatij v processe poznanija* (On the Role of Sense-Perception in the Process of Knowledge). IF. 1948/51. (d)

ZINOV'EV, A. A.:

(1) 'O razrabotke dialektiki kak logiki' (On the Elaboration of the Dialectic as a Logic). *VF* 1957, 4, 188–190.

(2) 'Sledovanie kak svojstvo vyskazyvanij o svjazjax' (Consequence as a Property of Statements on Bonds). *FN* 1959, 3, 84–88.

(3) 'K opredeleniju ponjatija svjazi' (On the Definition of the Concept of Bond). *VF* 1960, 8, 58–66.

ZINOVEV, A. A., REVZIN, I. I.: 'Logičeskaja model' kak sredstvo naučnogo issledovanija' (The Logical Model as a Means of Scientific Investigation). *VF* 1960, 1, 82–90.

ZOZULJA, A. M.: *Ob otnošenii meždu dokazatel'stvami i umozaključenijami v svete trudov klassikov marksizma-leninizma* (On the Relationship Between Proof and Reasoning in the Light of the Works of the Classics of Marxism-Leninism). MGU. 1953/54. (d)

ZVEGINCEV, V. A.: 'Neo-pozitivizm i novejšie lingvističeskie napravlenija' (Neo-positivism and Recent Linguistic Currents). *VF* 1961, 12, 92–101.

ZVONOV, L.: 'O knige M. Leonova "Marksistskij dialektičeskij metod"' (On M. Leonov's *Marxist Dialectical Method*). *B* 1947, 23, 65–72.

ŽELNOV, M. V.: 'Neotomizm i filosofija Kanta' (Neo-Thomism and the Philosophy of Kant). *V MGU* 1961, 5, 65–79.

ŽOŽA, AT.: 'O nekotoryx storonax dialektičeskoj logiki' (Some Aspects of Dialectical Logic). In *Problemy filosofii*. Moskva. 1960. 193–222.

ŽUKOVA, I. M.: 'Rol' analiza i obobščenija v poznavatel'noj dejatel'nosti' (The Role of Analysis and Generalization in Cognitive Activity). In *Process myslenija* ... (s. MATJUŠKIN, A. M.) 49–72.

WESTERN WORKS

ACTON, H. B.: *The Illusion of the Epoch. Marxism-Leninism as a Philosophical Creed.* London. 1955.

AHLBERG, R.: *'Dialektische Philosophie' und der Gesellschaft in der Sowjetunion.* Berlin. 1960.

BALLESTREM, K. G.: 'Soviet Historiography of Philosophy'. *Studies in Thought* III (1963) 107–120.

Bibliographie der Sowjetischen Philosophie. I–IV. Dordrecht, Holland. 1959–1963.

BLAKELEY, T. J.: *Soviet Scholasticism.* Dordrecht, Holland. 1961.

BOCHEŃSKI, J. M.:
(1) *Europäische Philosophie der Gegenwart.* Bern. 1947. (2nd edition: 1951). English: *Contemporary European Philosophy.* Berkeley. 1956.
(2) *Einführung in die sowjetischen Philosophie der Gegenwart.* Bonn. 1959.
(3) *Formale Logik.* Freiburg–München. 1962.
(4) *Der sowjetrussische dialektische Materialismus* (Diamat). Bern. 1960. English: *Soviet Russian Dialectical Materialism (Diamat).* Dordrecht, Holland. 1963.

BOESELAGER, W. F.: 'Recent Soviet Works on Neopositivism'. In *Studies in Soviet Thought* III (1963) 230–242, IV (1964) 80–83.

CASSIRER, E.: *Das Erkenntnisproblem in der Philosophie der Wissenschaft der neueren Zeit.* Berlin. 1922.

CORNFORD, F. M.: *Plato's Theory of Knowledge.* London. 1960.

FINDLAY, J. N.: *Hegel. A Re-examination.* London. 1958.

FLEISCHER, H.:
(1) 'The Limits of "Party-mindedness"'. *Studies in Soviet Thought* II (1962) 119–131.
(2) 'Die Idee der historischen Notwendigkeit im historischen Materialismus'. *Studies in Soviet Thought* II (1962) 181–203.
(3) 'Auf dem Bauplatz der materialistischen Dialektik'. *Studies in Soviet Thought* II (1962) 269–288.

JORAVSKY, D.: *Soviet Marxism and Natural Science 1917–1932.* London. 1961.

KLINE, G. L.: *Spinoza in Soviet Philosophy.* New York–London. 1952.

LOBKOWICZ, N.: *Das Widerspruchsprinzip in der neueren sowjetischen Philosophie.* Dordrecht, Holland. 1959.

SCHNEIDER, F.: *Die Hauptprobleme der Erkenntnistheorie.* München–Basel. 1959.

VRIES, J. de: *Die Erkenntnistheorie des dialektischen Materialismus.* München, 1958.

WETTER, G. A.:
(1) *Sowjetideologie heute I.* Frankfurt. 1962.
(2) *Dialectical Materialism. A Historical and Systematic Survey of Philosophy in the Soviet Union.* London. 1958.
(3) *Philosophie und Naturwissenschaft in der Sowjetunion.* Hamburg. 1958.

ZENKOVSKY, V. V.: *A History of Russian Philosophy.* London. 1953. (2 vols.)

INDEX OF NAMES

Abašev-Konstantinovskij, A. P. 146
Abelard 100
Abdil'din, Z. 146
Abramjan, L. A. 146
Ackerman, W. 108
Acton, H. B. 27, 193
Afanasev, V. G. 146
Ahlberg, R. 9, 193
Akperov, M. S. 86, 146
Albrecht, E. 174
Aleksandrov, A. D. 23
Aleksandrov, G. F. 89, 147, 156
Aleksandrova, S. E. 147
Alekseev, G. P. 147
   63, 66, 89, 108, 145, 147
Alekseev, V. I. 148
Anan'ev, B. G. 7, 50, 64, 77, 148
Anciferova, L. I. 148
Andreev, I. D. 4, 6, 27, 42, 45, 46, 47,
   49, 50, 51, 55, 57, 60, 64, 65, 66, 70,
   76, 77, 78, 88, 148
Andrjuščenko, M. N. 148
Angelelli, I. 139
Anisimov, S. F. 148
Anoxin, P. K. 45, 149
Anselm 114
Antonov, M. P. 149
Antonov, N. P. 149
Aquinas, T. 92, 108, 113, 114, 120, 123,
   132, 134, 135, 139, 165
Arisjan, L. 4, 149
Aristotle 1, 15, 35, 99, 110, 112, 113,
   120, 121, 135, 150, 176, 182
Artanovskij, S. N. 149
Artemov, V. A. 149
Arxangel'skij, L. M. 7, 8, 149
Arxipcev, F. T. 149
Arzamazov, V. P. 149
Asatiani, G. M. 149
Aseev, Ju.A 138, 139, 149
Askinadze, Ja.F. 150
Asmus, V. F. 8, 108, 138, 150, 176
Aszatjan, E. A. 7, 150
Augustine 110, 113, 121
Averroes 114, 120

Avicenna 114, 120
Axmanov, A. S. 150
Axmedov, E. K. 150
Axmedov, M. M. 151
Axundov, M. A. 151
Ayer, A. J. 123

Babajanc, M. S. 151
Babosov, E. M. 151
Bacon, F. 115
Bačmanov, V. S. 151
Bakradze, K. S. 5, 8, 24, 28, 61, 66, 137
   151
Ballestrem, K. G. 46, 137, 193
Baskin, M. P. 151
Batiščev, G. S. 151
Baxitov, M. S. 151
Bazarov, V. A. 16, 20
Baženov, L. B. 8, 74, 75, 151
Bechterev 24
Beemans, P. J. VII
Begiašvili, A. F. 8, 138, 152
Belavin, K. I. 152
Belov, P. T. 9, 152
Berg, A. I. 152
Berkeley, G. 16, 116, 118, 119, 121,
   126, 135
Bibler, V. S. 152
Birjukov, B. V. 139, 152
Birjukov, D. A. 152
Bjalik, B. 152
Blakeley, T. J. 11, 12, 88, 89, 145, 193
Bloxincev, D. I. 9
Bocheński, J. M. VII, 8, 9, 10, 27, 28,
   65, 88, 107, 121, 138, 145, 193
Bodnar, J. 138, 139, 152
Boeselager, W. F. 12, 138, 193
Bogdanov, A. A. 1, 9, 16
Bogdanov, G. N. 152
Bogomolov, A. S. 139, 152
Boguslavskij, V. M. 7, 152, 153
Bojarincev, A. L. 153
Bokarev, V. A. 153
Bol'šunov, Ja.V. 28, 153
Bol'šuxin, A. 153

Borisov, V. N. 153
Borisova, I. S. 153
Branskij, V. P. 153
Bridgeman, P. T. 137, 139, 154
Brodskij, I. N. 153
Brudnyj, A. A. 153
Brutjan, G. A. 8, 139, 153
Bueva, L. P. 154
Bunge, M. 108
Burov, A. I. 154
Burxard, A. I. 161
Buxalov, Ju.F. 4, 7, 154
Byxovskij, B. E. 2, 108, 139, 154

Carnap, R. 91
Cassirer, E. 94, 108, 193
Celiščev, V. I. 154
Cereteli, S. B. 154
Che Wen 154
Cimintija, A. B. 154
Coconava, B. S. 154
Comte, A. 118, 123
Confucius 112
Cornford, F. M. 94, 108, 193
Cornforth, M. 123, 155
Croce, B. 136, 139, 155
Cuprov, P. A. 155

Čalin, M. 139, 155
Čečin, M. N. 155
Čerkašin, P. P. 108, 154, 155
Čerkesov, V. I. 5, 6, 7, 9, 23, 61, 63, 65, 66, 148, 155
Černov, V. 16
Černyšev, B. S. 139, 155
Česnokov, E. N. 27
Čiknaverova, A. A. 155
Čilingarjan, A. S. 155
Čudov, A. A. 155
Čueva, I. P. 155
Čupaxin, I. Ja. 5, 7, 155
Čupin, P. P. 47, 77, 156
Čurakov, Ju. D. 156

Danilenko, D. I. 28, 156
Danin, D. S. 9
Davydov, Ju. N. 151
Deborin, A. N. 2, 9, 156
Dedov, K. M. 156

Demaev, D. I. 156
Demidov, M. P. 156
Democritus 189
Descartes, R. 110, 115, 118, 119, 120, 121, 150
Dewey, J. 129, 172
Dmitriev, A. T. 156
Dolgov, K. M. 156
Dolmina, I. G. 167
Dosev, P. 2, 156
Drozdov, A. V. 156
Dubrovskij, D. I. 138, 157
Dudel', S. P. 157
Dühring, E. 15, 27, 28, 157
Dynnik, M. A. 162
Dzjadik, L. K. 157
Džafarli, T. M. 157
Džibuti, G. A. 157

E. A. 45
Efimov, S. F. 157
Efirov, S. A. 139, 157
Elmeev, V. Ja. 164
Emdin, M. V. 157
Empedocles 111
Engels, F. 8, 10, 13, 14, 16, 17, 18, 20, 21, 22, 23, 27, 28, 37, 38, 46, 58, 66, 79, 80, 83, 84, 88, 89, 92, 143, 147, 148, 157, 164, 168, 172, 173
Erdmann, B. 65
Esenin–Vol'pin, A. S. 157
Evčuk, V. I. 157
Evdomikov, V. I. 157

Farber, V. G. 157
Fataliev, X. M. 85, 157
Feuerbach, L. 14, 15, 27, 157, 165, 172
Fichte, J. G. 118, 117, 119, 120, 125, 135, 177
Filatova, A. N. 159
Filimonov, N. P. 158
Folimonov, V. V. 158
Filippova, M. M. 158
Findlay, J. N. 27, 193
Finn, V. K. 158
Fišer, E. G. 158
Fleischer, H. 108, 109, 145, 193
Fomin, V. I. 158
Frege, G. 136, 139, 152

Frolov, I. T. 158
Frolov, Ju. P. 158
Furman, A. A. 158
Furman, A. E. 159

G. S. 47, 159
Gabriel'jan, G. G. 5, 159
Gagarin, A. P. 10, 108, 159
Gajdukov, Ju. G. 7, 50, 138, 159
Gak, G. M. 159
Galileo, G. 132
Galkina–Fedoruk, E. M. 159
Gal'perin, S. I. 159
Garadža, V. I. 159
Garaudy, R. 123, 159
Gazenko, V. I. 159
Gelasšvili, A. A. 159
Georgiev, F. I. 6, 65, 159
Gerasimov, I. T. 160
Getmanova, A. D. 152
Gevorkjan, G. A. 65, 78, 160
Gimel'štejb, E. X. 160
Glagolev, V. F. 160
Glezerman, G. E. 160
Goder, M. N. 160
Gokieli, L. P. 4, 160
Gonseth, F. 137, 139, 157
Gorbač, V. I. 147
Gorskij, D. P. 7, 59, 60, 66, 69, 139,
    160, 161
Graščenko, N. I. 45, 161
Graznov, B. S. 162
Grekova, A. Ja. 9, 161
Gricenko, I. I. 161
Grigor'ev, G. S. 161
Grigor'jan, B. T. 161
Grušin, B. A. 162
Gulian, K. I. 162

Hamann, J. G. 121
Hegel, G. W. F. 5, 8, 12, 14, 15, 27, 56,
    89, 100, 117, 118, 119, 120, 121, 134,
    137, 146, 151, 154, 162, 166, 173, 176,
    177, 188, 193
Hilbert, D. 108
Höfler, A. 65
Hume, D. 116, 118, 119, 120, 121, 125,
    135, 138, 173
Husserl, E. 139, 174

Il'enkov, E. V. 7, 77, 162
Il'enkov, F. I. 162
Iliadi, A. N. 7, 162
Il'in, V. V. 162
Ingarden, R. 108
Iovčuk, M. T. 162
Ivanov, E. A. 162
Ivanov, G. M. 162
Ivanov, M. A. 161

Jacobi, F. H. 121
Jakušev, A. A. 139, 162
Jakuševskij, I. T. 4, 7, 46, 138, 162
Janovskaja, S. A. 7, 12, 163
Jaroslavskij, E. I. 163
Jaroševskij, T. M. 139, 163
Jaspers, K. 92
Joravsky, D. 16, 27, 193
Judanov, A. A. 163
Judin, P. F. 10
Jurovskij, S. V. 163
Jusupov, E. 163
Juškevič 9

Kakavadze, Z. M. 163
Kalandarišvili, G. M. 89, 137, 188
Kal'sin, F. F. 50, 163, 181
Kammari, M. D. 10, 163
Kant, I. 8, 11, 12, 56, 94, 99, 100, 117,
    118, 119, 120, 121, 137, 138, 150, 164,
    177, 179, 187, 192
Kantemirov, D. S. 180
Kantorovič, S. G. 163
Karabanov, N. V. 163
Karapetjan, A. 1437, 163
Karapetjan, R. O. 163
Karasev, B. A. 163
Kardaš, A. D. 164
Karljuk, A. S. 164
Karpinskaja, R. S. 152
Kasymžanov, A. X. 7, 26, 164
Kazakov, A. P. 164
Kazakovcev, V. S. 77, 164
Keburija, D. M. 164
Kedrov, B. M. 4, 5, 6, 7, 8, 17, 27, 77,
    80, 82, 83, 84, 85, 88, 89, 162, 164
Kelle, V. 109
Kešelava, V. V. 165
Khrushchov, N. S. vii, 40, 41, 47, 63

196

Kičanova, I. M. 139, 165
Kirillova, E. G. 165
Kir'janov, G. F. 9, 165
Kiselev, V. 153
Kiseleva, N. A. 86, 165
Kiselincev, A. 50, 165
Kitov, A. I. 185
Kleene, S. C. 108
Klement'ev, E. D. 165
Kline, G. L. vii, 193
Knigin, A. N. 165
Koemets, E. X. 166
Kogan, L. A. 9, 166
Kolbanovskij, V. N. 166
Komlev, M. G. 161
Kon, I. S. 88, 138, 139, 149, 166
Kondakov, N. I. 24, 28, 166
Konstantinov, F. V. 6
Kopnin, P. V. 5, 6, 7, 8, 56, 57, 58, 60
   65, 66, 73, 74, 75, 85, 89, 166
Korčagin, A. A. 167
Korneeva, A. I. 138, 167
Kornilov, K. N. 24
Koršunov, A. M. 64, 77, 167
Korževa, T. S. 167
Kostjuk, G. S. 167
Koševoj, K. K. 167
Košin, A. G. 167
Koval'čuk, A. S. 10
Kovalgin, V. M. 147, 168
Koval'zon, M. 109
Kozeva, T. A. 168
Koz'jakov, P. S. 184
Koz'lov, V. K. 10
Kozlova, M. S. 168
Kremjanskij, V. I. 168
Kristostur'jan, N. G. 168
Kryvelev, I. A. 168
Kublanov, B. G. 168
Kuftyrev, A. I. 168
Kulagin, P. V. 168
Kuljabin, G. A. 168
Kuprikov, T. K. 168
Kuražkovskaja, E. A. 168
Kursanov, G. A. 4, 8, 10, 138, 168
Kuršev, I. K. 9
Kuz'min, A. F. 169
Kuz'min, V. S. 169
Kuznecov, B. G. 9

Kuznecov, O. P. 169
Kvizinadze, R. E. 169

Ladygina–Kots, N. N. 10, 169, 190
Ladenko, I. S. 169
Landshut, S. 27, 172
Lapšin, O. V. 169
Laxuti, D. G. 158
Lazarenko, T. M. 169
Lazarev, F. 169
Lebedev, L. P. 169
Lebedev, M. P. 169
Lektorskij, V. A. 139, 169
Leibniz, G. W. 116, 118, 119, 121, 125,
   168,
Lenin, V. I. 1, 5, 9, 11, 13, 14, 15, 16,
   17, 18, 19, 20, 21, 22, 23, 26, 27, 28,
   30, 33, 34, 36, 37, 40, 41, 45, 46, 47,
   49, 58, 64, 80, 89, 92, 107, 108, 119,
   124, 131, 137, 138, 143, 147, 148, 149,
   152, 153, 155, 157, 159, 160, 161, 163,
   164, 165, 168, 169, 170, 171, 172, 173,
   174, 176, 177, 178, 179, 181, 183, 184,
   185, 188, 189, 190, 191, 192
Leonhard, W. 108
Leonov, M. A. 10, 50, 161, 166, 170,
   190, 192
Levi, S. S. 170
Levin, G. A. 5, 170
Lingart, I. 107, 138, 170
Ljapunov, A. A. 185
Ljubimov, V. V. 170
Lobkowicz, N. 46, 193
Locke, J. 99, 116, 119, 120, 121, 138,
   180, 186, 192
Logvin, M. A. 45, 171
Lomov, B. F. 190
Lozovskij, B. I. 10, 171
Lysenko, N. F. 171

Mach, E. 16, 20, 118, 131
Majstrov, L. E. 171, 190
Majstrova, T. L. 171
Makarov, A. D. 27, 156
Makarov, V. T. 171
Makovel'skij, A. D. 171
Maksimov, A. A. 9, 171
Mal'cev, V. I. 171
Mamardašvili, M. K. 171

Mangušev, T. D. 172
Man'kovskij, L. A. 156
Mansurov, N. S. 10, 172
Mao Tse-tung 158
Marcuse, H. 108
Maritain, J. 92
Marmičev, E. A. 172
Markov, M. A. 2, 172
Martirosjan, G. A. 172
Marx, K. 11, 13, 14, 15, 18, 21, 27, 46,
    66, 80, 118, 119, 120, 128, 157, 162,
    165, 168, 171, 172, 178, 181, 190
Maslennikov, M. M. 172
Matjuškin, A. M. 172
Medvedev, N. V. 3, 172
Megrabjan, A. A. 172
Mel'nikov, K. F. 172
Mel'nikov, V. V. 172
Mel'vil', Ju. K. 138, 172
Meščerjakova, I. N. 172
Mežuev, V. M. 172
Mill, J. S. 76, 118, 123, 181
Mirošxina, N. M. 172
Mitin, M. B. 6, 107, 123, 138, 143, 162,
    173
Mitroxin, L. N. 172, 173
Mixailova, I. B. 173
Mixailovskij, G. V. 173
Mixajlov, S. I. 10
Mixajlov, V. A. 9
Mixalenko, Ju. P. 108, 138, 173
Mkrtyčev, G. G. 173
Modržinskaja, E. D. 108
Mogendovič, M. R. 173
Molodcov, V. S. 173
Moročnik, S. B. 152, 173
Morozov, E. I. 173
Moskalenko, F. Ja. 174
Motrošilova, N. V. 139, 174
Mšvenieradze, V. V. 174

Nabin, T. 174
Narskij, I. S. 8, 139, 174
Nasedkin, A. D. 175
Natadze, R. 2, 175
Naumenko, L. K. 175
Nazarov, I. N. 175
Nelep, A. T. 175
Nesterova, N. P. 175

Newton, I. 81
Nicholas of Cusa 100, 118
Nikitin, E. P. 138, 175
Nikitin, N. I. 175
Nikitin, P. I. 175
Nikitina, V. P. 176
Nikolaev, I. V. 176
Nikolaev, Ja. I. 176
Novik, I. B. 176
Novinskij, I. I. 176

Ockham 114, 121
Odueva, N. K. 176
Ojzerman, T. I. 50, 108, 176
Okulov, A. F. 177
Onuščenko, V. 169
Organova, L. 188
Orlov, V. V. 85, 88, 89, 177, 191
Os'makov, I. I. 23, 177
Ostroux, F. Ja. 177
Ovsjannikov, M. F. 177
Ovužejnikova, S. V. 177

Pancxava, I. D. 108
Panfilov, V. Z. 177
Pantin, I. K. 177
Paramonov, N. Z. 177
Pavlov, I. P. 3, 10, 30, 32, 50, 64, 150,
    158, 165, 172, 173, 175, 177, 182, 188,
    190
Pavlov, T. 2, 50, 156, 177
Pavlov, V. T. 177
Pažitnov, L. N. 178
Perederij, V. I. 178
Petlenko, V. P. 178
Petrov, I. G. 178
Petrov, V. V. 178
Petrovskij, A. V. 178
Petruševskij, S. A. 9, 10, 190
Piaget, J. 137
Plato 95, 108, 111, 112, 113, 120, 121,
    135, 179, 193
Plexanov, G. 1, 14, 17
Pletnev, D. V. 178
Plotinus 112
Plotnikov, A. M. 178
Podkorytov, F. A. 7, 89, 178
Podosetnik, V. M. 3, 4, 10, 41, 42, 47
Polikarov, A. 179

Ponomarev, Ja. A. 179
Popov, N. P. 179
Popov, P. S. 7, 46, 107, 179
Popov, S. I. 8, 179
Popovič, M. V. 139, 179
Presnjakov, P. V. 179
Protagoras 111, 112, 121
Protasjenija, P. F. 180
Pugač, G. V. 180
Pupunyrov, P. N. 180

Rajkova, D. D. 180
Raxubo, P. G. 180
Razmyslov, P. I. 180
Rejkovskij, Ja. 180
Revzin, I. I. 180, 192
Reznikov, L. O. 2, 8, 180
Rjakin, A. N. 181
Romanov, A. V. 181
Roška, D. D. 181
Rousseau, J.–J. 121
Rovenskij, Z. 181
Rozental', M. M. 2, 5, 6, 7, 12, 34, 46,
    47, 57, 59, 62, 65, 66, 77, 80, 85, 123,
    152, 161, 165, 166, 181, 190
Rožin, V. P. 23, 182
Rubin, A. I. 182
Rubinov, I. G. 182
Rubinštejn, S. L. 3, 7, 24, 45, 46, 68, 77,
    182
Rudov, A. G. 182
Russell, B. 91, 123, 130, 138, 184
Rutkevič, M. N. 3, 4, 7, 10, 12, 40, 41,
    42, 46, 47, 77, 182
Ruzavin, G. I. 77, 163, 182

Sadovskij, V. N. 179, 182
Sadykov, G. M. 183
Safonov, Ju. F. 183
Safrošin, V. G. 28, 153
Sagatovskij, V. N. 183
Sanaja, K. D. 183
Saradžjan, V. X. 183
Satybalov, A. A. 183
Savel'ev, M. N. 183
Savina, T. B. 183
Savinov, A. V. 183
Savonarola 133
Saxarova, T. A. 108

Sazonov, Ja. V. 183
Schelling, F. W. 117, 118, 119, 120, 121,
    134, 177
Schneider, F. 193
Scotus, J. 114
Scotus Eriugena 120
Sedov, B. M. 183
Selivanov, F. A. 183
Sellars, R. W. 123, 137, 139, 152
Semenčev, V. M. 184
Semenov, Ju. I. 184
Serebrennikov, B. A. 10
Serebrjannikov, O. F. 184
Seržantov, V. F. 184
Sidorov, M. M. 184
Sikorskij, V. M. 184
Sitkovskij, E. P. 184
Sivokon', P. E. 184
Skajsgiris, R. P. 184
Skočeljas, V. P. 184
Skrypnik, V. D. 184
Skvorcov, A. P. 184
Skvorcov, L. V. 184
Sladkov, V. S. 185
Slagnova, L. V. 185
Slavskaja, K. A. 185
Smaragdov, A. D. 185
Smirnov, A. A. 185
Smirnov, L. V. 185
Smirnov, V. A. 183, 185
Smirnova, E. D. 185
Sobolev, S. L. 185
Socrates 112
Sokolov, E. N. 185
Sokolov, V. V. 137, 185
Solgalov, G. V. 185
Soxin, F. A. 186
Spasov, D. 10, 186
Spinoza, B. 116, 118, 119, 137, 185, 193
Spirkin, A. 7, 186
Stalin, I. V. 2, 3, 10, 22, 47, 107, 147,
    148, 150, 153, 157, 170, 179, 185, 188,
    191
Starčenko, A. A. 76, 186
Stempkovskaja, V. I. 186
Stjažkin, N. I. 186
Storčak, L. I. 9
Strogovič, M. S. 186
Subbotin, A. L. 186

Sudarikov, A. A. 186
Sul'ženko, G. D. 187
Suško, N. Ja. 187
Suvorov, S. G. 187
Suxanov, I. V. 187
Suxov, A. D. 108, 187
Suxov, G. S. 187
Sviderskij, V. I. 9
Svincov, V. I. 187
Syčev, N. I. 154

Šaff, A. 187
Šarovatov, N. P. 187
Šaškevic, P. D. 187
Šaulov, D. D. 187
Šaumjan, S. K. 187
Ščedrovickij, G. P. 59, 66, 187
Ščurenkova, A. I. 187
Šejko, A. N. 188
Šemjakin, F. N. 10, 190
Šeptulin, A. 188
Šoroxova, E. V. 10, 188, 190
Štoff, V. A. 86, 89, 188
Šubina, G. P. 188
Šur, E. B. 188
Švyrev, V. S. 78, 188, 189

Tarski, A. 108, 123
Tarxova, M. A. 188
Tatulov, G. 188
Tavadze, I. K. 89, 137, 188
Tavanec, P. V. 60, 186, 188, 189
Teilhard de Chardin, P. 108, 141
Terent'eva, Ju. A. 189
Terleckij, Ja. P. 9
Tevosjan, A. M. 189
Titarenko, A. I. 189
Titarenko, V. E. 189
Tjuxtin, V. S. 45, 189
Tondl', L. 189
Tonojan, G. A. 189
Topčiev, A. V. 10
Topčiev, G. A. 189
Toporkov, A. K. 189
Traxtenberg, O. V. 162, 189
Trofimov, P. S. 9, 46, 190
Tugarinov, V. P. 190

Uemov, A. I. 181, 190
Uemova, E. 181

Ukraincev, V. S. 190
Uvarov, A. I. 171, 190

Val'd, G. 190
Valentinov, N. V. 16
de la Valla, L. 133
Var'jaš, A. I. 190
Vartanjan, G. M. 190
Vavilov, S. I. 9
Vekker, L. M. 190
Vel'cman, V. N. 154
Velikovič, L. N. 108
Veselov, M. G. 9
Veselovskaja, L. D. 190
Vetrov, A. A. 68, 89, 139, 191
Vievskij, A. F. 191
Vinogradov, V. V. 10
Vjakkerev, F. F. 191
Vladimirova, A. I. 139, 191
Vojšvillo, E. K. 191
Vojtonis, N. 191
Volčkov, M. I. 191
Vol'kenštejn, M. V. 9
Volovik, L. A. 191
Vorob'ev, M. F. 191
Vostrikov, A. V. 27, 191
Vries, J. de VII, 2, 193

Wetter, G. A. 9, 10, 27, 28, 88, 108, 193
Whitehead, A. N. 137, 139, 162
Wittgenstein, L. 130, 138

Xačaturjan, A. B. 192
Xanazarov, K. X. 108
Xasxačix, F. I. 2, 6, 9, 50, 192
Xorev, N. V. 192
Xvan Djan En 192

Zabotin, V. V. 192
Zaičenko, G. A. 138, 192
Zakarževskij, L. K. 192
Zenkovsky, V. V. 27, 193
Zinov'ev, A. A. 7, 12, 77, 88, 192
Zozulja, A. M. 192
Zvegincev, V. A. 192
Zvonov, L. 192

Želnov, M. V. 192
Žoza, At. 192
Žukova, I. M. 192

INDEX OF SUBJECTS

Absolute 117
absolute and relative truth 35–38, 137,
   144
abstract and concrete 69–72
abstract to concrete, ascent from 71
abstraction 69–70
act 135
agnosticism 121, 129
analogy 76, 145
analysis 130–131, 141
analysis to synthesis 68–69
ancient philosophy 110–114
Anti-Dühring 15, 37
ascent from abstract to concrete 71

Behaviorism 129
being 134

Central nervous system 32–33
church 132–133
classics 13–18
classification of science 80–84
coexistence, peaceful 63
common-sense 140
Communism, construction of 41
concept 33, 54–60, 114; fluidity of
   58–60; plasticity of 58–60
concrete, abstract and 69–72; ascent
   from abstract to 71
confusion 142
consciousness 33
construction of Communism 41
contemplation, living 49
contemporary philosophy 121–137
contradiction 105
correspondence, truth as 35–37
criteriology 38–42

Deduction and induction 72–73
description 75
dialectic 81, 100, 126; laws of 35; and
   logic and epistemology 19–24; 85,
   objective and subjective 33–35, 58–59
Dialectic of Nature 15–16, 18, 79
dialectical logic 4–5, 6–7, 22–24, 34,

56–59, 64, 69–70, 87–88, 124, 144–145
dialectical materialism 18
dialectical method 145
discussion on logic 23–24
doctrine, social 134
dogmatism 141–142
dualism 96, 120

East-West 141, 145
eclecticism 130, 143
empiricism 115
epistemological and social roots of
   religion and idealism 102–107
epistemology 95–97; and logic and dialectic 19–24, 85
essence 54, 76, 135, 136
excitability 31–32
existentialism 135–136
explanation 75
extension 62

Faith 135
first signal system 32
fluidity of concepts 58–60
form 134
freedom 136

General and singular 71–72, 105
generalization 67–68
God 135, 143–144

Hieroglyphs 1
historical and logical 42–44, 51
historical materialism 132
historical periods 110
history, of knowledge 110–137;
   of logic 8; of philosophy 8
hypothesis 73–75

Idea 75–76, 116
ideal 95–97
idealism 97–98; and religion, the epistemological and social roots of 102–
   107
image 33

imagination 53–54
immanence 95–97
immateriality 54
induction, deduction and 72–73
inference 62
instrumentalism 129
intellectual knowledge 54–77
interactivity 30
irrationalism 121
irritability 31
isomorphy 36

Judgement 60–62

Knowledge 33, 103; history of 110–137; intellectual 54–77

Language 3, 8
law 76
laws of the dialectic 35
living contemplation 49
logic 7, 26, 40, 112, 124, 129; and dialectic and epistemology 19–24, 85; dialectical 4–5, 6–7, 22–24, 34, 56–49, 64, 69–70, 87–88, 124, 144–145; discussion on 23–24; history of 8
logical, historical and 42–44, 51
logical proof 42
Ludwig Feuerbach 15

Marxism–Leninism 118
Marxist dialectical method 84–85, 143
materialism 82, 98–99; dialectical 18
Materialism and Empirio-Criticism 1, 16–17, 80, 92, 124
mathematics 86
matter 18, 29–30, 95, 103–104,
meaning 126–127, 136
mental and physical work 106
Messianism 90–91
metaphysics 99–100, 124–126, 133, 134
method 79–88; dialectical 145
methodology 7–8, 79–88
mind-body 24–26
models 86
modern philosophy 114–121
monad 116
monism 96, 120
motion 83–84

Neopositivism 8, 123–132
neo-realism 129–130
nervous system, central 32–33

Object and subject 136
objective and subjective dialectic 33–35, 58–59
objectivity 82
ontology 95–97
ontologism 93
operationalism 137

Party-mindedness 90–91, 143
peaceful coexistence 63
perception 51–52, 104, 116
periods, historical 110
personalism 137
Philosophic Notebooks 1, 17–18
philosophy, contemporary 121–137; history of 8; modern 114–121; Russian 13
physical 25
physical and mental work 106
physiology 24–25
plasticity of concepts 58–60
positivism 123–132
practice 3–4, 7, 38–42, 53–54, 128, 144
pragmatism 127–129
presentational immediacy 137
process, truth as 37–38
propositions 131
psychic 25
psychology 2–3, 7, 24–25, 95–97, 142

Rationalism 115, 133, 120–121
real 95–97
realism 140
reasoning 62–64
reflection 29–35, 140–141
reflex 32
relative and absolute truth 35–38, 137, 144
religion 132; and idealism, epistemological and social roots of 102–107
representation 52
roots, epistemological and social of religion and idealism 102–107
Russian philosophy 13

Scepticism 121, 129
scholasticism 113–114, 132
science 8, 13, 73–74, 85, 106, 124, 132;
    classification of 80–84
second signal system 33
semantics 131–132
sensation 32, 49–51
sense-data 131
sense-knowledge 48–54, 104
senses 32
sensibility 31
sensualism 121
signal system, first 32; second 33
singular, general and 71–72, 105
social doctrine 134
social and epistemological roots of
    religion and idealism 102–107
sovpadenie 19–24, 86–87, 142–143
spirit 29–30, 95, 117
subject, object and 136
subjective and objective dialectic
    33–35, 58–59
subjectivism 128
subjectivity 37
subordination 81 f.

syllogism 64
synthesis, analysis and 68–69
system 140; central nervous 32–33;
    first signal 32; second signal 33

Terminology 93–97
theory 75–76
Thomism 132–135
'third path' 97f., 121, 126, 130
transcendence 95–97
truth 61, 105, 127, 131, 136, 141; abso-
    lute and relative 35–38, 137, 144; as
    correspondence 35–37; as process
    37–38

USA 127
universal 69

Verification 127

War 135–136
West, s. East
word 32–33
work, mental and physical 106

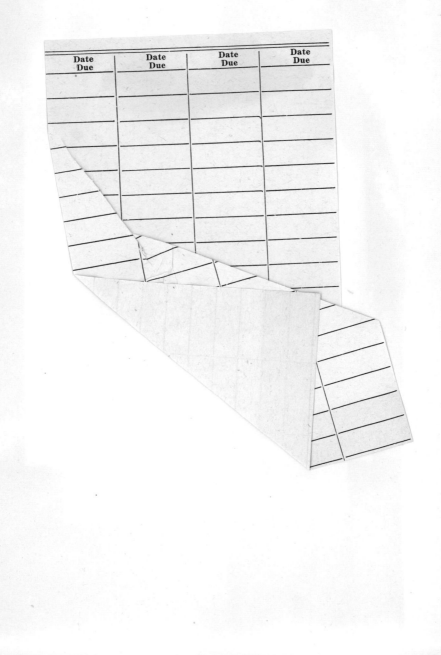